Andrew P. Peabody

Reminiscences of European Travel

Andrew P. Peabody

Reminiscences of European Travel

ISBN/EAN: 9783337210212

Printed in Europe, USA, Canada, Australia, Japan

Cover: Foto ©Andreas Hilbeck / pixelio.de

More available books at **www.hansebooks.com**

REMINISCENCES

OF

EUROPEAN TRAVEL

BY

ANDREW P. PEABODY.

BOSTON AND NEW YORK
HOUGHTON, MIFFLIN AND COMPANY.
The Riverside Press, Cambridge.
1896.

Copyright, 1868 and 1896,
BY ANDREW P. PEABODY AND MARY R. PEABODY.

All rights reserved.

PREFACE.

THE author was invited, last winter, to deliver twelve Lectures on what he saw in Europe, before the Lowell Institute. The chapters of this book are those Lectures, with hardly a verbal change, except the occasional substitution of *readers* for *hearers*. The author has not thought it necessary to interpolate or add a narrative of those portions of his tour not embraced in the Lectures; for his way seldom diverged from the wonted highway of travel, about which enough has been written.

One word more. The Lectures were, for the most part, transcribed from letters written to the author's own family, without the remotest reference to publication either by voice or through the press. In many instances, in which his taste might have dictated a change, he has preserved the very words of his letters, in the belief that the form in which one describes new scenes and experiences while his impressions are still fresh and vivid, can only become less graphic by the attempt to improve it.

HARVARD UNIVERSITY, *June* 5, 1868.

CONTENTS.

CHAPTER I.

OLD ENGLAND.

First Impressions of England. — Chester. — Tokens of Antiquity. — Sherwood Forest. — Haddon Hall. — Fountains Abbey. — Boston. — Houses of Parliament. — Dinner Speaking. — Lord Brougham. — The English Pulpit. — Spurgeon. — Newman Hall. — Martineau 1

CHAPTER II.

LONDON.

Municipal Organization. — Climate. — Police. — Literary Associations. — Parks. — Contrasts. — The Bank. — The Royal Exchange. — The Thames. — The Tunnel. — The Tower. — Westminster Abbey. — St. Paul's. — The British Museum. — The South Kensington Museum 25

CHAPTER III.

SKETCHES OF TRAVEL IN THE BRITISH ISLANDS.

Scottish Lakes. — Highland Scenery. — Ben Nevis. — Killarney. — The Jaunting-car. — The Gap of Dunloe. — The Irish Lakes. — Mendicancy. — The English Lakes. — Memorials of Wordsworth. — Sheffield. — Manufactures of Iron and Steel. — Edinburgh. — Old and New City. — Scott's Monument. — Dublin. — St. Patrick's 50

CHAPTER IV.

ART.

Superiority of Ancient and Mediæval Art. — The Ministry of Art. — The Sistine Madonna. — Other Pictures at Dresden. — Titian's Assumption of the Virgin. — Raphael's Transfiguration. — Rubens' Pictures. — Wood-carving. — Pulpit at Brussels. — The Dying Gladiator. — Michael Angelo's Moses. — The Milan Cathedral. — Goldsmith's Work. — Reasons for the Decline of Art 76

CHAPTER V.

SWITZERLAND.

Swiss Roads. — Inns. — People. — Basle. — Lucerne. — The Rigi. — Lake Lucerne. — Pass of St. Gotthard. — The Furca. — Glacier of the Rhone. — The Grimsel Pass. — Lake of Brienz. — Falls of the Giessbach. — Interlachen. — The Jungfrau. — Swiss Music. — Bern. — Geneva. — Lake of Geneva. — Lausanne. — Baths of Saxon. — Ruins 100

CHAPTER VI.

CHAMOUNY AND NORTHERN ITALY.

Routes to Chamouny. — The Valley. — The Flégère. — The Montanvert. — The Mer de Glace. — The Glacier des Bossons. — Sunrise at Chamouny. — The Simplon. — First Views of Italy. — Domo d'Ossola. — Lake Maggiore. — Lake Lugano. — Lugano. — Lake of Como. — Como. — Market-scene. — Milan. — The Last Supper. — Church of St. Ambrose. — Golden Altar. — Ambrosian Library 124

CHAPTER VII.

PARIS.

Manysidedness of Paris. — Its Exterior. — Industry. — Manufactures. — Holidays. — Charities. — Education. — Paternal Government. — The Boulevards. — The Madeleine — The Pantheon. — Notre Dame. — Chapelle Expiatoire. — Chapel of St. Ferdinand. — Père la Chaise. — Tomb of Napoleon. — The Louvre. — Jardin des Plantes. — Jardin d'Acclimatation . . 148

CHAPTER VIII.

NAPLES AND ITS VICINITY.

Naples. — Views. — People. — Modes of Living. — Vesuvius. — The Solfatara. — Monte Nuovo. — Lake of Agnano. — Stufa di Nerone. — Virgilian Sites. — Avernus. — The Acherusia Palus. — The Elysian Fields. — Cave of the Cumæan Sibyl. — Road to Sorrento. — Sorrento. — The Blue Grotto. — Capri. — Palace of Tiberius. — Road to Amalfi. — Amalfi. — Salerno. — Peasants' Costume. — Present Condition of Italy. — Protestantism in Naples and Florence 174

CHAPTER IX.

POMPEII, PISA, PERUGIA, AND BOLOGNA.

Destruction of Pompeii. — Its Streets, Shops, Houses, and Temples. — National Museum at Naples. — Unrolling of Manuscripts. — Relics of the Buried Cities. — Pompeii a Commentary on the Classics. — Pisa. — The Cathedral. — The Baptistery. — The Leaning Tower. — The Campo Santo. — Perugia. — The Staffa Madonna. — Pietro Perugino. — Bologna. — Raphael's St. Cecilia. — Guido's Madonna della Pieta. — The Campo Santo 201

CHAPTER X.

ANCIENT ROME.

First Impressions. — The Seven Hills. — The Capitol. — The Forum Romanum. — Trajan's Forum and Column. — Baths of Caracalla. — The Colosseum. — The Pantheon. — Aqueducts. — The Tarpeian Rock. — The Mamertine Prison. — The Cloaca Maxima. — Ancient Sculpture. — Inscriptions. — Church of St. Clement. — The Catacombs. — Hadrian's Villa. — Tivoli. — The Campagna. — The Tiber. — Vestiges of the ancient Roman Race. — Saturnalia on the Eve of the Epiphany . 229

CHAPTER XI.

MODERN ROME.

St. Peter's. — The Vatican. — Sistine Chapel. — The Last Judgment. — Raphael's Creation. — Etruscan Museum. — Hall of

Maps.—Vatican Library. — Manufacture of Mosaics. — Christmas at St. Peter's. — The Cardinals. — The Pope. — Christmas at the Ara Cœli. — Scala Santa. — Church of St. Stephen. — Vault of the Capuchins. — Monks in Rome. — State of the City. — Palaces. — Artists. — Houses of the Poor. — Beggars. — Chestnut Venders.— Bad Police. — Fox-hunt. — Protestant Cemetery. — Falls of Terni 258

CHAPTER XII.

GERMANY.

Nuremberg. — Aspect of Antiquity. — Fountains and Markets. — Instruments of Torture. — Old Curiosity Shop. — Honor to Distinguished Natives. — Prague. — Hymns to the Virgin. — Cathedral of St. Vitus. — The Judenstadt. — Old Synagogue. — Church-customs. — Heidelberg. — Castle. — Fair. — Market. — Baden-Baden. — Castles, Old and New. — High Play. — Hot Springs. — Freiberg. — School of Mines. — Practical Mining 285

REMINISCENCES

OF

EUROPEAN TRAVEL.

CHAPTER I.

OLD ENGLAND.

First Impressions of England. — Chester. — Tokens of Antiquity. — Sherwood Forest. — Haddon Hall. — Fountains Abbey. — Boston. — Houses of Parliament. — Dinner Speaking. — Lord Brougham. — The English Pulpit. — Spurgeon. — Newman Hall. — Martineau.

HEAVEN's richest boon to a traveller is the presentific power of memory. Mere recollection would give us little pleasure or profit, nay, might awaken a comfortless yearning for what we had once seen, or a life-long regret that the beautiful visions could never be repeated. It would be worse than unsatisfying to recall places, names, and the mere details of an itinerary. But what we have once beheld is thenceforth ours. In a profounder sense than the poet meant,

"A thing of beauty is a joy forever."

We admire, and cannot admire to excess, the photographic art in its various modes of presentation. It is an unspeakable privilege to bring together on our tables scenes from every land, sun-pictures, too, of world-renowned master-works, and to make our tour in every zone and clime by shifting the slides in the stereoscope. But how immeasurably more precious is the gallery of photographs, taken on the retina of our own vision, deposited where they never grow dim, stored away in countless numbers, as vivid by night as by day, found at the very moment we seek them, the slide shifting as rapidly as the thought, — photographs, too, not with the mere lights and shadows, but polychromatic, retaining every hue of the sunset clouds, every delicate tint of the painter's brush, every bright color of the peasant's costume! I propose to describe in part a series of these photographs taken during a European tour, in the years 1866 and 1867.

It is fitting that I should begin with England, both as our mother country, and as the land in which almost every American obtains his first foreign experiences. *Old* England we learn at once to say with intense emphasis; *New* England acquires a fulness of meaning which it never had before, and the two centuries and a half of our history no longer carry us back to an appreciable antiquity.

The steamers that ply between the two countries have arrangements specially adapted to produce this impression of contrast. The American embarks at Boston or New York on Wednesday, and in the ordinary course of navigation, reaches Liverpool on

Saturday morning of the following week. Liverpool seems to him like New York without an Astor, St. Nicholas, or Fifth Avenue, — a vast wilderness of docks, shops, and warehouses, opulent, crowded, tumultuous, with some magnificent edifices, and some quiet and homelike streets, but without an inn that looks either restful or attractive. London is too remote for a Saturday's journey, and one who would economize his time prefers approaching the metropolis by stages that will enable him to visit various intermediate points of essential interest, without retracing his steps. Chester, within half an hour by railway, is, therefore, chosen for Sunday's repose; and there the traveller finds himself transplanted into the Middle Ages, with not a few memorials of an antiquity to which they are modern.

Chester, a corruption of *Castra*, (a camp,) was a Roman military station from the time of Julius Cæsar until the Romans left the island. The wall, which entirely surrounds the old city, and is broad enough for a promenade, was commenced under their auspices, and completed nearly a thousand years ago. The principal streets are distinguished by a style of architecture which some antiquaries refer to a Roman origin, and which undoubtedly belongs to a period prior to any continuous history of Great Britain. The sidewalks rest upon the basements, and are roofed by the second stories of the houses. The covered ways thus formed are lined with shops of every description, under, behind, and above which are the dwelling-houses, each upper story projecting over the one next lower, — so that occupants of the fourth floor on opposite sides of the street are brought into a proximity which must make them either strong friends or very bitter enemies. From these streets lead all manner of narrow lanes and alleys, through the oddest places, among queer, antique houses, shops, and inns, glazed with miniature diamond-shaped panes in leaden sashes. There are no two buildings alike, and hardly one which does not look as if it had a history; while several of the taverns carry us back at least three centuries, and can hardly have been new even then.

The Cathedral befits the city. It is partly in ruins; the whole exterior wall is in slow decay; and huge, ancient trees grow where some of the cloisters of the once adjacent abbey stood, and over vaults and crypts still occupied and frequented. Here may be found mosaic altar-pieces, and pavements, and painted glass, with figures indicating an age prior to the use of perspective in grouping; while the grim forms of knights and churchmen and dames of high degree, in gray stone, look down from the walls, or lie in rudely ambitious sculpture on the floor.

Age and the consciousness of it form the most prominent characteristic of England and of the English people, and are the prime source of all their idiosyncrasies. No token of antiquity that can be preserved is obliterated. Restoration is preferred to renovation. An old building is not disused so long as it admits of occupancy; nor is a dilapidated member of a building removed simply because it is untenantable. The Church of St. John the Baptist, in Chester, built in the tenth century, and now in full use for a large congregation, has, lying behind the chancel, the ruins of the lady-chapel, which was crushed by the fall of the tower several centuries ago, and the tower that succeeded the one that fell has long been a ruin. An Englishman has no reverence for modern architecture. In London, the buildings erected immediately after the Great Fire are the latest in which the citizens take pride, and these are new compared with the cathedrals, colleges, castles, and manor-houses that are the glory of the land.

The manners and habits of the people have their roots " in the time whereof the memory of man runneth not to the contrary." Table etiquette retains, for the most part, the stateliness and formalism of earlier days. In dress and furniture, glaring colors and showy fashions are an infallible sign of vulgar breeding, abjured by all who have, or pretend to have, ancestors. Precedent is imperative law, and the only way to dislodge a precedent that has become obsolete, is to conjure up the similitude of one still older. Steam, elsewhere revolutionary, here innovates but slowly, even in the departments that lie most open to its influence. Not only the rural inns, but those at important railway stations and in large provincial towns, and even many in London, retain the staff, appointments, and customs, made familiar to us by the literature of Queen Anne's reign; and the *table d'hôte* dinner, universal on the Continent and very common in Scotland and Ireland, has been introduced, so far as I know, into but one English hotel.

Above all, England manifests everywhere the accumulated opulence of an age of many centuries. Solidity and massiveness, regardless of cost, characterize constructions of every kind, — roads, bridges, railways, fences, public edifices, private dwellings. There are no makeshifts, no lath and plaster buildings, no cheap ornamentation, no imitation of mouldings and cornices in limewash, no mockery of precious woods in paltry pine. Wealth is not ostentatiously displayed; but it is stowed away in masses that constantly protrude into sight, and impress the fresh beholder with perpetual amazement. England may have reached and passed her climacteric: but if so, her decline must be slow and long; for her hoarded resources may sustain her national strength for many generations.

Even the forms of vegetation that constantly meet the eye in England sustain the prestige of venerable age. Yews through whose decayed trunks a coach and six may be driven without collision on either side; hedges of thick-set trees, once shrubs; ivy with stalks as large as a man's body; parterres of flowering moss and yellow house-leeks springing luxuriantly from the roofs of old farm-houses and barns; single grape-vines whose fruit is reckoned by the ton; avenues of box that screen a tall man from the sun or shelter him from the sudden shower, — these and many like objects conspire to sustain the feeling that we are in an older world than our birth-world.

I spent a day in Sherwood Forest, where there is not a tree that might not have been a shelter for Robin Hood and his merry men. The very oak on which he used to hang his venison is pointed out. I dined under another oak beneath which I fancied he must have often dined, and in whose shade fifty men might hold high festival. Except those destroyed by lightning, not a tree has been taken from this forest for four or five centuries, nor has one been added to it. No undergrowth is suffered, except a tall and beautiful fern. The trees are wreathed into all manner of fantastic shapes, gnarled and knotted, bulging out with huge excrescences, many of them with hollows in which children might play hide-and-seek, and yet with foliage as rich and full as in their prime.

Of ancient houses, the most remarkable in the kingdom is Haddon Hall, belonging to the Duke of Rutland, for a century and a half occupied only by its custodians, kept in perfect repair, and wholly unaltered from the time when it harbored full seven score of servants, and kept incessant revel with open doors from Christmas to Twelfth-night. It differs from a Pompeian house in having been preserved without being buried. There remains the kitchen, almost as large as the parish church, with two fire-places, in either of which an ox might be roasted whole; adjacent to it is the bakery, with immense ovens, the very thought of filling which, makes one feel poverty-stricken; and this opens into the butchery, with its murderous apparatus, and the meat-block for cutting up the slain beasts. On the other side of the rude, stone-floored hall is the great dining-room, with the dais at the upper end where the master of the house sat with his more distinguished guests. Still chained to the wall is the iron handcuff that used to be employed for the punishment of the guest who would not or could not drain his bumper. By this contrivance the hand was fastened at a painful height, while water was poured down the recusant's sleeve from time to time, until either he desisted from his obduracy, or his tormentors became too drunk to do their duty. The chapel contains some painted glass more than four centuries old, and reading-desk, family pew, and servants' seats, all bear tokens of an age when personal comfort was wholly dissociated from the rites of public worship. Besides a great number of mere kennels for guests and their servants, too small for half the paraphernalia of a modern toilette, there are several state-chambers. One of these contains two very deeply embayed windows, with panes but little over an inch square set in lead. In another of these chambers is preserved a once most magnificent state-bed, with canopy and hangings in tatters, in which royal personages have often slept, and which was transported to Beaver Castle, the usual residence of the Duke of Rutland, when George IV. once made him a visit. In the garden attached to this house, I saw the finest specimens I have ever seen of the topiary-art, — the training and clipping of trees and shrubs so as to represent various figures. There was one clump of shrubbery so cut as to reproduce in great perfection the form of a peacock with bill, crest, and tail complete; another equally good, representing the heraldic cognizance of the bear and staff.

With the prevailing love for antiquity, ruins are of course cherished in England as nowhere else. So strong is the passion for them, that brand-new artificial ruins are found, not only on the grounds of *parvenus* of cockney extraction, but, incongruously enough, on the estates of some of the oldest families in the kingdom, — showing that taste does not appertain of necessity to noble lineage.

Of all the actual ruins I have seen, those of Fountains Abbey are the most extensive and the most interesting. They cover sixty-four acres, a space about as large as the Boston Common; and they are set in a framework of lake, stream, lawn, grove, and forest, unsurpassed in that quiet, slumberous beauty, which is the dominant type of English scenery, and which accords most perfectly in tone with the memorials of long-vanished generations. The tower of the convent-church, two hundred feet high, is still standing, together with fragments of its walls, arches, and pillars, sufficient to enable one to trace its contour, to determine its several divisions, and to form a distinct conception of its architecture. It was of the upright Gothic, highly ornate, and yet massive enough to survive in its dismantled condition from the time of Henry VIII., when it was first exposed to human violence, through several succeeding centuries in which no efficient measures were taken for its preservation. The walls of the abbot's house, too, are in great part standing, and his magnificent dining-room is distinctly traceable, with portions of its splendid double colonnade. Least of all to be forgotten are the convent kitchen, with its chimney sixteen feet broad, and the dining-room of the brethren hard by, with the high little gallery where one of the fraternity was doomed to read while the rest ate. Then there are cloisters enough to lodge a little army of cenobites, almshouses, reception-houses for strangers, supplementary edifices for divers uses, sacred and secular, all unroofed, shattered, and dismembered, yet in such a condition that the reconstructive fancy is seldom baffled or perplexed. The walls are heavily festooned with ivy; the brook that turned the abbey mill winds murmuring among the displaced flagstones; venerable yews, beeches, and sycamores curtain all the avenues; and in the park through which the tourist's access lies, vast herds of deer, so tame that they suffer the near approach of man, are, no doubt, the lineal descendants of those whose haunches were wont to smoke on the abbot's table.

On the same journey from London on which I saw Fountains Abbey I visited Boston, which, in the air of venerable antiquity, is second only to Chester. It lies somewhat aside from the usual route of travellers; but when I was at Cambridge, I could not resist the temptation to make my almost daily home-passage "from Cambridge to Boston."

The greater part of Lincolnshire — the fen-country — looks like a tract borrowed from Holland. By diking and draining it has been reclaimed from the sea, which, but for unnumbered windmills that work pumps in times of inundation and freshet, would long since have taken back what it gave. It abounds in canals much wider than most of the English rivers, which, great in song and with crowding historical and literary associations, are generally smaller than the nameless rivulets of our country. This whole region is on a dead level, with scarce a hillock, and it has a dreary, chill, waterlogged aspect; but it is profusely fertile, and its crops of grain and grass are the richest on the island.

In this region is Boston, about five miles from the sea, on both sides of the river Witham, — an estuary almost dry at low tide, but swollen into a deep and vigorous stream by the rapid and high tides that set in from the German Ocean. The most remarkable object in Boston is the Church of

St. Botolph, which is, I think, the largest, and is regarded as the most magnificent parish church in England. By a coincidence singular, if not designed (and it can hardly have been designed), it has as many doors as there are months, as many windows as there are weeks, and as many stairs in the ascent of the tower as there are days in the year. The tower, which is most elaborately finished, is as high as the church is long; and in the lantern near its summit, in early times, a beacon fire was kept up for the guidance of travellers by water, whether on the open ocean or among the adjacent marshes. The eastern chancel window is one of surpassing beauty, representing a series of subjects connected with the ancestry, the earthly sufferings, and the celestial glory of the Saviour. The Cotton Chapel, used as a vestry and a depository for records, was put into its present neat, but by no means elegant condition, by contributions from Boston, Massachusetts, and has a mural tablet of brass, with a highly classical inscription in Latin to the memory of John Cotton, written by the late Mr. Everett. I confess I was but ill-satisfied to find so scanty memorials of a name which had there become illustrious for learning and piety, long before it was heard in the New World. Indeed, the inconspicuousness and smallness of the tablet, and the reticence as to this chapel of the otherwise very communicative sextoness, led me to believe that there was at least a willingness to ignore the Puritan vicar.

Among the many old houses in Boston is the birth-house of John Fox, the martyrologist, — long, low, with broad latticed windows, and with heavy cornices projecting over each story, — evidently in its time the house of a family of ample substance and a highly respectable position, but now kept as an ale-house and dram-shop. There are many other family mansions that must have been old in John Cotton's time, and yet seem incapable of decay; and there is one mediæval tower, windowless and roofless, the only remaining portion of the splendid residence of an ancient and extinct family, whose lands somehow fell into the ownership of the municipal corporation, and were conveyed by that body to a citizen of Boston, with the truly English stipulation, that he should "keep the tower in its present form as a ruin."

There was a time when Boston maintained a very extensive commerce in fish, corn, salt, wool, and woollen goods; and in King John's reign it was the second commercial town in the kingdom, having about nine-tenths as much trade as London. The only remaining tokens of this thriving condition are certain quaint, massive, low-browed warehouses, too dark and mouldy for any possible use, too thoroughly soaked in brine to be ever burned, and seemingly too solid for mastication by the mordant tooth of time.

The streets of Boston are narrow and very crooked, and there are many lanes hardly wide enough for a wagon-path. The houses of the poorer sort have brick floors, generally a little below the level of the sidewalk. The town is neat and orderly; but there are few indications of enterprise or of wealth. Indeed, Boston has been stranded during the whole lifetime of her New England namesake, and now claims our interest chiefly on account of the daughter, who, with her name, robbed her of her brightest jewels.

I have selected for description certain places and objects associated together solely on the score of age. I propose in the residue of this chapter, to give my remembrances and impressions of Parliament and Church, of English oratory and public speaking; and though all I have to say does not fall naturally under the text of "Old England," still the differences between English and American oratory are chiefly those which would naturally exist between an old and a young people, while there is a not unlike contrast between the organism and ceremonial both of Church and State on this and the other side of the Atlantic.

Westminster Palace includes the new Houses of Parliament, with old Westminster Hall incorporated into the structure as a vestibule. The entire building, old and new, covers a surface of eight acres. Westminster Hall is an immense apartment, about three hundred feet long, and is rendered memorable as the scene of the great state trials for many centuries, from that of Sir Thomas More to that of Warren Hastings. Here Charles I. was condemned to die. Here have been enacted the most momentous tragedies in the history of the kingdom. The architecture of this hall is solemn and impressive, as befits the theatre of transactions involving the destiny of a nation. In apartments opening from the hall on either side still sit the four great law-courts of the kingdom. The Houses of Parliament are built of Yorkshire limestone. They are of a modernized Gothic, with three huge and lofty towers. The edifice is splendid and beautiful, yet unsatisfying to the eye; for it lacks symmetry, — it suggests no idea but that of a costliness beyond calculation. It is immense without grandeur, exhausting all the resources of art save the genius which alone can vivify and harmonize its creations. The ante-rooms to the Chambers of Parliament are interesting chiefly from their historical frescos,[1] among which I was glad to see one representing the embarkation of the Pilgrims from Delft Haven for New England. The Chambers of the Lords and the Commons are richly decorated with gilding and carved work, but are smaller and much less convenient for their uses, than most of the legislative halls in our state capitols.

[1] I use the word *fresco* in its common acceptation. It properly belongs only to pictures in which the colors are laid on fresh plaster, into which they sink so deep as to be indelible; while almost all the modern and many of the mediæval pictures that bear the name of *frescos* are paintings on dry walls.

In the House of Commons the Speaker and the clerks wear (as do all the judges and barristers in the several courts) gowns, bands, and gray flaxen wigs, — the wigs being made of flax as fine as silk, with rows of puff-curls, and two curls pendent behind. The Lord Chancellor, in presiding over the House of Lords, wears a huge flaxen wig which entirely covers his cheeks, and hangs over his shoulders like a vandyke. His seat looks like a scarlet woolsack (whence its name), with another smaller sack as a pillow for the back, but with no support for the arms, — the very acme of discomfort for a long session. The bishops appear in the House of Lords in white robes, with full lawn sleeves.

In the House of Commons I heard Mr. Gladstone's valedictory speech on retiring from the ministry. His elocution was plain and dignified, but with no display of oratory. The speech would have fallen dead upon an American audience. His manner could hardly have been other than it was, had he said the same things in his own library to two or three intimate friends.

In the House of Lords I heard a singular debate, which seemed to belong to the dark ages. A bill was introduced which ran somewhat in this wise: " Whereas in the year 1814, the parish church of Sunbury, having fallen into decay, was repaired and remodeled, and the altar was placed ten feet six inches from its former site; whereas this change in the position of the altar remained unnoticed until it was recently discovered in the examination of plans of the church in its original state; and whereas many persons have been married at that altar, supposing it a place legally consecrated for the celebration of marriage,— therefore be it enacted, that such marriages be declared and deemed legitimate." This bill was opposed by one of the bishops, on the ground that, were it passed, due care might not hereafter be taken in the repairing of churches to preserve the site of the altar unchanged,— a possibility, the very thought of which seemed to fill him with holy horror, and to avert which he was willing to throw into chaos the property, domestic relations, peace, and well-being of an entire community. The bill was passed by a large majority; that on such a question there should have been a minority in the negative, unless in an assembly of idiots, is to me inconceivable. The epithet which best characterizes the speaking in the House of Lords is *gentlemanly*. It is not merely courteous in form; but it is manifestly the natural, spontaneous utterance of high-bred men, who would not know how to be coarse, rude, or vulgar.

I had several opportunities of hearing the best English after-dinner speaking, which is so utterly unlike ours, that the lovers of one could not even tolerate the other. At an English dinner-table the spread-eagle element is entirely wanting. There is no talking against time, no oration making, none of that kind of speaking which has primary reference to the next day's newspaper report. It is literally table-talk, only loud enough to be heard by the whole company, — as free, simple, unartificial as the *tête-à-tête* conversation of fellow-guests, but withal rich either in wit, wisdom, or both. It seemed to me that on such occasions men did not talk for the sake of saying something, but because they had something to say. The only dinner-speaker whom I heard that approached the studied oratory to which we are used on similar occasions, was a deaf man, Napier, late Lord Chancellor of Ireland, who evidently had adopted an almost rhythmical style of utterance as the best mode of governing the voice without the aid of the ear.

It was my happiness to receive an invitation to the last dinner at which Lord Brougham presided, the annual dinner of the Association for the Promotion of Law Reform and Social Science. Lord Brougham was too feeble to walk across the room without assistance; yet he spoke with all the vigor and earnestness of youth. Age has had no mellowing influence upon him, but has manifestly toughened and indurated him. His face is as hard as flint, with the deep furrows of strong thinking, but without a line suggestive of kind feeling or of ordinary human sympathies. I suppose that he has been a not ungraceful speaker; but, if so, no grace is left. His speech is abrupt, vehement, torrent-like in its rapidity, — like a torrent tumbling among rocks that roughen its flow. On the occasion on which I saw him, he made, as President, the opening speech, and followed several other speakers with shorter addresses expressive of approval or dissent. I cannot dispel certain canine associations with his face and voice. He certainly has, with nobler elements, no little of the bull-dog.

At a dinner of the Society of Political Economists, I heard, among other distinguished men, John Stuart Mill, who cannot of course speak otherwise than ably and pertinently, but whose utterance is feeble, hesitating, and unimpressive, while his bearing indicates extreme timidity and diffidence.

English pulpit eloquence, in general, seemed to me utterly unworthy of its office, and entirely below the demand of the times; and I always found the most meagre preaching where the apparatus for the highly artistical performance of religious services was the most ample and elaborate. I attended, one Sunday evening, one of the meetings for the people of which we have heard so much, under the dome of St. Paul's. There could not have been less than three or four thousand persons present. The preacher had come from Edinburgh, and was announced by placards all over the city for eight or ten days beforehand. His sermon was just fifteen minutes long, consisted only of desultory remarks by which I thought he was groping his way toward a subject, and while

I was listening with some solicitude for the announcement of his theme he broke off with the closing doxology. The sermons that I heard at the Temple Church, Westminster Abbey, and sundry cathedrals, were, in general, admirably written, but jejune or trite in thought, and cold as an iceberg. The ministers of the parish churches, especially those of the evangelical party, impressed me much more favorably. They preach like men thoroughly in earnest; but they have not yet found the most efficient way of doing their work. They are very much in the habit of preaching from partially written sermons, extemporizing at frequent intervals, with a small Bible in the hand from which they read illustrative texts, often naming the chapter and verse. Their evident sincerity and earnestness greatly interested me; yet it seemed to me — I know not if it were so — as if they were in a transition state, — as if this method had but lately come into use; they had not yet become accustomed to it, and were forfeiting the advantages of the fully written sermon, without having acquired due freedom and power in extempore utterance.

Of course I heard Spurgeon, and I regard it as a great privilege to have heard him. His Tabernacle is on the Surrey side of the Thames, about a mile and a half from Temple Bar, an immense building, severely simple in style, with a row of Doric pillars and a Grecian pediment in front. Within, two deep galleries extend along all four sides of the edifice. There is no pulpit. The preacher stands surrounded by hearers, on a semicircular platform which projects from the lower gallery, opposite the entrance-doors. The church, when I was there, was entirely full, and it is said to contain not less than four thousand persons. The audience were breathlessly still, except at the close of the prayers and the exposition, and at pauses between the heads of the sermon, when there was a tumultuous explosion of suppressed breathing, coughing, and analogous processes. The service was two hours and a half in length; yet no one seemed to be fatigued. There were three hymns sung by the congregation without any instrumental accompaniment, and the sound was "as the voice of many waters." There were two prayers, and a reading of Scripture with an able and copious exposition. The sermon was strongly Calvinistic, and I could not entirely sympathize with its doctrinal statements; but it was real preaching, and the preaching of the church dignitaries seemed child's play as compared with it.

Spurgeon has a physiognomy full of strength and beauty. The ordinary engravings of him are like him, yet unlike. They give him a somewhat coarse, sensuous look, which he may perhaps have, when his features are in repose; but in preaching his countenance is radiant, spiritual, and wonderfully vivid in its play and in its prompt adaptation to the thought he utters. His voice is the finest I ever heard. Every syllable could be clearly distinguished by every ear in his vast audience, and his tones were all those of easy, colloquial discourse, with no rant, and no striving for effect. There are in his early printed sermons passages revolting for their coarseness and irreverence, poor jokes, stale anecdotes, illustrations drawn from low life; but I am inclined to think that these were due to his then imperfect culture. He has evidently been a rapidly improving man, and he must have made himself familiar with the best models of style. When I heard him, there was not a word which could offend the most fastidious taste. His language was pure English, with a predominance of the Saxon element. His words were singularly well chosen. There is a rare intensity and lifelikeness in his mode of stating religious truth, which arrests and enchains the attention. Without degrading spiritual themes, he makes them seem almost visible and tangible. His imagery is sensuous, as appealing to the perceptive faculties, yet pure and elevating to the thought. He translates, as it were, the language and the narratives of Scripture, the parables and similes of the Gospels, into the things that most nearly correspond to them in our own time, and says just what it may be supposed the apostles would have written in England in the nineteenth century, in lieu of what they wrote in the first century in Palestine. Such preaching teaches the common people as they can be taught in no other way; interprets to them what would else be unintelligible. One cannot hear Spurgeon without being not only convinced of his sincerity, but impressed with the entire absence of self-reference, his complete identification with his work, and his burning zeal in the cause of his Divine Master. There can be no doubt that he is now exerting a more extended influence than any other preacher in the kingdom, and is second to none among the moral forces in the great metropolis.

Next to him in his power as a popular preacher, his superior by far in culture, his equal in self-devoted zeal, is Newman Hall, whom many of my readers have recently heard. I heard him preach at St. James's Hall, to an immense audience, composed almost wholly of the poorest classes, — of persons who are never seen in any church. His sermon was remarkable for its entire freedom from dogmatic subtleties, its directness, simplicity, and intense earnestness. Spurgeon speaks as though he were wholly absorbed in his subject; Hall, as if he took up into his own strong emotional nature the needs, wants, trials, infirmities, and sorrows of his entire audience. With his hale and bluff manhood there is a wonderful closeness and tenderness of sympathy, and the coarse, rude people hang upon his words, as if a brother, who felt all that they feel, were pleading with them for their highest good.

At the widest possible distance from these men is another great preacher, well known by his writings on this side of the Atlantic, — Martineau. I heard but one sermon from him, and that was a discourse of very extraordinary power and merit. It was undoubtedly occasioned by his then recent rejection as a candidate for the Professorship of Intellectual Science in the London University, in effecting which the decisive weight was thrown into the adverse scale by well known positivists. The sermon was a profoundly philosophical vindication of the Divine Providence against the postulates of the positive philosophy. So much, so deep, and so fructifying thought can seldom have been condensed into the same space; and though his hearers listened intently, as if accustomed to highly concentrated spiritual nutriment, there are few congregations in Christendom which such a discussion would not have overtaxed. With the philosophy there ran along a rich vein of devout sentiment, so that to recipient minds there was edification no less than instruction. But the preacher's manner was chilling. His voice is clear and strong; but his delivery is almost monotonous, — not the monotony of indifference or dullness, but of suppressed feeling, — still less the monotony of feebleness, but of reserved and smothered power. His oratory is eminently that of a commanding mind, weighty and impressive; but at the same time it is heavy and unexciting.

I have space only to add, that Martineau approaches the normal type of English oratory much more nearly than Spurgeon or Hall. Old England prefers in her orators, with the gravity and wisdom, the subdued and quiet tone and style of mature, if not of senile age.

CHAPTER II.

LONDON.

Municipal Organization. — Climate. — Police. — Literary Associations. — Parks. — Contrasts. — The Bank. — The Royal Exchange. — The Thames. — The Tunnel. — The Tower. — Westminster Abbey. — St. Paul's. — The British Museum. — The South Kensington Museum.

WE complain of Englishmen for never understanding the complicated and interacting machinery of our state and national governments. It is equally difficult for an American to comprehend the municipal organization of London. London lies in three counties, and is a confederation of cities, parishes, and precincts, each autonomous to a certain extent, and the whole united by a common system of administration rather than under a common central government. But in the different sections of the metropolis, while there is a community of system, there is a wide diversity of form. In some districts, churchwardens and vestries discharge precisely the same functions that in others are vested in municipal officers.

The jurisdiction of the Lord Mayor does not extend beyond London proper, which comprises not more than a tenth part of the territory called London, and not more than a twentieth part of its inhabitants. Adjacent to this is the ancient city of Westminster, in which are Westminster Abbey, the Houses of Parliament, St. James's Palace, and almost all the buildings belonging to the national government. London, in its restricted sense, small as it is, includes much more than the Londinium of the ancients, the territory embraced within the wall probably constructed by Constantine, hardly a vestige of which now remains except in the names bequeathed by its gates — such as Newgate, Ludgate, Bishopsgate — to the streets upon which they opened. Temple Bar, at the western extremity of the old city, separating it from Westminster, is the only gateway now standing, and this was built by Sir Christopher Wren, after the Great Fire. The gate at Temple Bar is never closed, except when the sovereign is going to enter the old city, — a rare event, occurring only on some religious ceremonial of national significance at St. Paul's, or on some great civic festival. Then a herald sounds a trumpet before the closed gate; another herald knocks; after a parley in prescribed and ancient forms, the gate is thrown open; the Lord Mayor surrenders his sword of office to the sovereign, and receives it again from the hand of royalty.

In going westward from Temple Bar into Westminster we enter the Strand, now one of the most crowded and busy streets in London, with short and densely peopled streets leading to the river, and numerous streets and thoroughfares parting from it on the opposite side. The name has adhered to it from the time when it was a mere river-strand, — a narrow, thinly-settled suburban lane, washed by the Thames. The Strand terminates at Charing Cross, near which is the spacious and stately parish-church of St. Martin's-in-the-Fields, originally built, as its name implies, for a suburban and almost rural population. But Charing Cross is now the chief centre not only of London, but of cosmopolitan travel, omnibus lines radiating from it to every part of the city, and railways communicating, directly or by intersecting lines, with every portion of the island, and across the Channel with the Continent. What has taken place with the Strand, has equally taken place with the whole territory of London. Its different sections were formerly separated by sparsely inhabited spaces; but now the whole ground, of more than a hundred and twenty square miles, is one continuous city; there is hardly room for new streets; and if the population of nearly three millions is to have any considerable growth, it must be outside of the present limits.

The climate of London is that of England in general, modified by the coal smoke and soot from unnumbered chimneys. In summer this is not annoying. There is then a slight haze in the atmosphere, much less, however, than hangs over our great manufacturing cities in the West. I have never enjoyed more genial summer days than in a London midsummer. Yet on the brightest day there are generally sudden and brief showers, and an umbrella is as essential a part of a Londoner's apparel as his coat or hat. The summer heat is seldom oppressive. Indeed, the fashionable season lasts through midsummer. In the winter a heavy coal-mist hangs continually in the atmosphere. For an hour or two before and after noon, on a reputedly fair day, the sun may be seen, blood-red like a full moon, floating as in a sea of melted tallow. There are a few severely cold days, but the winter temperature is generally mild. I spent the first fortnight of February in London, and during that time there was not a day colder than the average of our New England May days. During that fortnight I did not once see a star. I suppose that most of the nights were fair; but starlight has not penetrating power sufficient to break through so opaque a medium as the London winter sky.

London is an admirably governed city. The police are omnipresent, and the officers on duty are the most courteous and helpful of men, giving promptly and explicitly all local information that may be desired, and taking the utmost pains to direct the wayfaring stranger. I should start without hesitation from any point in London for any other point however obscure or distant, in the full assurance that by the aid of these functionaries I should be put and kept upon the shortest and best route.

There are indeed districts where one might encounter peril by night; but in the streets which a stranger is likely to frequent, one is conscious, at any hour, however late, of entire safety from assault or molestation. Indeed, it is difficult to know when the London night begins. If there be a " dead of night," it is the hour before sunrise. But there is hardly an appreciable interval between the roll of the late coaches and the rumbling of the early market-wagons. The latest hours of my experience were dinner at eight o'clock, supper at one, and a retreat among the first from a party at half past two; and, *per contra*, I found it very difficult to coax together the materials of a breakfast before nine, and I never felt sure of accomplishing any out-of-door purpose till the sun was at least half-way to the meridian.

One of the great charms of London to an American consists in the identification of the very spots familiar to him as often recurring in English books, or associated with the great names in English literature. Thus, in Fetter Lane we find the dwelling-house of Dryden, — a high, narrow building, in the quaintest style, entirely unchanged, except that the ground-floor is fitted up as a beer and ale shop, — a use which would not have been unwelcome to the poet in his life-time. The old Fleet prison, the not infrequent home of poets and authors for many generations, is indeed taken down; but, in standing on its site, it is easy to see how its publicity made it at once a scandal to the city, and a place of the most facile communication with the outside living world. Houndsditch, at first a canine cemetery, we know through books as centuries ago inhabited almost wholly by Jews. It is still their abode, and over every one of its numerous beer-shops is inscribed, " Rum and shrub during the whole of Passover," during which period fermented liquors, as well as leavened bread, are forbidden to the faithful. Little Britain remains the site of book-stalls and kindred branches of traffic. Covent Garden Market is, as of old, the greenest place in London, no flesh being sold there, but only vegetables, fruits, and flowers. Smithfield, after having been for centuries renowned for jousts and tournaments, then for other centuries alternately desecrated by criminal executions and hallowed by martyrdoms, became the greatest cattle-market in Europe, and is now awaiting I do not remember what other mode of occupancy. The present building for the Blue Coat School is new, and we cannot define the precise *habitat* of each of the men of world-wide fame who studied, starved, and suffered there; but the boys may be met every day in the neighborhood of Newgate, in the cruelly grotesque apparel ordained at the foundation more than three hundred years ago, and then intended as a menial livery, namely, a short blue gown, white bands, yellow petticoat and stockings, red girdle, and a black yarn cap, or rather mat, of the circumference of a small saucer. St. Sepulchre's Church was injured in the Great Fire, and restored in an altered style; but its magnificent and intensely sombre Gothic steeple frowns, as of old, over the sad precincts of Newgate, and its bell still tolls the final hour of those under sentence of death. Beneath the floor of this church lies the body of the great American navigator, marked only by a slab bearing the name of JOHN SMITH. The old Bow Church, so called because it was the first church in the city that was built on stone arches, perished in the Fire; but the Bow Bells, on its now venerable successor, hang in Cheapside just where Whittington heard them, and give voice to a clock that juts out from the church over the crowded sidewalk.

The parks of London form one of its most striking geographical features. There are some eight or ten of these in the very heart of the city, the smallest twice, the largest more than seven times as large as the Boston Common. Victoria Park, the newest and most beautiful, is in the extreme East End, the poorest section of the city, and was expressly designed for the health and recreation of the common people. Some of the parks are, indeed, frequented by the aristocracy. This is especially the case with Hyde Park, and the world can produce no more gorgeous show of dress, horses, and equipage, than may be seen in the afternoon (the morning of the fashionable world) on Rotten Row (a corruption of *Route du Roi*), and on the drive along that very straight sheet of water misnamed the Serpentine. But at all hours, in fair weather, you may find in the parks the very kind of persons that most need them, — invalids, students, nursery-maids, children, family groups, and worn looking men and women out on a rare holiday, — large numbers of people whose whole aspect and mien show that their express object is to breathe in fresh air, and to feast their eyes on trees, flowers, and running water. These grounds are laid out with very great beauty and in a wide diversity of style, combining forest, fountain, lawn, and flower-garden, and some of them containing rare exotics among the trees and shrubs. They must have an immense sanitary efficacy, in interposing such large open spaces between different sections of the city, no less than in their special ministry to the thousands upon thousands of their daily visitors.

In addition to the parks, there are numerous squares of various dimensions, from two to eight or ten acres, which open for many hundreds of dwellings, avenues to the light and air of heaven, and which, in the more aristocratic quarters, are laid out and planted with adequate taste and skill.

It is impossible to describe London by any general terms. No other great city is so heterogeneous, or presents so many contrasts in close proximity. The most squalid street I ever saw,[1]

---

[1] Called Church Street, no doubt from the edifice opposite to its entrance.

commences almost under the shadow of St. George's Church in Hanover Square, so noted for fashionable marriages. Similar streets, too narrow for carriage-ways, offensive to every sense, peopled with beings whose age might be determined by the depth of the deposit of filth upon their persons, wind in and out hard by the Inns of Court with their shaven lawns and their air of learned repose. In some quarters of the city, broad and deeply shaded streets, lined with stately dwellings, hear not even the distant echo of busy, tumultuous life. Some modest districts are as rural in their aspect as a New England country village; each house with its little garden. The eastern portion of the city is crowded with buildings, new, cheap, and mean. The buildings occupied by the great merchants and bankers are, for the most part, massive, substantial, but by no means showy, and many of them of venerable age. The shops, though commodious, are seldom magnificent, and none of them can bear comparison with the most attractive shops of Boston and New York. The Strand, Fleet Street, Cheapside, and Cornhill — in fact one continuous street, and the main artery of the city circulation — are thronged with such a closely stowed, multitudinous life as can be seen nowhere else in the civilized world, — a double line of pedestrians, omnibuses, carriages, and drays pressing up and down in so dense array, that the corkscrew movement is the only practicable mode of progress, and that not without frequent stoppage, and such choking of the pavement that the interlocking of wheels can be avoided only by consummate vigilance and skill. In this otherwise straight thoroughfare, St. Paul's stands as a vast barrier, and the narrowed passages around it are a maelstrom from which it seems as if the floundering vehicles could never emerge sound and whole.

The Bank of England is the centre of commercial life. It is a sombre building of gray stone, with no pretension to architectural beauty, with no windows on the outside, and, so far as it admits the light of day, receiving it through windows overlooking an inclosed court-yard. Some idea of the immensity of this institution may be formed from the fact that no less than eleven hundred people, including armed sentries, are employed on the premises. All the printing for the Bank is done within the building. The notes are never reissued, and the notes returned are cancelled, registered, filed, and kept seven years, so that if there be any question about any individual note, it can be answered at the Bank. Nearly a hundred persons are employed on the notes that come in from day to day. Here, and at other English banks, gold is not counted, but weighed. You present a check for twenty pounds, and the teller takes up gold in a shovel and throws enough into a scale for the index to point at the right weight. From this weight there cannot be the deviation of a grain. There are, in the Bank of England, several machines for testing gold pieces, in constant operation. The pieces are put into a cylinder slightly inclined. If a piece be too large, as it probably will be if a counterfeit of lighter and baser metal, it will not take its place in the cylinder; if one be too small, at a certain point of its descent it is jerked out as if by unseen fingers. At a lower point each piece drops into a balance from which, if too light, it is jerked out; while the pieces of normal size and weight fall into a hopper below.

The Royal Exchange stands not far from the Bank, the third building on the site, its predecessors having been destroyed by fire. It is an immense building, with pillars and pilasters of the Corinthian order, with a light and graceful central tower, with ample space on the principal floor for the congregating of merchants and bankers, and with spacious and elegant apartments, occupied by Lloyds' and other similar establishments. Here and at the Bank one is overwhelmed with the evidence of wealth in perpetual transit, beyond the power of thought to measure or of figures to designate.

The same impression of multitudinousness, vastness, opulence, and intense activity that is made upon the stranger as he passes through the principal streets and marts of the city, rests upon him equally as he rows or steams on the Thames. At Liverpool one sees the still life of commerce, — such forests of masts lying tier upon tier in the dock, and jammed together as if there were neither exit for the imprisoned ships, nor room for the entrance of another. But the Thames is hardly less a crowded thoroughfare than the Strand. Its consistency of swirling mud might leave you almost in doubt, on a windy day, whether the dust that flies in your face is blown off from the shore, or rises from the river on whose bosom you are floating. But, however this may be, there is incessant motion. There are London steamers leaving and taking passengers at frequent stairs; for the expedition and cheapness of this mode of transit — a penny fare for several miles — make it a preferred method for a large proportion of the city travel. There are steamers to cheap watering-places and places of amusement, swarming with passengers; and steamers to various Continental ports. The flags of all nations may be passed on the stream, and laden vessels are arriving and departing every moment, while unnumbered row-boats are threading their serpentine way, surging in the wakes of steamers, darting under the bows of merchantmen, shooting out into the mêlée from docks and landing-stairs.

The river is crossed by several bridges of the most solid workmanship. It is a myth that

"London Bridge is broken down."

A more substantial piece of masonry the earth bears not on its bosom. An army of elephants might trample over it, and it would not vibrate under their tread.

The Thames Tunnel is a magnificent mistake. It was designed as an avenue for foot travel; but it is so far below the centre of the city, that it accommodates very little travel of business or necessity, and those who pass through it are principally strangers from the rural districts, or foreigners. It is the most lonely, I might say the only lonely place in London; and I can hardly conceive that the paltry toll of visitors can more than pay for the lighting. I took a boat at London Bridge, and was rowed two or three miles to the site of the Tunnel. Then I descended several long flights of steps, found myself in a gas-lighted corridor, and thence crossed the river under its bed by a narrow arched way about half a mile in length, gloomy, damp, almost slimy. Along the walls are numerous booths for the sale of beer, lemonade, eatables, and paltry trinkets, all at fancy prices. There are two of these ways. One only was then open to the public. A city railway company has since purchased the Tunnel, and is about to lay its track over one or both of the roadways. Satisfied with my submarine passage, I very gladly emerged into daylight by another series of staircases on the Wapping side, and took a steamer thence to Charing Cross.

In professing to describe London, I ought not to omit the buildings identified with it in history. But here I must run the risk of describing what many of my readers have seen, and many more have often read about. However, as I shall draw my materials from my own notes, I may chance to specify what others have overlooked.

I will first say a few words concerning the Tower of London. This lies on the north bank of the Thames, at the eastern corner of the old city. There must have been a fortification here in the Roman times; for it is a point which could not have been left unguarded. But the oldest part of the present pile is the White Tower in the centre, known to have been built by William the Conqueror. What is now called the Tower is a confused cluster of buildings, most of them extremely old, and some of them very lofty and imposing, though without any striking architectural beauty, surrounded by a turreted wall, — the wall surrounded by a moat now dry and grass-grown, and containing within its inclosure a park or parade-ground of moderate extent. It was formerly relied on as the chief military defence of the city, though, should England's floating wooden walls and iron bulwarks fail, it would present but feeble resistance to the improved modes of modern warfare. It is, however, manned by a considerable body of troops, and contains the principal supply of all arms, except artillery, for both the army and the navy. It is interesting mainly for its relics, curiosities, and historical associations. The crown-jewels are kept here, — the *koh-i-noor* among the rest. This immense diamond of course challenges admiration;

but it is too large for any conceivable use, and therefore its very magnitude detracts from its beauty. In one apartment are the suits of steel and chain armor that belonged to all the English kings that ever wore such armor, as also suits bearing the names of many renowned knights and nobles. These are arranged as if in battle-array, the figures representing the former owners on horseback, the horses also in full plate armor, and the squires, similarly encased, each standing at his master's side. There are also in the armory materials for a complete history of the art of war, — specimens of ancient, antique, and foreign weapons and defensive apparatus of every description, and from almost every nation under heaven. In another apartment are preserved thumbscrews, boots, racks, and divers instruments of torture, — a sight cheering and gladdening to those who believe in human progress, and know that such instruments can never be employed again by civilized man; arousing, too, some ancestral pride, for the modes of torture here indicated are humanity and mercy, compared with those the mementos of which are to be found in Nuremberg and other continental cities.

I felt no little interest in seeing the octagonal chamber in which Sir Walter Raleigh was confined for twelve years, with his bed-room, excavated in the prison-wall, which is here seventeen feet thick. The room, for many centuries used principally for state-prisoners, bears unerased on its walls the inscriptions made by its inmates, many of them very elaborate, some poetical, some pictorial; and a list of the names here written would comprise not a few who wore out their lives in duress or closed them on the scaffold, because the world was not worthy of them. The block and axe used for the execution of the two wives of Henry VIII. and of Lady Jane Grey, are shown to all visitors. But I need not proceed with this enumeration. There is no end of the memorials of tyranny and violence treasured up in this sad spot; while beneath the floor of the plain and gloomy chapel, still used for Divine service, lie the remains of almost all that were beheaded within these walls.

I pass from the Tower to Westminster Abbey. This majestic pile has been the work of eight centuries, and hardly a year elapses without additions or restorations, all in keeping with the solemn grandeur of the original design, though it is easy to point out incongruities, and marks of the prevailing taste of successive ages. But a Gothic building needs not perfect symmetry. Its vast outlines, its depths of shadow, its innumerable details, of which only a small part can be taken in at any one view, permit much of the diversity which makes a landscape beautiful; and not a few of the European cathedrals present, like this, a history of architecture, and are only the more grand and impressive, because they seem less the conception of one mind than the growth of centuries. The main building of Westminster Abbey is a perfect church, with choir, nave, and transepts; and within the church are numerous chapels, partly closed, yet so far open that in certain positions one can get a full view of the entire length and breadth of the edifice. The church occupies one side of a quadrangle, of which the other three sides are lined with rows of cloisters. There are numerous painted windows of various styles and ages; and the stone-work of the interior is elaborately carved from the ceiling to the floor.

The church and the cloisters are full of monuments and of monumental inscriptions. One can hardly step without treading on a name, and frequently an illustrious name. The walls are covered with memorial tablets, often of great elaborateness and beauty, often more venerable than beautiful. On the floor are innumerable structures of greater or less artistical pretension, — many of them temples in themselves, — of every conceivable style, in brass, iron, bronze, alabaster, marble, — with life-size figures in every possible position, — frequently groups representing a numerous family; for instance, a father laid out in state, his wife weeping over him, a troop of children arranged on either side of the couch. There are many royal monuments, remarkable at once for their sumptuousness, the multitudinousness of their details, and their skillful execution, which generally far exceeds the artistical merit of the design. Some of the most costly monuments, of alabaster, with gilded mouldings and bands, have become utterly black with age.

Among so many memorial structures there are, of course, the widest diversities of artistical genius and no-genius. Many of them are rude in conception by reason of their antiquity. Many are showy and gaudy by reason of their newness. Not one is worthy of the world-wide celebrity which belongs to such works of the kind as may be seen in Vienna, Venice, Florence, and Rome. Some of the most ostentatious, some of the most genuinely beautiful, commemorate names else unknown, and some, names only too well-known. The inevitable John Smith, as the Latin epitaph has it, *de prosapia Smithorum Northumbriensium* (from the stock of Northumberland Smiths), has his many virtues transmitted to posterity in a lofty and elegant marble structure large enough to be generic in its purpose. The Poets' Corner is profoundly interesting, as containing the dust or cenotaphs of some thirty or more of the most illustrious poets of the kingdom, from Chaucer downward; but interspersed with these are memorials of about an equal number of persons whose claim to a sepulture so honored, however valid, has faded from the memory of man. Not only there, however, but in every part of the edifice, one is amazed by the affluence of the foremost names in science and literature, arts and arms, state and church. Few names are wanting of those which History could not spare, nor Fame erase from her scroll. It is, if I mistake not, an entirely unique cemetery, — the only national place of sepulture in the world, — the only spot whose monuments epitomize a people's history. Most appropriately, as under a guard of honor drafted from the centuries of the dead, are kept in the Abbey the coronation-chairs of the sovereign and the royal consort, — the former having fastened under the seat the huge stone of Scone, on which the Scottish monarchs were crowned. Had I been left to my own judgment, I should have supposed these to be penitential chairs, belonging to the old conventual régime, so cruelly straight, stiff, and hard are they, rude and unsightly too, without a particle of ornament. Happily, coronation occurs but once in a lifetime.

The choir of the abbey-church is screened in part, is handsomely fitted up in a somewhat modern style, and is used for daily and Sunday services, making an auditorium about as large as the average of our city churches. The nave has no furniture except some thousands of plain flag-bottomed chairs, which are stacked during the week, and arranged on Sundays for one of those evening services for the people, which are among the aggressions upon the heathenism of the great city, inaugurated by the present energetic Bishop of London.

St. Paul's is, undoubtedly, in many respects a

splendid failure. A temple or cathedral is even more the work of its age than of its architect. It embodies the sentiment of the generation at whose bidding it has birth. No genius, however exalted, can impose upon a people a house of worship unsuited to its conceptions of grandeur and devotion. St. Paul's was built too late, — at a period when the religious sentiment, however sincere, had ceased to embody in material forms its whole energy and fervor, thus petrified into enduring life. It was erected after the Great Fire, toward the close of the seventeenth century. The architect, Sir Christopher Wren, was thwarted in his plans by the condition of the kingdom. It was in his heart to build, on the site of the immense cathedral that had been burned, a church that should be especially fitted for Protestant worship, and should, at the same time, be worthy of its place as the cathedral of the great metropolis. But his plans were made under the last of the Roman Catholic kings, a little before the Revolution of 1688; and James, determined that the Protestant ritual should be abolished before the completion of the edifice, overruled the architect in almost all essential points. The result was a compromise, which Romanism would accept with great hesitation, and which Protestantism finds but imperfectly availing. Add to this, that by court cabal Wren was dismissed from public employment before the building was finished, and that his incompetent successor made additions against which he vehemently protested.

The edifice suffers, also, from its situation. There is no point from which it can be seen in perspective, nor yet can the front be seen in full at a distance of more than a hundred feet. St. Paul's Churchyard has long since ceased to be, except in name; Paternoster Row, Amen Corner, and Ave Maria Lane, are, I apprehend, resonant of more curses than prayers; and the cathedral retains little more than the ground it stands on. It suffers, too, from the foul atmosphere. Tradition says that it was built of white marble. Large portions of it are now of continuous black; other parts are slightly streaked with a dingy white. But the dome, which is seen at a very considerable distance, is surpassed in grandeur only by that of St. Peter's, being at once massive and airy, and as it looms up through a dense fog seeming to float upon the clouds. There are, also, at the corners of the front or western portal, two steeples of exquisite grace and beauty, of a style, I think, peculiar to Wren, and repeated by him with variations, but with the same general effect, in all his churches.

The interior is symmetrical and grand in its design, but very unequally finished. The choir is elaborately and beautifully fitted for worship, and here are performed the regular daily and Sunday services. The space under the dome, capable of seating an audience of four thousand, is used for a people's service on Sunday evening, furnished only with flag-bottomed chairs, and lighted by jets of gas springing from the circumference of the dome. In a loft in one of the transepts is an immense organ, played only on state occasions; that in common use stands in the choir. A large part of the interior — adapted to the paraphernalia of Roman Catholic worship — contains only monuments and memorial tablets; and the architectural effect is greatly impaired by the superabundance of unoccupied and dreary space in the floor and on the walls. The style of the edifice is Composite, with a preponderance of the Corinthian order, wherever the conditions imposed on the architect admitted the employment of that order.

Among the institutions of its kind in the British empire, and indeed in the whole world, no one takes precedence of the British Museum. The library alone contains nearly a million of volumes, with room for half a million more. The most noteworthy part of the establishment is the reading-room, a rotunda one hundred and forty feet in diameter, and of a height nearly equal to the diameter, from the floor to the summit of the dome, which has a larger span than any other dome in existence. In this room, on aisles which radiate from the centre, are seats for about five hundred readers, each seat being furnished with a desk and writing materials. Any properly introduced and certified person, of either sex, may frequent this apartment. On a central desk is a manuscript catalogue of the library in many volumes; and in cases set in the circular wall of the reading-room are reference books, to the number of twenty thousand and more. Any authorized reader, by writing on a card his name, the number of his desk, and the titles of the books he wants to read or consult, can send for any book in the whole library, however rare or costly, and can have the use of the same secured to him from day to day, by inserting his card in it when he leaves his desk.

Another department of the Museum is devoted to the colossal bulls and lions, and the many other objects of curious interest, brought from Nineveh; another, to similar massive works from Egypt. In another are the Elgin marbles, with a vast collection of architectural and sculptural fragments from Athens, among which are some of the reputed works of Phidias. There are also immense collections in every department of Natural History; collections, too, of British antiquities, and of antiquities and curiosities of all ages and nations, costumes, weapons, culinary utensils, ornaments, skulls, in fine, everything that can illustrate history or ethnology.

In the basement are sitting-rooms and refectories, so that one may pursue his studies till nightfall without neglecting those more material needs, the regular supply of which the normal Englishman never omits or postpones. The whole building is open daily for all registered readers, and on certain days in the week for the entire public, not only without fee, but with printed notices that any attendant known to receive a fee is peremptorily dismissed from the service.

Of this institution the National Museum at South Kensington is, in some respects, a duplicate, in others a supplement. The buildings and grounds at South Kensington are on the most extensive scale, including a large botanic garden with greenhouses; a collection of models of patents; the National Portrait Gallery; a gallery of paintings, containing large collections of Turner's and Landseer's works, and, above all, Raphael's original cartoons for the Vatican; specimens of the products of all the arts in all times and lands; models of artistical objects, from Trajan's Column downward: models, drawings, and studies for pupils in the arts. But I must pause. It is easier to say what is not there than to tell what is there.

In the style of the old divines, I want to close this chapter by a "practical application." These institutions are sustained, regarded, treated, and used, not as mere show-places, but as educational institutions for the people. One cannot visit them without seeing more persons who come to learn than who come merely to gaze. Now any and every institution which essays this educational office has emphatic claims on the support of a people whose sole safety lies in the intelligence of its voters. We have one such institution — local only because it must have a definite locality, national, nay, cosmopolitan in its purpose and administration — the Zoölogical Museum at Cambridge, already superior in many respects to the corresponding department in the British Museum. It is largely and generously educating our youth in the science which it illustrates, and is yielding to the State, for the funds which have built and endowed it, the most ample return in the liberal culture which it imparts. Shall it be suffered to languish by a community whose annual waste of wealth would suffice for its permanent support, its rapid growth, and its ultimate superiority to any other similar collection in the civilized world?

CHAPTER III.

SKETCHES OF TRAVEL IN THE BRITISH ISLANDS.

Scottish Lakes. — Highland Scenery. — Ben Nevis. — Killarney. — The Jaunting-car. — The Gap of Dunloe. — The Irish Lakes. — Mendicancy. — The English Lakes. — Memorials of Wordsworth. — Sheffield. — Manufactures of Iron and Steel. — Edinburgh. — Old and New City. — Scott's Monument. — Dublin. — St. Patrick's.

The lake regions of the three kingdoms of Great Britain are all attractive and charming; while each has its own peculiar characteristics. As the order in which I saw them may have affected my impressions of them, I will preserve the same order in my description.

The Caledonian Canal is the name given to a series of cuttings and locks, by means of which Scotland — before deeply indented by the Friths of Moray and Clyde, and with several lakes and rivers between them — is completely bisected for ship-navigation, from the German Ocean to the Atlantic, Inverness and Glasgow being the usual termini, at least for pleasure travel. On this route I took passage in a steamer from Inverness, the capital of the Highlands, passed through Lochs Dochfour, Ness, Oich, and Lochy, then, to avoid the delay of a long series of locks, made a detour of a mile in an omnibus, and reëmbarked on Loch Eil for Oban, where I passed the night.

This day's navigation carried me through the heart of the Highlands. No wonder is it that here has been found so rich inspiration for poetry and song. The route lies through constantly varying mountain scenery, much of it intensely beautiful, much of it hardly less grand, solemn, and majestic than the wildest mountain regions of Switzerland. We left the steamer for an hour to visit the Falls of the river Foyers, a sight which Professor Wilson declared worth a walk of a thousand miles. We have, indeed, immeasurably grander falls in America. This is a mere thread of a cataract; but it descends through the most picturesque of chasms, with such a setting of rock and forest scenery as makes the tiny white sheet transcendently lovely. While the lower portion passes into Loch Ness in a shadow too dense to be pierced by the beams of noonday, the upper part is open to the sun's rays, and the spray presents the full spectrum of prismatic colors.[1]

[1] Burns commemorates these Falls in a passage remarkable for the almost prosaic accuracy of the description, and, at the same time, not destitute of poetical beauty.

"Among the heathy hills and rugged woods,
 The roaring Foyers forms his mossy floods;
 Till full he dashes on the rocky mounds,
 Where, through a shapeless breach, his stream rebounds·
 As high in air the bursting torrents flow,
 As deep receding surges foam below,

Of all the mountains Ben Nevis is the sovereign. Viewed from the lakes it has the aspect of a colossal elephant, crouching on the summit of a lower mountain, while its color in the shade is that of the elephant's hide, which it resembles also in seams and corrugations, — deep fissures, doubtless, but which reminded me of the wrinkles in the animal's skin. In many of the clefts near the summit are patches of perpetual snow, and they lie at such an angle as in the morning sunlight to present the roseate hue often seen among the Alps. Ben Nevis is but one of a myriad of Bens of all shapes and dimensions, almost numerous enough to represent the old tribe of Benjamin, man by man. Some of them are wooded to their summits, some covered with ferns and mosses, the lowest with grass. Some are tilled for several hundred feet from the base; many have bare crowns and precipitous sides; and many are tumbled about in such tumultuous raggedness and desolation, as to remind one of the day when the earth-born giants " piled Ossa upon Pelion, and leafy Olympus upon Ossa."

We passed many of the sites most famous in legend, tradition, and poetry, and by several ruined castles that had borne a distinguished name and

> Prone down the rock the whitening sheet descends,
> And viewless Echo's ear, astonished, rends.
> Dim seen through rising mists and ceaseless showers,
> The hoary cavern wide surrounding lowers.
> Still through the gap the struggling river toils,
> And still below the horrid cauldron boils."

part in Highland warfare. The old castle of Urquhart, which was captured by Edward I. in 1303, still frowns from a bold promontory over Loch Ness. On a rock on the margin of Loch Oich is the dismantled castle of Invergarry, which was the rallying point of the clan subject to the " Lord of the Isles." We passed near a boulder of several tons' weight which the peasantry of the neighborhood still believe to have been thrown by Rob Roy when hard pressed by his pursuers; and the skeptical are silenced by the question, " How then came it here ? " It differs, in point of fact, as to its geological structure, from all other rocks in the vicinity. Inverlochy Castle, built by the Banquo of Macbeth's time, covers a large area on the shore of the river Lochy, and a path below its walls still bears the name of " Banquo's Walk." We went far up into Glencoe, the most sombre of glens, deeply wooded, with the wildest of mountains frowning over it, — a fit scene for one of the most horrible massacres that ever defiled the records of humanity. We saw the very ferry over a rapid current, where Lord Ullin's daughter was lost. There is a lighthouse hard by it now, built, no doubt, to prevent the recurrence of a like calamity to runaway maidens. I inquired whether she had ever been heard of, and a Scotch gentleman, who seemed very intelligent, surprised me by saying that he had never heard of her. As his residence was near the ferry, I concluded that since her father " was left lamenting," there had been no tidings of her. But there is no end to the exciting associations and memories connected with that day's voyage.

Oban, where we landed for the night, is the usual starting-point from the South for a Highland tour, and a place of fashionable resort, well worth visiting for its lake and mountain scenery. Oban lies on Loch Linnhe, and the first two or three hours of the next day's voyage were on that lake. We passed through the Sound of Lorn; but no one could show me "the house of fair Ellen of Lorn." The Island of Mull, which is very mountainous, with some peaks nearly as high as Ben Nevis, was in sight for several hours. We emerged from the Lake region by the Crinan Canal, and after navigating a series of inlets from the sea, came into the broad Frith of Clyde, verdure, cultivation, and beauty taking the place of the sterile and awful grandeur of the Highlands so gradually, that it was hard to say where the one type faded and the other began to predominate.

Of the Scottish lake region, wild and solemn sublimity is the prevailing characteristic; awe and adoration give the key-note to the traveller's thought; and beneath the rude, bold, colossal outlines of nature, man and his works are utterly dwarfed and almost lost from sight.

I visited the Killarney Lakes on a charming day in July. There was a slight haze, like a veil of the thinnest gauze, between the sun and the earth, and just clouds enough to cast ever varying and flickering shadows on the hills and waters. I started from the town of Killarney in that peculiar Irish institution, a jaunting-car, which it may be worth a parenthesis to describe. The jaunting-car is roofless, and has two seats placed back to back, like the seats of an omnibus reversed, each seat fitted to hold two persons. If there be two or four passengers, the driver is perched in some inscrutable way in front; if one or three, he preserves the balance by occupying one of the seats, placing himself at an angle of forty-five degrees with his horse. One not "to the manner born" finds it necessary to hold on, by one hand at least. The jolting is indescribable, — a compound motion for which I would defy the most astute mathematician to construct the scientific formula.

A drive of five or six miles from Killarney, through scenery gradually rising from beautiful to grand, brought me to the Gap of Dunloe, through which a pony, evidently aboriginal, took me, for four miles, over what merits to be called a bridle path, only because it is actually thus used every pleasant summer's day. The Gap is a notch or cleft between mountains more than three thousand feet high, — in some places so narrow that three men would ride abreast with difficulty, with precipitous walls that admit only the midday sun; in other parts, in its increased breadth and the gentler acclivity of its sides, reminding me of the Franconia Notch in New Hampshire. It terminates in what is called the Black Valley, by far the broadest part of the defile, but with so nearly perpendicular cliffs frowning over it as to keep it in perpetual shadow.

From this valley I suddenly emerged upon the upper of the three Lakes. While far from presenting the multitudinous panorama of mountains which I had admired in the Scotch Highlands, this is more closely walled in by mountains than any of the Scotch lakes, and by mountains offering a very great diversity of scenery,— some bald, craggy, and precipitous; most of them, however, glowing with a rich purple tint from the heather that clothes them from the summit to the base. There are several deeply recessed bays, with tall cliffs projecting over them. Nothing can be more picturesque than this lake; but on its bosom one is shut out from the whole world beside,— the position is almost like that of the crater of a volcano. In one of the bays lies the last of the serpents, which St. Patrick enticed into a box by false representations, then shut the lid upon him, and threw the box into the water. I questioned our boatmen about the story, and found that they had no doubt of its truth. They said that on the approach of a storm the snake always makes a great commotion in the water by attempting to get out of the box. I learned from other authorities that the water at that point is very deep, and therefore very turbulent when a storm is impending. The passage from the upper to the middle lake is by a river five or six miles long, more than serpentine in its convolutions, and so narrow that flowers might have been plucked from both sides of our boat at the same moment.

The middle, or Muckross Lake, is less wild than the upper, but no less beautiful. It has mountain scenery on one side, contrasted, on the other, with the richest *Irish* views of alternating hill, valley, meadow, wheat-field, grass-field, forest, and sheep-walk. I emphasize *Irish;* for the green of Ireland is so intense a green, that I could not have imagined it without seeing it, and had I previously chanced upon a picture representing it as it is, I should have supposed it overwrought, unnatural, and impossible. The tint can be matched in vividness only by those brilliant dyes which we sometimes see in shells from the ocean.

A very short passage leads into the lower lake, or Lough Leane. This is by far the largest of the three, and the least picturesque, yet inexpressibly beautiful, — its surroundings consisting wholly of park, lawn, and forest, planned, cultivated, and adorned with consummate skill, and maintained at heavy cost by the two titled proprietors. On a peninsula between the middle and lower lakes, are the charming ruins of Muckross Abbey, richly festooned with ivy, — the floor and walls of the church retaining numerous monuments of the dead of earlier centuries, while the gentry and people of substance in the neighborhood still use the sacred inclosure as a cemetery. On an island in the lower lake, close by the shore, are the ruins of Ross Castle, which was anciently a celebrated stronghold in Irish warfare, and in the great Civil War was the last of the Irish fortresses to surrender to the Parliamentary forces. So much of this castle remains, that one might easily construct a plan of it, as it was when fully occupied and defended. The peasantry believe that its original proprietor, the great chieftain O'Donoghue, still lives in the lake, and makes his appearance every first of May.

I ought not to forget the human part of the scenery of this beautiful region. In and to more senses than one I found there a verification of the familiar lines of Bishop Heber's hymn,

> " Where every prospect pleases,
> And only man is vile."

It is impossible to estimate the multitude of men, children, and especially women, who live chiefly as beasts of prey, and almost drive the desperate traveller into the water, where alone he can be quit of them. Some have ponies to let; some, bugles to blow; some, guns to fire. Then there are numerous venders of bogwood ornaments, and of articles manufactured from the wood of the arbutus. There are blind men, with wives to hold their hats; and legless men, with children to run after pennies; and idiots who, incapable of learning anything else, are adepts in the science of mendicancy. The women bring out goats' milk and *mountain-dew*, (the Hibernian euphemism for whiskey), and run along with their bottles as fast as the car or pony can go at full speed,— always so civil and good-natured that you cannot speak rudely to them, and opposing the resistance of a laugh or an attempted joke to every rebuff. And

> "O, did ye ne'er hear of Kate Kearney?
> She lives by the Lake of Killarney,"

and a granddaughter of hers was among the most eloquent and persistent of my tormentors. I had heard much of Swiss and Italian beggary. Its pressure and urgency bear no comparison with the leechlike tenacity of the Irish mendicant. Language, or even gesture, can convey a negative to the sturdiest Continental beggar; the Irish mind is impermeable to a negative. Even if you aver that your silver and copper are exhausted; if you show your empty purse, or turn your pockets inside out, the secretive habits of the people preclude their belief in your veracity, and sustain their faith in some recondite hoard which their importunity may open.

The Killarney lake region, exclusive of the Gap of Dunloe, is more weird than grand, *bizarre* rather than wild, a fit scene for fairy revels, but not for the sanguinary legends of fierce gods and savage men that seem the indigenous growth of the Highland lake country.

The English lake region is preëminently slumberous in its character. Everything about it suggests repose and indolence; even literary *activity* seems out of place there; and De Quincey might have revelled there in waking dreams without the aid of opium. The waters are surrounded by mountains, as they are called, and they are high enough for the clouds and mist-wreaths to rest and play upon their tops and sides; but the clouds seem rather to stoop to the hills, than the hills to rise to the normal altitude of the clouds. The clouds do undoubtedly hang low; for it rains there almost every day in summer. And I have never had glimpses of beauty surpassing those that broke in upon me there in lucid intervals between showers, when the mist-wreaths became rainbows, and the clouds masses of silvery smoke, while the mountain-tops and hillsides shot out light-beams of dazzling green, as the sun was reflected with intensest brilliancy from grass, ferns, and foliage. The mountains are all green, and nowhere else have I seen vegetation so rich. The trees are such masses of leafage, that one can hardly see their limbs, while close-clinging vines mantle their trunks and hide the bark. The walls, houses, and stables seem mere frames for ivy to climb upon, and it requires no little use of the shears to keep unobstructed window-room enough to let daylight into the dwellings. There are very few rocks, and they are, all but one, covered with moss, and hung with ivy.

The houses are dotted round in the most charming spots, now on a peninsular tongue of land, then on a spur of a hill, with a steep acclivity behind, then in some dell, by the side of a rivulet, with a garden or a serpentine walk climbing a hill in the rear. There are many fine cascades, some falling from a great height.

The lakes are all small. Windermere, the largest, is ten or twelve miles long. Rydal Water is hardly larger than many artificial ponds in private grounds. Grasmere may cover some two or three hundred acres. Conistone, which is not much larger, is navigated by a steamer so liliputian that it looks like a model for the shelf of a museum. Six passengers would crowd it; a dozen would sink it.

Of course, the memorials of Wordsworth are a prominent object of interest. His home was a small, thin, plain two story house, of rough stone plastered with a grayish stucco, almost hidden by trees and shrubbery, and almost wholly covered with ivy. It is on the brow and near the summit of Rydal Mount, which is a spur of Nab Scar, — the highest mountain in that vicinity. Behind it is the poet's favorite walk, — a narrow footpath, first ascending, then descending toward the highway. On the opposite side of the road, just over Rydal Water, reached by a short flight of steps, is the rock where Wordsworth wrote a great many of his poems. He would sit there, day after day, close by the highway, yet screened from it by the intervening foliage, with the little lake just under his feet, and with scenery of tropical luxuriance and beauty all around him. This is the one bare rock to which I just now referred. The frequent feet of pilgrims will not let the moss or ivy grow upon it. Grasmere church-yard, two or three miles from his house, was his family burying-place. There lie the bodies of Wordsworth, his sister, and his children, and of his wife and her sister, — their resting-places marked by head and foot stones of plain black slate. Hard by is the grave of Hartley Coleridge, with a simple, graceful monument of white marble. In the Grasmere church, on the wall of an arch against which Wordsworth's accustomed pew is built, is a mural monument to him, of Italian marble, with an excellent bust of him in alto-relievo below the inscription. The church is, in its exterior, massive and imposing; in its interior, rude in the extreme, — the general structure having undergone no change for seven or eight centuries, and the present pews having been built in the sixteenth century.

Among the many dwellings hallowed by personal associations, I had peculiar pleasure in visiting Fox How, Dr. Arnold's favorite retreat. The house is moderately large and very pretty, not, however, quaint or picturesque, close by a little winding river (*brook* we should call it in America), deeply embowered in trees and shrubbery, with a high hill directly in front, — as completely shut out from all the world's sights and sounds as Robinson Crusoe's home could have been.

But I need not multiply descriptions of particular sites. What I have said may suffice to illustrate the peculiar charm of the Lake country for men of unworldly habitudes, and to show why it is that the literature to which it has given birth, is less renowned for strength than for beauty.

On my tour to the English lakes, my point of departure and return was Sheffield, and, though with no other association, except it be that of contrast, I will make the transition in my narrative. The existence of this city of more than two hundred thousand inhabitants is an item of assured belief, rather than an observed fact. It can be seen only during a general and prolonged strike. A dense cloud of smoke and soot hangs perpetually over the city, slightly relieved on Sunday, yet not then admitting any clear sunlight. The richer citizens emerge from the smoke at nightfall, and live on cheery, healthy heights in the suburbs, in sumptuous villas, from whose windows and grounds the cityward view is precisely what that of Sodom and Gomorrah was, the day after they were burned. I had my domicile with a kind friend in that favored region; but I had previously dined at the *Black* Swan Inn, — most appropriately so called; for not even a swan could keep white there.

The whole neighborhood is beautiful. From the rich valleys of the Sheaf and Derwent the ground rises into heath-covered moors, from which the eye can range over a vast extent of territory, while the lungs inhale an atmospheric tonic with every breath.

There is, within the city, very little of architectural splendor or beauty, and an American manufacturer would be amazed at the generally paltry and shabby aspect of the great establishments whose names are known all the world over. The extensive manufactories are unified, not by the builder's original act, but by bridges or covered ways that connect neighboring edifices else unrelated, or by unsymmetrical extensions and outbuildings.

Cutlery is nominally the staple of Sheffield; but steel and all possible manufactures of iron and steel are made here. There are not a few immense forges and foundries, and the manufactories of Bessemer steel would seem on too large a scale to be worked except by Cyclopean artisans, till we see how deftly the steam-giant tilts the huge cauldron of molten metal, and poises on his finger's ends red-hot bars as large as rafters. Of course, gold and silver electroplating, as among the iron arts, is to be witnessed here. I need not describe the process, it has been so recently and so ably portrayed by Mr. Parton in the "Atlantic Monthly"; but the great diversity of objects to which it is applied, the uniformity and completeness of the work, and the nicety with which the thickness of the plating can be predetermined and tested, filled me with wonder and delight.

No name is better known in America than that of the Messrs. Rogers, in connection with every form of cutlery. Their show-room is magnificent, exhibiting a large assortment of electro-plated ware, as well as of cutlery, together with no small amount of goods in gold and silver. The firm, however, makes nothing but cutlery, and my readers may form some idea of the magnitude of its operations, when I say that its complement of operatives exceeds six hundred, and that for knife-handles alone, a ton of ivory is used every month, the ivory bearing a very small proportion to the horn and bone consumed. A pocket-knife that is sold for sixpence, passes through more than twenty different hands. The operations are performed, for the most part, in small, dingy, mean-looking apartments, each large enough for from two to six workmen. Steam-gearing is carried through all the rooms, and steam-power is put into requisition where it would seem the part of idiocy to reject it; but a great many of the processes, which in this country would be conducted by machinery, are performed by the unaided hand. Indeed, I think that from a third to a half of the time and labor of man that it costs in Sheffield to make any given piece of cutlery, would make it in America. I said so to the foreman of the Rogers firm. He replied that he was well aware of this, but that the intense jealousy of new machinery and of labor-saving processes on the part of the operatives, made it dangerous to introduce improvements, — experiments of that kind having frequently resulted in the extensive destruction of property and life. I noticed the same difference, due, undoubtedly, to the same cause, between the Sheffield nail, tack, and screw factories and those which I have seen in Taunton and in Providence.

From Sheffield I went north to Edinburgh, and I will ask my readers to go thither with me for a little while. Edinburgh has a weird, unreal look, like a city in cloudland or dreamland. It is made up of two distinct portions, the Old and the New City, separated by a broad and deep ravine. In the New City are wide streets, fashionable hotels, genteel houses, handsome shops, public squares, monuments, statues in bronze and marble. In the Old City are a few streets of moderate width, some good houses, most of the churches, and the University; but the greater part of it is in narrow streets, with old tumble-down houses (many of them once palaces), from six to ten stories high, — these streets intersected by *closes* and *wynds* (that is, lanes and alleys), so narrow that two persons cannot meet in them without contact, often mere tunnels, and when open above, so dark from overhanging walls — it may be fifty or sixty feet high — that their midday is feeble twilight. These portions of the city are so offensive to the nostrils, that one cannot conceive of human life being sustained in them. Yet it is sustained in such swarms that it is hard to believe one's own eyes.

I have nowhere else seen or imagined such tokens of a redundant population as in the Old City of Edinburgh. The women and children live, not merely on the sidewalk, but in the middle of the streets, and do their knitting and sewing seated in the very carriage-way, moving a little to make room for an occasional dray or wagon. In London I do not know that I saw a barefooted woman; in Edinburgh I saw none but well dressed women that were not barefooted. The poor women in Ireland dress redundantly, heap rag upon rag, and often look as if a ragbag had been emptied on their backs; in Edinburgh the poor women wear as little as they can, and, though less depraved than corresponding classes in other cities, they seem to have less of the instinct of decency than can be found in any other part of the civilized world. The only mark of cleanliness to be seen in these poorer quarters is the vast quantity of clothes always hung out to dry; for the week seems to be a continuous washing-day. The clothes are suspended on poles projecting from the windows, and are to be seen on every story, from the tenth downward.

In the Old City the poorest houses are, of course,

as elsewhere, let in single apartments. The better sort, and many also in the New City, are let in flats or half flats, and it is very common to see on each side of the street-door of a respectable house, five, six, or eight bell-pulls, with as many name-plates.

The Old City is considerably higher than the New, and there are, in some parts of it, streets under streets, making, literally, a two story town. On the side of the Old City, the intervening ravine is very precipitous. This ravine is beautiful, — a part of it as wild as Nature left it, part converted into a park or public garden, very prettily laid out, and crossed at a high level by bridges.

The royal castle, the chief military post in Edinburgh, is on the summit and brow of a precipice in the Old City, and is a confused pile of buildings of different ages, with no pretence to symmetry or beauty. The principal objects of curiosity there are the crown, sceptre, and other regalia of the Scottish kingdom; the little room in which James VI. of Scotland and I. of England was born, with a curious metrical inscription in black letter, commemorating the event and invoking blessings on the child; and, above all, a quaint little private oratory, built for her own personal use by Queen St. Margaret, in the eleventh century, and restored by the present Queen.

Holyrood Palace has so many historical and such deeply tragic associations connected with it, that one treads its halls and staircases almost with awe.

While there is much that meets the eye which tends to deepen those associations, there is very little that can feed the sense of beauty or of grandeur. There is a large gallery of portraits of royal and eminent Scotch personages who lived before the union of the crowns; but most of them are poor paintings, are less than two centuries old, and are not certainly known to have been copied from previously existing portraits, but are suspected of being inventions and not likenesses, so that they have the attraction neither of antiquity, authenticity, nor merit. Queen Mary's and Darnley's apartments are preserved as they were when they occupied them, with the very same tapestry-hangings, and much of the same furniture. Queen Mary's bed remains, with a portion of one of the blankets, and there are shown some little articles of her toilette, and her work-table. There are still distinctly visible the stains, made by Rizzio's blood, as he lay all night in the ante-chamber. Attached to the palace are the ruins of the chapel of Holyrood Abbey, which must have been, in its time, far more magnificent than any ecclesiastical edifice now left entire in the city.

Close in the rear of the Palace rises Arthur's Seat, — a hill nearly a thousand feet high, commanding from its several acclivities and from its summit, a series of surpassingly beautiful views, embracing the city, the surrounding country, the whole of the Frith of Forth, and the sea beyond its mouth. On a spur of this hill are the very picturesque ruins of St. Anthony's Chapel, and beneath it is a pellucid, living spring called St. Anthony's Well, which affords to the American his daily refreshment at home, — the rarest of all luxuries in Great Britain, — a draught of ice-cold water, the only luxury which money cannot purchase, ice being so grudgingly used that it is almost impossible to procure at hotel or restaurant water that is not tepid.

On the west of the city, and somewhat lower than Arthur's Seat, is Calton Hill, which also is rich in its views of city, country, frith, and sea, and which has, on or near its summit, the Observatory, a very tall and ungainly monument to Nelson, part of a Grecian colonnade designed to surround a temple commemorative of the heroes of Waterloo, left unfinished for want of funds, and monuments to Playfair and Dugald Stewart; while from it and near its base are seen the monuments of Hume and Burns. On the New City side of the ravine, opposite the mean and shabby house where he lived in the Old City, is a graceful monument to Allan Ramsay.

The most splendid architectural structure in Edinburgh is the monument to Sir Walter Scott. It is a Gothic edifice, terminating in a spire whose apex is two hundred feet from the ground. The lower story is an open space, in the centre of which is a magnificent marble statue of Scott, seated, with his favorite dog at his side. In the four principal niches over the lower arches, are figures in marble of prominent personages in Scott's poems and novels, and there are fifty-two other niches, designed to be similarly occupied. The monument has already cost more than fifteen thousand pounds, and the design may probably be completed by an additional expenditure of four or five thousand.

The churches of Edinburgh are, for the most part, plain, but commodious, and well adapted to Protestant worship. St. Giles' Cathedral is, externally, a vast and splendid Gothic structure; but it is now divided into three places of worship, neither of which has enough of taste or ornament within its walls to distract the attention of the worshippers.

But if the churches are plain, they are well filled and well manned. Sunday is a Sabbath-day in Edinburgh. The streets are still; there is no visible pleasure-seeking; places of business are all shut; and, except at the beginning and close of public worship, hardly a footfall is heard on the sidewalk. It was refreshing to listen to the able, elaborate, vigorous, earnest preaching of the Scotch divines, after a sojourn of several weeks in England, and to mark the rapt attention of the full audience, young and old, Bible in hand, turning to the texts quoted by the preacher, and always designated by chapter and verse. I heard Dr. Alexander, the minister of an Independent church, and Dr. Hanna,[1] of the Scotch Presbyterian Church. The Presbyterian

---

[1] The son-in-law and biographer of Dr. Chalmers.

churches have no instrumental music, and still sing the rude version of the Psalms used in the time of the Covenanters. Placards designating the tunes to be sung, are suspended in sight of the whole congregation, and all join in the psalm, with no perceptible discord, and, as seems to me, much more to the edification of the worshippers, than when the service of praise is delegated to a hired quartette.

I will close this chapter by a few words about Dublin. This is one of the most splendid cities in Europe, yet to me uninteresting, perhaps because I visited it shortly after my high enjoyment of the picturesque site and environments of Edinburgh. The streets — those that have any appreciable breadth (for there are many narrow and filthy lanes) — have a very generous width; the public buildings are numerous and imposing; there are several squares and promenades of great beauty; and the dwelling houses on the principal streets and squares look solid, ample, and opulent. The city lies on both sides of the Liffey, which is a mere estuary, and grows, as one ascends it, "beautifully less," so that of the seven or eight graceful bridges by which it is spanned, the uppermost is not half as long as the lowest. The largest building, and by far the handsomest secular building, is the Bank of Ireland, formerly the Parliament House. The Castle, where the Lord Lieutenant has his residence, and where the most important functions of government are discharged, is a strongly fortified group of buildings, of various ages and styles, but with no one edifice or apartment that claims special mention. The Custom-house, Exchange, and Post-office are spacious and elegant modern structures, of style and proportions adapted to their uses, rather than conformed to any architectural order or idea. Among many monuments and monumental statues, the principal is Nelson's Monument, noteworthy, not for its beauty, but for its conspicuous position and its massiveness. It is a huge marble cylinder, surmounted by a colossal statue of Nelson. By the way, there is hardly a place in Great Britain that possesses any work of the kind, which has not one commemorative of Nelson.

The oldest church is Christ Church, which was begun more than a thousand years ago, and exhibits traces of the workmanship of every age from then till now. One of the original entrances has been preserved. It is so low that it would seem to have been built by a race of troglodytes, and yet it bears vestiges of no mean architectural taste and ambition.

The Cathedral of St. Patrick is in the most wretched district of the city, surrounded by the dirtiest lanes and the foulest population. It stands on the spot where, according to tradition, St. Patrick baptized the king. It was built in the twelfth century, and for nearly three centuries was one of the most magnificent churches in Europe; but it was much injured in the civil disturbances of the fifteenth and sixteenth centuries, then was secularized and surrendered to the law-courts, and finally was occupied as a stable by Cromwell's soldiers. Though subsequently given back to sacred uses, it remained in a dilapidated and almost ruinous condition till within a few years. It has now been restored, virtually rebuilt, at the cost of a hundred and forty thousand pounds, by the munificence of Mr. Guinness, a citizen of Dublin, who has made an immense fortune by the manufacture of the malt liquor called Dublin Stout. This is, I believe, the only cathedral in Great Britain that has a modern interior. The floor and walls are crowded with monuments, among which Swift's, of course, arrests special attention. But I was more interested in the monument of Archbishop Whately, — a coffer-shaped marble structure, with a full-length statue of him in a recumbent posture.

I attended the daily morning service here. There were present, a canon who intoned the service, a choir of eighteen men and boys in dirty and ragged surplices who sang gloriously, two vergers in full official dress with gilded staves, and a congregation of ten persons, including myself, seven of which ten were strangers, and remained to inspect the building. This, so far as I had the opportunity of observing, is about the average of week-day attendance upon cathedral service in every part of Great Britain. Now I rejoice to have the devotional services of the church performed for ten, or three, or even for one hearer; but this apparatus of daily worship is sustained at a cost for which there can be no justification on rational or Christian grounds, especially when, as in the case of St. Patrick's, there are unevangelized thousands under the cathedral's shadow, whose redemption from ignorance and depravity would be an immeasurably more worthy offering than can rise from the lips of a mercenary choir.

CHAPTER IV.

ART.

Superiority of Ancient and Mediæval Art. — The Ministry of Art. — The Sistine Madonna. — Other Pictures at Dresden. — Titian's Assumption of the Virgin. — Raphael's Transfiguration. — Rubens' Pictures. — Wood-carving. — Pulpit at Brussels. — The Dying Gladiator. — Michael Angelo's Moses. — The Milan Cathedral. — Goldsmith's Work. — Reasons for the Decline of Art.

ONE of the convictions forced upon a traveller in Europe is, that the arts of form and design attained their highest grade of perfection several centuries ago, and that no modern works can be brought into comparison with the ancient and mediæval. It is common, but unjust, to speak with emphatic contempt of American art. I am inclined to think that, as regards artists now living, our country would bear a not unfavorable comparison with the most cultivated nations of Europe. I never saw a poorer collection of paintings than one containing works of living artists at Dresden, within a few rods of the world-famed gallery. In the Louvre, Luxemburg, and Versailles palaces there are several acres of canvas, which, I am sure, could have been fully as well covered in Boston or New

York as in Paris. Of the sculptors who are now enjoying a high reputation in Rome and in Florence, there are Americans who are regarded as second to none. At Rome, where the very stones might be expected to cry out against an artistical deformity, there is now building a Church of St. Paul, nearly as large as St. Peter's, sumptuous beyond all precedent, its materials so precious as to make its pavements of veined and variegated marble look mean, which yet is true to no idea or sentiment, is immense without being great, handsome without being beautiful, exquisite in detail and in finish, but wholly unimpressive, — in fine, very much such an edifice as a plain New England carpenter would erect, if you told him to build a meeting-house four or five hundred feet long, and gave him marble, porphyry, and alabaster instead of pine-lumber, and portraits in mosaic instead of paint for the walls.

I rejoice to recognize, not so much human genius, taste, and culture, as the Divine inspiration in art. Not alone in mountain, waterfall, lake, and river has God wrought. We see Him no less in dome and pillar, frieze and cornice, in forms of beauty that grew under the patient toil of artists who built, and painted, and chiselled far better than they knew, and have left for the ages copies of thoughts and visions immeasurably transcending the models before them, — an ideal perfectness and beauty which had no earthly prototypes. Moreover, as the Divine inspiration, attested by miracle, and made availing for the religious culture of coming generations, had its peculiar epochs not to be repeated, so is it with the *gifts* — I use the word significantly — which create preëminence in the arts. And I think we can see why it was fitting that such gifts should have been conferred on ruder ages than ours. The more advanced stages of progress can be best realized by the agency of the voice and the pen; while in earlier periods, grand and beautiful forms, vast cathedrals, marble glowing with the Promethean fire, pictures that were gospels for men's faith and reverence, had the very same mission which now belongs to the written and spoken word. These master-works of art were God's ministers for intenerating the rude hearts of fierce and wild men; for bowing in adoration the stubborn necks and stiff knees which no inferior power could have bent; for shaping the gentler virtues; for infusing the amenities and charities of domestic and social life; for nourishing the very faith which no longer needs, but perhaps too rudely spurns their aid.

I cannot here separate the Divine from the human; and if we praise God in those heights and depths of infinite power and wisdom in which He has wrought alone, all the more should we praise Him in and for the great creators, whose genius was kindled by His own breath, whose archetypes lay in the treasury of His own beauty-teeming spirit, whose work was wrought in patterns shown them from above.

Most of all have I felt the presence of this Divine element in the great pictures that are shrines of pilgrimage for travellers from the whole civilized world. Their mission is all Godward and Christward. I spoke of them as gospels, and they do rehearse to their beholders now their several portions of the Redeemer's life and aspects of His character, with a vividness and power which words cannot approach. But if they are fresh evangels, with a vivifying force else unexperienced, to those who have always had the sacred record in their hands, what must they have been when the Scriptures were a sealed book to the multitude, and the redemption-story was published only through these wonderful creations? It is worthy of our grateful acknowledgment that the inspiration of art runs parallel with revelation, and culminates in the great moments of sacred history, so that the highest office of human genius has been the interpretation of the Divine Word, — of the Word that " was made flesh, and dwelt among men."

I am conscious of the impossibility of adequately describing the great works of which I have spoken; nor yet can engravings or photographs enable one to anticipate the joy of seeing and of having seen them. I can compare it only to the creation of a new sense, and of an entirely new class and range of sensations through its ministry.

It seems to me that there can be but one voice as to the preëminence of the Sistine Madonna at Dresden over all other pictures. The Virgin with the infant Saviour in her arms is represented as standing on luminous clouds, in a light at once intense and soft, — with a countless multitude of angel-faces in the background, as if in obedience to the command, "Let all the angels of God worship Him." Beneath, at her right hand, kneels the Pope, St. Sixtus, an old man, with a face expressive equally of awe and of loving reverence, — his tiara lying on the ground at his feet. On the other side kneels St. Barbara, — her eyes cast down as if dazzled by excess of glory, and her beautiful countenance indicative of rapt devotion. At the bottom of the picture are two child-angels — their forms but half-revealed — whose faces cannot have been copied from the fairest of the children of men; but if the spirits nearest the eternal throne have visible forms, one would almost think that Raphael must have been prepared for his work by being caught up into the third heaven. Where everything is wonderful, what amazes me most is the expression of the eyes of each member of the group. The Virgin's eyes are those of a happy mother, yet with a prescience of far-off sorrow, — full, beaming, gladsome, yet with a slight but indelible touch of pensiveness. St. Barbara's eyes are those of a beatified spirit, crowded, whelmed and dazed by the multitude and richness of heavenly visions and experiences. The old Pope looks entranced and overwhelmed, and in his eye trembles the *Nunc dimittis*. The eyes of the little cherubs are so broad and bright that they appear to be looking in every direction at once; they seem to pierce the beholder's very soul, yet all the while they are turned intently heavenward. They are eyes which we feel can never be for an instant closed. They are brimming over with joy; they are full of praise. One can think only of the spirits that cease not, day and night, to cry, " Holy, holy, holy Lord God of Sabaoth." But the eyes of the infant Jesus,— how can I describe them! In everything else He is a human child, thus in striking contrast with the infant cherubs below. His eyes, too, are those of a human child, and yet it seems as if they already looked through immensity and eternity. Such knowing eyes, yet not piercing, but self-contained; sweet too, full of loveliness. If He in His tender years gave presage of what He should be, we must conceive of Him just as Raphael has painted Him. The enjoyment of this picture is well worth the double Atlantic voyage. I have fed upon it ever since I saw it. There is not a waking half-hour, during which it does not reproduce itself in sight-like reminiscence. Yet more, I feel as if this picture will, for my life long, stand between me and that coarse, unappreciative rationalism of our time, which seems to find an especial joy in eliminating the Divine element from the birth and infancy of our Lord. It is an argument to the reason and the understanding, no less than to the æsthetic nature; for surely a mode of manifestation, which, in its artistic guise, thus lifts the soul into an ecstasy of praise and adoration, cannot be unworthy of the Divine wisdom and love.

There is, in the Dresden Gallery, another remarkable Madonna, by Holbein. It was painted to the order of one Jacob Meyer, burgomaster of Basle, to commemorate the restoration of a sick child to health, as was supposed, through the intercession of the Virgin. The burgomaster, his wife, his wife's mother, and his daughter are introduced, all kneeling before the Virgin. It is said that they were all portraits from life; and for a more dowdy-looking family the artist might have searched the Continent in vain. There is, however, in the father's face, coarse and heavy as it is, a look of earnest supplication, such as I have sometimes witnessed in the profoundly devout, in their crises of severest need; and his lifted eyes glow intently with loving and admiring faith. The Virgin stands, superbly attired and crowned, with a countenance full of ineffable compassion. She has put down her own child, and has taken into her arms the poor, lank, wasted, almost dying child, for whom the group are praying; and a little son of the burgomaster has risen partly from the kneeling posture, to play with the infant Jesus. The picture is full of contrasts, — the transcendent beauty of the Virgin, blending at once queenly majesty, a mother's tenderness, and the surpassing sanctity belonging to the mother of Jesus, with the almost painful uncomeliness of the family; the round, rosy, healthy, gleeful form and countenance of the Christ-child, with the wan frame, pinched face, and skeleton hands of the sick child; the profound gravity of the father and the females of the group, with the mirth, frolic, absolute roguery of the little boy, who can think of nothing but the beautiful child he is playing with.

Next to these pictures, I saw none in the Dresden Gallery that interested me so much as Titian's picture of the Saviour and the Tribute-money. This is, and was meant to be, unique as a specimen of artistical handwork. Even on examining it with a strong microscope, it is impossible to trace the marks of the brush, and the colors look as if they had grown on the canvas, as they grow on the petals of the lily. But the great charm lies in the two faces. That of the Pharisee who brings the denarius, is perfect in its kind, expressive of low cunning in every line and angle and rounding of the countenance. Though no representation of the Saviour's face can ever seem fully adequate, yet this picture contains and suggests more of the strength and majesty of His character than, had I not seen it, I should have supposed capable of artistical expression. The countenance is not only calm and self-collected, sweet and gentle; but it bears the tokens of immeasurable superiority over the Pharisee, even with his own weapons and on his own low plane. It bespeaks one who is equally at home on earth and in heaven, — equally versed in the mole-paths of human guile and treachery and in the way of the upright, — one whom no wiles can betray into an utterance or a look not in sacred harmony with His teachings and His mission among men.

In this same gallery is to be seen the original of Correggio's Magdalen Reading, with which the common engravings have made us familiar. No words can express the exquisiteness of the tints in this work, and the perfectness of the *chiaro-oscuro*, as if the sun itself had brooded over the finished picture long enough to fix its light and the corresponding shadows there; while the face is, as it should be, young, beautiful, witching, yet with the abstracted, introspective air of one who has taken her farewell of the world, and is henceforth the bride of Heaven.

But I must not linger at Dresden. The most noteworthy picture in Venice is Titian's Assumption, or ascension to heaven, of the Virgin, — one of the accredited myths of the Romish Church, and a favorite subject of mediæval art. This picture is remarkable mainly for its coloring. It may be safely said that it could have been painted by no man but Titian, and nowhere but in Italy. In his colors there is an indescribable charm. They not only arrest, but usurp the attention, blunt the critical acumen, make one unaware of the details of form and figure, incapable of detecting blemishes, even when he knows that they exist. Then too, every scene, group, or figure that he paints is bathed in an Italian sky, about which let me say a word in passing. It is often asked, Can there be anything in Italy to be compared with our autumnal sunsets? I answer, No, — not to be compared with them, because in every way unlike. The Italian heavens are less splendid, less brilliant than ours, have less diversity of coloring. All their tints are a lighter or a deeper azure, or such hues as might naturally melt into this pervading azure. But the term *sky-blue* acquired for me in Italy a meaning which it never had before. I no longer wondered that, in the Latin classics, every person and thing that is gloriously beautiful is liable to be called *cerulean*. Then there is always in the atmosphere a delicious haze, translucent indeed, so that objects can be seen at a very great distance, — light and thin too, so as to make the very air more intensely ethereal, — yet robing the entire panorama, the hills, and waters, and clouds, and stars, in its own azure gala-dress, than which Paradise can offer none more enchanting. It is this atmosphere which gives tone to Titian's pictures, and in the Assumption of the Virgin it is intensified, as it should be, worthily to represent so great a miracle. In the transcendently luminous clouds through which she is rising, in the drapery that wraps her form, in the light which from the central figure is radiated over the whole group, I recognized the tints which I had admired in that same morning's sunrise, and the hackneyed figure of dipping the pencil in the sunbeams, seemed a metaphor no longer.

The Gallery of the Vatican at Rome contains comparatively few pictures; but, unlike the others, it affords room to none but master-works. Among these, I cannot conceive that any one should fail to give the precedence to Raphael's Transfiguration, — his last work, not quite finished when his hand was arrested by death, and hung over his bier at his funeral. It presents the scene on the mountain, and that at its foot, simultaneously, — the Saviour floating in fleecy clouds between Moses and Elias, with His awe-stricken companions at His feet; and below, the multitude gathered about the epileptic boy as he writhes in agony, — his father, mother, sister, each in look and action indicating the relationship, — the disciples perplexed and dismayed by the demand made on their healing power, — the Jews around them, sneering at their discomfiture. There is not, in the whole group, a face which does not fully define itself, and the beholder is drawn into the most intense sympathy with the distressed family, longs for the Saviour to emerge from " the excellent glory," and listens with the inward ear for the shout so soon to go up from the assembly beneath, " God hath visited and redeemed His people." This work has been criticised as lacking unity, — as being two pictures on the same canvas.

To me it does not seem so. The two portions belong together, are part and parcel, each of the other. The most impressive and touching feature of the gospel narrative is the Saviour's plunging at once from the splendor and joy of the heavenly communion into the wild confusion and bitter anguish that awaited His descent and craved His loving ministry; and in the picture there is, to my eye, no break, no harsh contrast, but a perfectly natural transition from the celestial glory to the human suffering and sorrow for whose relief it was kindled.

Not to dwell longer on the Italian painters, I will ask my readers to go with me to Antwerp, and look at the world-famous pictures of Rubens. The works of Rubens are more numerous than those of any other of the great painters, and are to be found in every gallery in Europe. He must have often painted hastily and carelessly, and many of his pictures have nothing but his name to recommend them. He had two wives, both of them stout, coarse, blowzy-looking women, of a low type of sensual beauty, and they seem to have been his perpetual study; for we find one or the other of them disfiguring almost every one of his groups. But, in his sacred themes, his æsthetic nature seems to have taken on a refinement and delicacy which we can hardly trace in his other works; and not even Raphael brings before us the great moments of the Saviour's life with profounder feeling or effect. In the church of Notre Dame, formerly the

Cathedral of Antwerp, are the great pictures of the Elevation of the Cross, and the Descent from the Cross. Each of these occupies a space about twelve feet square, and each has, connected with it, two side-pieces of about the same height and half the width, — those of the former being the Crucifixion of the two Thieves, and the Women at the Cross, — those of the latter, the Meeting of the Virgin Mary and Elizabeth, and the Presentation of the Infant Jesus to Simeon in the Temple. These pictures are on wood, which Rubens preferred to canvas, and which, certainly, in his use of it, showed its superiority, and justified his choice.

The Elevation of the Cross represents Jesus as already fastened to the cross, which His executioners are lifting to an upright position. The painter seems to have thrown his whole artistical genius into the faces of the executioners, and if subjects had come up from Pandemonium to sit to him, these might have been their likenesses. The wretches are made all the more fiend-like, in contrast with the blended terror and pity of the women in the side-piece. There is the Virgin Mother, uniting the firmness of an assured faith with the profoundest awe and grief. There is her mother, St. Anna, an old, shrivelled woman, with the sharpest angles in her face, looking as if the climax of horror had been reached, yet as if she, for the sake of the younger women with her, must not utterly give way to her sorrow. Then there is a young mother letting her infant drop from her bosom, and falling back as in a deathlike swoon, — with several other figures, all equally expressive of the emotions of the scene.

The Descent from the Cross represents the disciples and the faithful women taking our Saviour's lifeless body down from the cross, — the men having mounted on ladders so as to let down the head and the upper portion of the body, while the women are helping the apostles in sustaining the precious burden as it approaches the ground. In this wonderful picture there are two chief points of interest. One is the perfectness with which death is painted, and this, not only in the face, but in every part of the flaccid form, so that there is not a limb or an angle of the body, which, if all the rest were covered up, would not speak of death. It is the more touching, because the Saviour's countenance resembles so closely that in the other picture, with the omission of all lifelike expression, that it suggests all that was there before life was extinct. The other striking feature is the intense tenderness portrayed in the group busy about the cross. This is seen, not in the faces only, but in posture, hand, and movement, — their looks and gestures showing how anxious they are that the body shall sustain no rude touch or jar, and how profound are both their reverence and their grief.

The execution of these pictures is fully adequate to their conception. The coloring is soft and mellow with age, while the tints are as fresh and vivid as if they had been painted yesterday.

In another church in Antwerp is the Flagellation of Jesus, by Rubens, a most painful theme, so lifelike in its rendering as to make one feel, as we cannot possibly feel in reading the narrative, the horrible indignity and outrage; but this is more than redeemed by the godlike meekness and gentleness in the Saviour's countenance, as if the Divine in Him shone out only the more resplendently from the lowest depth of His humiliation.

There is at Brussels a picture of Rubens, which impressed me as fully equal, in every trait of surpassing excellence, to those in Antwerp. It is the *Via Dolorosa*, the Way to Calvary. It represents the moment when, Jesus having fallen under the burden of the cross, it is forced upon Simon of Cyrene. The Saviour is in the attitude of one who has just fallen forward, and has thrown out His hands to save Himself, too weak to rise without assistance; while one of several women in the crowd is tenderly wiping His brow, the others are looking on with pity and dismay, and the Jews behind are scowling with malice and rage. The Saviour's face expresses the keenest suffering, yet mingled with sweet patience and resignation, and with a look of gratitude, which seems a Divine benediction, directed to the woman bending over Him. Her face is hardly less remarkable, blending adoring reverence with the tenderest compassion, and though devoid of anger, yet flushed with a vivid sense of foul indignity and wrong. Nowhere have I beheld a picture of any scene in the Saviour's life which entered so profoundly into my soul, and so became, as it were, a part of my own being.

But it is not my intention to confine myself to pictures. There is another art, deserving our passing notice, of which Belgium furnishes by far the most remarkable specimens, namely, that of carving in wood, — now a mere handicraft, but, for a season, elevated in Belgium and Holland into one of the fine arts, and holding a position not one whit beneath the more ambitious members of the sisterhood. Of the capacity of this mode of representation, I may give my readers some idea by describing a pulpit in the principal church in Brussels. The structure is a huge mass of carved oak, without a finger's breadth that does not form part of the design. The trunk and body of the pulpit represent the Fall of Man, while the portion above the rostrum tells the story of Redemption, so that we have Paradise Lost and Paradise Regained in one. The base of the structure is the garden of Eden, — a cluster of large trees laden with the most luxuriant foliage and fruit. These trees are densely peopled with beasts and birds of almost life size, — such as a monkey munching an orange, a squirrel cracking a nut, a peacock with full-spread fan, a cock in the attitude of crowing, an eagle perched on a solitary branch. In front of this scene, as if just leaving it, are Adam and Eve in their "coats of skins:" Eve with the fatal apple in her hand; Death, in skeleton guise, shaking his long, fleshless fingers over her; and the angel with the flaming sword, hovering in the rear. Behind the rostrum is a crucifix, with Faith and Hope beside it. Over the sounding-board is a queenly image of the Virgin Mary, supporting the infant Jesus as He is just learning to walk, and his naked little foot is laid on the head of an immense monster, half serpent, half crocodile, whose frame seems quivering with agony under the touch predestined for his destruction. Around them are various angel forms, one of which is letting down the golden chain that is to draw man heavenward. In the only place where there is room for an inscription, these words stand in letters of gold, *Ave Maria mutans Evæ Nomen;* or, in English, The *Ave* addressed to Mary is but the name of Eve (*Eva*) reversed. I sat under this pulpit during a Sunday morning's high mass, and it was to me prayer, anthem, sermon, and, most of all, benediction. I could attend to nothing else. Indeed, the ritual going on in the church, however significant to the initiated, was to me devoid of meaning and interest; but for once I found "tongues in trees," and more came into my soul from that clump of trees, than could have found utterance by the tongue of man, however eloquent. **Must** not such a work have been to the rude minds of earlier generations, a perpetual instructor and monitor of things Divine, endowed with a didactic power far beyond any homily that priest or monk could have droned from its inclosure?

Sculpture, in general, has less power over the emotional nature than painting; yet there are works of the chisel whose mere presence in a city or a land, would, of itself, be a refining and elevating force of incalculable momentum. Among the many statues which, in more or less perfect preservation, have come down to us from remote antiquity, there is none, as it seems to me, to be compared for expression and effect with that called the Dying Gladiator. Whether it is rightly so called, it is impossible to determine. All that we are certain of is that it represents a young man who has been engaged in a conflict of arms, and is dying of his wounds. He wears a collar, which may denote a captive obliged to fight at his master's will, or it may denote a Gaul; for the Gallic warriors all wore collars. The face bears not a trait of anger or vindictiveness, but indicates a native nobleness of spirit, calm and firm endurance, and, at the same time, profound sensibility. In two words, its expression is manly tenderness; and this is so inwrought in the marble, that no living countenance in the death-agony could call forth deeper sympathy or warmer admiration. Withal there is, in the eyes, that which inevitably suggests the idea of one dying on a foreign soil, and dwelling in his last thoughts on home and the friends from whom he is forever separated.[1]

The master-work of mediæval sculpture is Michael Angelo's Moses. This represents the great law-giver, seated as in the presence of the hosts of Israel, giving them the law which he has received on Mount Sinai. The figure is colossal, massive, of the most majestic aspect; the beard hanging in immense curls below the waist, the arms vast masses of corrugated muscle, the whole form betokening unparalleled strength, hardihood, and prowess. Saint, sage, seer, ruler, warrior, — all are united in look, mien, and attitude. No other personage in history could have given his name to this statue; but it fulfils every condition of a statue of Moses, and epitomizes his years of physical training in the deserts of Midian, his holy vigils on the mountain, his kingly place and office among men. One singular feature is a pair of horns protruding from the brow. This was in accordance with a mistranslation from the Hebrew of the book of Exodus, perpetuated in the Latin Vulgate,— the only Scriptures to which the artist had access. The face of Moses, in our translation, is rightly said to have *shone* when he came down from the mountain; in the Vulgate, it is said to have been *horned*. In other hands these horns would have

---

[1] " Sternitur infelix alieno volnere, cœlumque
　　Adspicit, et dulcis moriens reminiscitur Argos."

been a deformity, and they are so in miniature copies of the Moses. But, in the original, they are what the horn always is in the symbolism of the Old Testament, — a token of power, intensifying the massiveness of the brow, and giving the last touch of completeness to the heaven-breathed vigor and energy of him who must ever remain unequalled among the children of men.

I shall give here but a single specimen of ecclesiastical architecture, and it shall be the Cathedral of Milan, which seems to me the most impressive of all the great churches of Europe. It is nearly five hundred feet long, more than three hundred and fifty feet high to the top of the colossal, gilt, star-crowned statue of the Virgin which surmounts the spire, and more than a hundred and fifty feet from the floor to the upper eaves. It is of white marble, in part slightly discolored by time, but at a little distance, of a pure and dazzling white. It has a mosaic floor of a very rich pattern, and a ceiling of fretted stone-work, which looks from the floor as fine and delicate as the most skilful carving in ivory. There are five aisles, separated from one another by four rows of clustered columns, their capitals richly carved and adorned with statuary. The nave has three stories, — the central aisle having rows of windows at a very great height; the aisles adjacent to it forming a clearstory with its own tiers of windows; while the long windows which give the principal light belong to the outer aisles. The exterior has a somewhat Saracenic aspect. It shoots up in unnumbered pinnacles, each pinnacle surmounted by a statue of apostle, martyr, or saint, — the martyrs all bearing palms. Every niche that can be so filled, is occupied by human or angelic figures; while from the angles of the several roofs, peer out gargoyles of strange aspect, eagles' heads, dragons, nondescript monsters. The statues number more than three thousand. They are all of life size; all of the most perfect finish, and many of them by world-famous sculptors. One may ascend almost to the top of the highest tower; and, as I looked down from the three successive roofs and from the landing-places of still loftier staircases, the forest of pointed turrets, statuary, and carved work, like a peopled forest petrified, seemed even grander, more splendid, more luculently Divine than the glorious view in the not very remote distance, of Monte Rosa with its vicinage of snow-crowned Alps, which can nowhere else be seen in such peerless vastness and brilliancy. I said *more luculently Divine;* for what can be more fully fraught with the Divine than the inspiration of human art? And while the pencil and the chisel may lend themselves to more various and richer forms of beauty, and may awaken profounder emotions of love and sympathy, the sublimity of art culminates in these vast mediæval temples, in which we behold man's least finite copy of the infinite.

I might, did my proposed limits permit, add illustrations of the ministry of art from the golden altars, and the numerous specimens, still extant, of an ability and skill which gave to Benvenuto Cellini and other illustrious goldsmiths of his age, a world-wide and world-enduring fame. While in mechanical finish we can imagine nothing more perfect than these works, in conception, grouping, perspective, and all the details of complicated design, they manifest a transcending genius, and a wealth of resources which commands our highest admiration. In this department, originality has ceased. The most hopeful movement of our own day has been a retrogradation to Etruscan forms. Some slight novelty of style or pattern may, indeed, from time to time be introduced, in a pitcher, salver, or vase; but no man who has an epic in his heart, would now think of chasing it in gold or silver.

In the seeming miscellaneousness of this chapter, I have had a unity of purpose. I have wished to show what art has done and can do for the culture of thought, sentiment, and character, for the development and elevation of human nature, for the growth of faith, worship, and devotion. But how are we to account for the stagnation and decline of art in these latter days? I answer that art has ceased to advance, nay, in some departments has retrograded, mainly because the needs, the demands, and the receptivity of civilized man now are essentially different from those of earlier centuries. Genius includes impulse no less than capacity. It cannot remain as "a fire in the bones," but it will somehow utter, that is, *outer* itself, put itself forth, get its grasp on the imagination, sentiment, faith, enthusiasm of the race. It is, in a certain sense, universal. Though it may have one chief mode of self-utterance, the others are open to its choice. But its tendency is to choose the mode of utterance, by which it can best reach the mind of its age. When royalty could not write, and few noblemen could read, and those mysteries which, according to Dogberry, come by nature, were confined to the cloister, genius, of necessity, seldom sought expression in books; nor yet, except in times of fierce political tumult, was there an open arena for popular eloquence. Form and color were the chief modes of communication between the master-minds and their contemporaries whom they were born to teach and train and elevate. The poet, the *maker*, would he enrich the world by his creations, was constrained to paint, or chisel, or carve, or build them, so few could read or hear them, were they clothed in measure or song.

The art of those ages was not, however, of spontaneous growth, any more than is the higher literature or eloquence of the present time. Genius is not the capacity of producing without toil, but the capacity of working greatly and gloriously. Among the most interesting objects of curiosity in the European art-centres are the studies and tentative sketches of the great masters, which show that they passed through the processes of careful training, that eye and hand were thoroughly educated for their work, and that they had learned, as the condition precedent of their fame,

"To scorn delights, and live laborious days."

By like culture, the genius which now puts before the mind of the age the images of things unseen — gorgeous, beautiful, grand — in words that make our hearts leap and glow and burn, might have learned to place the same images before the outward eye. Genius, like physical force, is one and convertible. God gives its power; the age, its aim and object.

CHAPTER V.

SWITZERLAND.

Swiss Roads. — Inns. — People. — Basle. — Lucerne. — The Rigi. — Lake Lucerne. — Pass of St. Gotthard. — The Furca. — Glacier of the Rhone. — The Grimsel Pass. — Lake of Brienz. — Falls of the Giessbach. — Interlachen. — The Jungfrau. — Swiss Music. — Bern. — Geneva. — Lake of Geneva. — Lausanne. — Baths of Saxon. — Ruins.

I PROPOSE in this chapter to give some sketches of Swiss travel. But before entering on the scenery, let me say a few words of the roads and the people.

The Swiss railways are well-built, well-stocked, and well-managed, making somewhat slower time than the English and French, but much faster than the German railways, which realized for me, as nothing else ever did, the old philosophical definition of motion as a series of rests. Steam-carriage must, however, be abandoned in the wildest and grandest regions, and forms, therefore, but a small part of the tourist's experience.

The carriage-roads in the mountainous districts of Switzerland, are the most magnificent specimens of engineering that I have ever seen or can conceive of. Some of them attain a higher altitude than the summit of Mount Washington, where the snow never wholly melts, and the summer is but a mollified winter. A mountain is generally climbed by a series of inclined planes, which terrace its face obliquely, and are just as steep as can be safely descended with locked wheels and the constant use of a brake. Such roads are shelves hewn in or built upon the mountain-side, often with precipices of thousands of feet above and below. They are precisely wide enough for the passing of two carriages without collision, — the road-bed firmly laid and smoothly gravelled, and its outer margin guarded by a wall of solid masonry some four feet high. The several cantons keep these roads in excellent order during the travelling season, charging no tolls, but remunerating themselves by the influx of foreign gold, which must, of necessity, bear a close proportion to the ease and security of travel. Of course the winter snows obstruct, and the spring rains gully these roads, so that they are sometimes impassable or dangerous; and every season requires for them thorough and costly repairs. Good carriages and careful drivers can be had everywhere at a moderate charge, always with an addition for *backshish* or *Trinkgeld* to the driver.

There are many important routes, over which a wheeled carriage cannot pass. On these, in every case, as good bridle-paths as the nature of the ground will permit are maintained, and sure-footed mules can always be hired. But an able-bodied man will generally prefer his own feet, and he can, at any station, procure for his baggage a trusty porter, who will serve him also as a guide and nomenclator, and who, under a back-load of fifty pounds, will lead him at as vigorous a pace as he can easily maintain. The stages which a pedestrian will find it convenient to make, vary from ten to thirty miles; and the pure, bracing mountain air renders foot-travelling much less wearisome than I have ever found it in quite extensive experience in New England.

In the principal cities and towns, such as Bern, Interlachen, Lausanne, Geneva, the inns are hardly equalled, not surpassed in comfort and luxury anywhere in the world. In the less important villages, and especially at the mountain stations, there is much to be desired on the score of neatness and cleanliness; but I found no place at which the table d'hote was not well served.

The Swiss people are honest and intelligent, but dull and heavy-witted. Property is nowhere safer than among them. It is almost impossible to lose even the smallest article. Indeed, loss, could it occur, would often be great gain. Whatever a traveller leaves on his route is sure to be sent after him, but by such slow stages, that it may cost him more than it is worth by the time it reaches him.

But if the people will not steal, they are sturdy and persistent beggars. All the children in a hamlet dog the traveller's footsteps with clamorous solicitation; and one can hardly pass a farm-house, however affluent in its surroundings, without having a hat or hand held out for alms.

The Swiss are not neat. They are not offensively uncleanly in their persons. On Sundays and holidays, their gala attire — varying much in the different cantons — though sometimes grotesque, indicates great regard for personal appearance, and in some quarters, is even beautiful. On working days, the men are decently clad, and nothing can be more charmingly picturesque than the costume of the women at hay-making, — broad straw hats with bright ribbons, white sleeves, and dark bodices. But they love to heap all the litter they can in and about their houses. I have been in cottages built with exquisite taste, and presenting at a distance the most inviting aspect, which were not nearly so clean as a well-kept stable. Indeed, the cellar of a farm-house is generally used as a stable, and the smaller live stock have the unchecked liberty of the whole house.

The women are subjected to a very great amount of severe out-of-door toil. In the cities, the street-sweepers are all women. All over the country, besides performing most of the agricultural labor, the women carry heavy burdens on frames or in baskets fitted to their backs, and the girls are inured to this task from very infancy. They thus acquire a uniformly stooping gait, as if born under the curse written in one of the imprecatory psalms, "Bow down their back always." Yet the severity of their lot is due, not, as in Saxony and Austria, to the comparative degradation of women in the social scale, but rather to the brevity of the working season, which compels all the members of a family to the maximum of effort, to provide for the long period of inaction. Over heights which no wheeled carriage can surmount, and at times when all attainable mules are required for the use of travellers, the human back is the only medium of transportation; and if the women bear heavy burdens, the men bear still heavier. Many of them are employed as porters, carrying enormous articles of baggage, and frequently their feeble or indolent owners, to the summits of the highest mountains. Others take care of the herds that are pastured far up among the clouds, and bring down the products of these aerial dairies to the level of terrestrial markets. For all of them, too, the cutting and transportation of firewood alone, make a severe demand upon their strength.

I will now give some of my remembrances of the country. I entered Switzerland by the way of Basle, a place lying on both sides of the Rhine, which rushes through the city with a noise like that of a mill-race. With a great deal else that is curious and attractive, I was most interested there in the numerous works and memorials of

Holbein, who passed there his boyhood and early manhood.[1]

I first found myself in the Switzerland of my lifelong dreams, at Lucerne, a charming little city, on the river Reuss, at the point at which it enters Lake Lucerne. Arriving there late in the day, I watched the sunset on the Alps. The snowy summits were first bathed in rose-tints, which slowly faded as the stars came out, till they gleamed in pure white, and shot forth rays that vied with the moonbeams on the quiet waters at their feet, and over the valleys in their deep shadows. I rose at early dawn, and there was not a vestige of the mountain panorama. At sunrise the veil began to part. Here and there a summit peered out of the ocean of undulating mist, then a few flecks of snow, green patches, and rough, craggy shoulders, from the mountain-sides. Then the mist, dispelled from the higher regions, lay in azure belts midway between the base and the crown of each separate Alp. Then it was cut into fillets and streamers, which slowly floated away and vanished. The lake is inexpressibly beautiful, — cruciform, with unnumbered bays and inlets, with nooks of the richest verdure, with Mount Pilatus — stern, rugged, precipitous — on the right of the city, and on the left, Rigi, a mass of variegated green, densely wooded, and dotted, for its whole height, with white farm-

[1] Holbein was born in Augsburg.

houses and chalets, that seem to cling to the mountain-side.

I ascended Mount Rigi, and spent on its summit the last hours of daylight. Here, from the north to the west, covering three fourths of the entire view, is an ocean of Alps, looking almost as close together as the crests of billows in a storm, — many of them twice as high as that on which I stood, — many of them snow-crowned, with glaciers stretching from peak to peak across immense ravines. On the north side the Rigi is precipitous, and at its foot lie the Lake of Zug and numerous smaller lakes, traceable in their entire outline, with the city of Zurich, the town of Schwytz, and many intervening villages and hamlets; while beyond them, the horizon is bounded by lesser Alps, yet all high enough to be mountains of renown in any other land. The sun sank beneath our horizon long before it ceased to shine on the distant hills, so that we had every possible variety of light and shadow, — the last sun-rays being broken into all the hues of the iris by one of the far-off snow-peaks. I stayed to see the mountains put on their night-clothes. Some wrapped themselves in thick black robes, — presage of the coming storm; others, in a purple such as no Tyrian dye can ever have approached; others, in a pure white drapery hardly less radiant than the beams of the half-full moon; while the snow-peaks slumbered with no other covering than their day-dress, — they being too cold for the moisture about them to assume the form of vapor.

I had hardly been an hour in my chamber, when the rain fell in torrents, with eddying winds which made our hostelry a very cradle, but a cradle whose spasmodic rocking banished sleep. Suddenly there was a lull of the wind and rain. I arose, and put my head and hand out of my window. I could not see my hand. The mountain was wrapped in so dense a cloud, that I doubt whether I could have seen a light in the next window. Yet the cloud was so warm, so near the temperature of my own body, that my head and hand were not moistened by it. The storm was renewed toward morning, and I commenced my descent in a whirlwind of rain and driving mist, in which I could hardly see my mule's head. Soon the storm abated; vistas of lake, rock, and forest appeared fitfully at intervals; the sun — not yet shining on us — began to gleam from the distant mountains, making ghastly rents in their night-dresses; then it came out full and warm on us, converting the raindrops into jewels, and making the grass greener than before, — and there is no grass, not even in Ireland, more intensely green than the Swiss.

That day's route carried us — first on the lake and then on land — by the most memorable spots in the history of Switzerland, — Tell's chapel, birthplace, monument, statue, Schiller's monument, the vale of Rütli where the Swiss Confederacy had its birth, — all of them romantic sites, worthy of their associations. The lake scenery is rendered sublime by the surrounding Alps, while its waters assume forms of ever varying beauty; and the quaint villages, hill-side cottages, and rustic chapels, always in spots which invest them with a wondrous charm, make the navigation a joy to be remembered for a life-time.

I disembarked at Fluelen, and took the road which leads to the Pass of St. Gotthard, with the River Reuss constantly at my side. This river averages a descent of more than a hundred feet in a mile, so that its whole flow seems to be over falls and rapids, always noisy and impetuous. Its water is of deep green, with a crest of milky white. At the Devil's Bridge (Teufelsbrücke) is the principal fall of several hundred feet in height, through a chasm so wild, so terrific, so strewed with the débris of elemental conflicts in pre-adamite ages, that it might seem the rallying place for the infernal gods of some rude mythology. The road, rising by more gentle acclivities to Hospenthal, thence scales the mountain of St. Gotthard by a series of those wonderful terraces already described, till it reaches the height of eight thousand feet above the sea. At its summit I found deep snow-banks, so condensed by the impact of the summer's rains, that it was difficult to thrust a staff to the depth of more than two or three inches.

From the St. Gotthard hospice I looked down

into Italy, and then returned to Hospenthal, whence I took the road to the Furca, — a mountain-ridge nine thousand feet high, between two peaks which rise like the tines of a fork, and give the pass its name. The road winds up the Galenstock. We gradually rose among the clouds, into the region of perpetual snow. At one time we had nothing but cloud and mist visible below us, the sinking sun sending up his broken rays through the mist in gold, violet, purple, and orange, while only snow-tipped pinnacles were seen above the clouds. We spent the night at the Furca inn, perhaps the highest house in Europe, though two or three others contest that distinction with it on nearly equal terms. In the morning we descended to the Glacier of the Rhone, which, for hours of our zig-zag path, lay in full view beneath us, a vast sea of snow-covered ice — discolored by the detritus of the adjacent mountains — from which the river issues a slender, milky rivulet.

From the Glacier I ascended the Grimsel Pass. The Grimsel Hospice is in a valley about six thousand feet high. Behind it are the See der Todten (Lake of the Dead), so called from a great battle that took place near it, and Grimsel Lake, in which the Aar has its rise. There is here a thin and scanty crop of grass, with many of our own familiar flowers, — the dandelion, the hawkweed, the buttercup, and a very beautiful bluebell. Unnumbered goats are pastured here, and at sunset crowd around the hospice to be relieved of the burden of the day. Directly in front of the hospice, my hostess pointed out with evident satisfaction, among the multitudinous brotherhood of hoary summits, the honored name of Agassiz.

The next morning I descended the Pass to Meiringen. The road — a mere bridle-path for sixteen miles — is close along the course of the Aar, with mountains from four to eight thousand feet high on either side; and it looks as if the whole chain had been cleft for the little river to tumble through. And it does not flow; it rushes, so that its sound, seldom a mere murmur, often a roar, never dies upon the ear. Sometimes there is just room for the river to pass, and for the road — hardly wide enough for two men to walk abreast — to creep along a rocky shelf at its side; and then the valley widens sufficiently for a few farms to nestle under the hills. Sometimes there is a dell so deep and so heavily overarched by trees that it seems like the valley of the death-shadow; and then, in a moment, the traveller emerges into the clear sunlight, gleaming gloriously from the snow-peaks and the cascades. The cascades are numberless. They are never, for an instant, out of sight. Sometimes I could count ten or twelve within view at the same moment, issuing from the snow on the mountain-tops, and pouring down in sheets of chased silver into the river.

The Falls of the Handeck on this route are entirely unique, and unutterably grand. The Handeck, a pure, transparent mountain-torrent of great volume, is here precipitated more than two hundred feet, half of the way in an unbroken sheet, then broken by projecting points of rock into feathery spray. The Aar — like most of the Swiss rivers, of a whitish green — has here a considerable fall; and the two rivers meet at right angles in mid-air, wreathe and twine their waters, with the most gorgeous intermingling of the transparent and the turbid stream, and plunge together into the abyss below.

The mountains on this pass are generally covered with trees and clothed with vegetation as high as plants can grow, and then shoot up in huge pinnacles, or in sharp teeth, or in irregularly clustered pyramids, and often seem hewn into rude architectural forms, looking like ruined castles of antediluvian giants.

Arrived at Meiringen, not a little foot-weary, I took a carriage to Brienz, and embarked in a dapper little steamer upon the Lake of Brienz. I wonder that they did not call it *Himmelsee* (Lake of Heaven); for no one can see it and not think of the waters of Paradise. Emerald-green, with just the faintest ripple on its surface, surrounded by Alps of every form and tint, the snow-capped, the bald and bare, the toothed and jagged, the intensely green and verdant, with villages on the margin and straggling up the hill-sides, and single cottages climbing to still higher altitudes, — I could have spent a summer on that deck without a moment's weariness.

I landed at the mouth of the Giessbach, whose falls combine loveliness and grandeur to a degree in which they are rarely united, even in Switzerland. The river here pours into the lake from a height of eleven hundred feet, over a stairway of seven nearly equal steps, — each separate cascade having, therefore, a greater altitude than that of Niagara. A steep path leads to the summit, and thence, and from a series of bridges thrown across the several cascades, the visitor can have an indefinite variety of views; while only so much of the native forest is cut away as to open from each of the falls glimpses of those above and below. With these, however, are let in the most charming vistas of lake, mountain, and woodland. The whole scenery harmonizes in tone with the lake into which the river falls. The several cascades, though surrounded by a dense forest, lie singularly open to the sunlight, are clear, limpid, bright, with spray like showers of diamonds; and the last leap into the lake is radiant to the eye and jubilant to the ear, as if there were conscious and ecstatic gladness in the mighty plunge. If we could imagine a waterfall in Eden, we might seek its type in the Giessbach; nor would there be one terrific or sombre association to remind us of a Paradise laid waste.

I reëmbarked for Interlachen, which, as its

name indicates, lies between the lakes of Brienz and Thun. This is a beautiful, even splendid city, created and sustained by the influx of summer tourists and residents, — a city of vast hotels and *pensions*, magnificent pleasure-grounds, attractive bazaars, and halls for various amusements, — in fine, the great watering-place of Switzerland: by the predominance of English guests assimilated very closely to Leamington and other fashionable English watering-places, while its environments make it more lovely than words can describe.

I went thence to Lauterbrunnen, so called from the multitude of springs (*Brunnen*) that have their issue here. It is a deep and slumberous valley, so deep that the shadows in it have a weird, fantastic look. On the longest day the sun does not rise here till seven o'clock, and on the shortest day sunrise and sunset are not more than two hours apart. Yet the valley is verdant and fertile. Several beautiful cascades fall over its impending mountains, the most noted of which is the Staubbach (Dust-Brook), a fall of about a thousand feet, in which the water is so broken as to look for its whole height like a shower of finely pulverized silver.

Hence I crossed the Wengern Alp, which, on its ascent and from its summit, brought me face to face with the Jungfrau. It was, indeed, a most solemn interview. The Jungfrau (the maiden-mountain) towers in bare and bald sublimity from a base about as high as the summit of the Wengern Alp, to an

8

altitude above it nearly equal to the height of that summit from the sea. Her head (or rather, her heads, for she has two chief heads, besides several smaller ones), and her neck down to the waist, are covered with pure, dazzlingly white snow, and stripes of snow descend to the point where vegetation begins. Below the snow is an immense mass of brown rock, from which there stretch down into the valley numerous sheets of rocky débris, the scars and relics of frequent avalanches from her sides. No other mountain, not even Mont Blanc, has ever impressed me so profoundly as the symbol and shrine of the Creator's power and majesty. In its vastness, and its intense whiteness and brilliancy, it made me think continually of the "great white throne" in the Apocalypse.

I descended to Grindelwald, — a little village, close upon the brink of an immense glacier, which every year approaches a few feet nearer the homes of its inhabitants. Here is a magnificent array of ice-needles and crystalline forms in boundless variety.

On this route and on several others, I enjoyed most richly the mountain echoes from the Alpine horn, — an instrument as long as the man, longer than the boy, who plays it, from which a single strong, sweet note is caught by and sent back from scores of Alps, first nearer, then more distant, till at length it dies away in the faintest whisper of melody. This was the only good Swiss music I heard. The national singing is a guttural yelping, to my ear very offensive. The people, however, seem proud of it, and it is one of their favorite forms of mendicancy, — those who will not purchase their songs being ready, perhaps, to pay double for their silence.

My sojourn at Interlachen closed, I took an omnibus to Neuhaus (so called when the old hotel of which the place consists was new), and embarked on the Lake of Thun, another *Himmelsee*, larger than the Lake of Brienz, equally picturesque, commanding glorious views of the Jungfrau and her companions, and having on its shores numerous castles, villas, and hamlets. Landing at Thun, I went by rail to Bern, — the most grotesque of cities, with more of mirthfulness and drollery in its architecture and its permanent features than I should have deemed possible but for the sight. In the principal streets, the houses are built on arcades, thus affording the shelter of covered sidewalks, which are lined throughout with shops, many of which are attractive from the indulgence of individual caprice in the arrangement, combination, and display of their contents. There are very numerous and copious fountains in the squares and at the street-corners, all of them adorned with statuary, and some with designs expressly adapted to promote laughter. The most ludicrous of all is the figure of an ogre in the act of devouring a child, with his pocket and girdle full of children in keeping for future use. Below him is a group of bears in armor. The bear, the scutcheon of the city and the canton, appears everywhere, and in every possible guise, — at fountains, on pediments, over gateways, on the summits of towers.

The clock-towers of Bern are among its curiosities. Of these there are three, remarkable for quaintness and venerable for age. One of them not only receives special attention from strangers, but gathers under it, every hour in the day-time, a multitude of wonder-stricken children. In this a very complicated puppet-show is connected with every striking of the clock. A cock comes out, claps his wings, and crows twice before and once after the striking of the hour; the figure of Time, with the usual insignia, turns an hour-glass, and keeps even rhythm with the clock-hammer by the movement of his jaws and of his scythe; and a large troop of bears dance in pantomime.

Besides the unconsuming bears to be found on every hand, the city sustains several huge living bears at the public expense, in a magnificent den, into which a municipal ordinance, solemnly placarded, forbids, under a heavy penalty, that anything except bread and fruit shall be thrown. Bread is daily thrown to them in such quantities as to attract myriads of sparrows that feed among the bears, and take promptly to their wings, when, at frequent intervals, Bruin rushes and snaps at them.

The Cathedral in its present condition, seems adapted to minister to the appetite for the ludicrous, here so thoroughly catered for. It is well proportioned and imposing in its exterior design, and the carving of the Last Judgment, with the Wise and Foolish Virgins, in its deeply recessed portal, is a work of surpassing merit. But the unfinished tower is covered with a tiled roof so gaudy, so ill-shaped, so mean, as to seem a burlesque of the building below. Behind the Cathedral is a terrace, once a churchyard, directly above the Aar, and from the height of a hundred feet presenting a most extensive range of scenery, of rich and varied beauty, which would be grand also, anywhere but in Switzerland.

Geneva was my next stage. This city lies, as my readers well know, at the point where "the arrowy Rhone" emerges from the Lake of Geneva. It is remarkable for the extent of its water-front, its best streets being built on the margin of the lake and on both sides of the river. It is a splendid and sumptuous city, with some quaint streets and nooks, and many memorials of mediæval men and events, but with a predominant air of newness, style, ostentation, and conventionalism. I was glad to see in the Cathedral — which has a grand and impressive exterior, and an interior prettily and expensively, yet inadequately finished and furnished — the ancient pulpit in which Calvin preached; and, in my heretical way of thinking, I was not unwilling that Calvin's pulpit should be an antiquity.

One of the most curious sights in the city is the

army of washerwomen. For nearly a mile, boats, each about a hundred feet long, are moored close to the river-bank, and in these the women stand in as intimate juxtaposition as is consistent with the free use of their arms. Such a splashing as they make, and such a deafening din with their tongues! If Nausicaa's washing-day was not unworthy of Homer's song, the washers of Geneva surely deserve better commemoration than in my unambitious prose.

The Lake of Geneva is not a *Himmelsee;* but for an earthly lake it has beauty enough to awaken an unutterable admiration and delight. It is reported, under favorable atmospheric conditions, to afford a transcendently fine view of Mont Blanc; but though I crossed it in different directions, on two nearly cloudless days, the requisite conditions were not fulfilled in my experience. The lake is almost entirely surrounded by vine-growing slopes and hills, with ranges of mountains in the distance, and sometimes approaching the shore. Its waters are of a deep blue. On its banks are some of the most beautiful cities and villages in Europe.

The Castle of Chillon is on a rock a few feet from the eastern shore. It is a huge and massive pile of masonry, that looks as if it might yet weather twice the centuries that have passed over it, — gloomy and sombre, lighted by the narrowest possible slits in the walls, — as dreary a prison as man could build, yet surrounded by gorgeous beauty.

The beam still remains, from which the victims of tyranny and bigotry used to be suspended.

Next to Geneva, Lausanne is the largest city on the lake. It is a city developed almost as much vertically as horizontally, — tunnels, bridges over deep ravines, and long flights of steps, leading to several successive stories of streets; while straight lines are wholly abjured, and if one wanted to go west, he would be most likely to effect his purpose by starting with his face toward the rising sun.

The Cathedral, a venerable, low Gothic building, stands almost directly over the principal market, — a mean wooden staircase of more than a hundred steps leading from one to the other, and being, perhaps, the most frequented thoroughfare in the city. The Cathedral has a very beautiful interior, the aisles being separated by clustered columns of singularly fine proportions; but, like several other similar edifices in Protestant cities, it illustrates the inexpediency of putting "new wine into old bottles." The great continental cathedrals were all built for, and adapted to the exigencies of the Romish ritual, and Protestantism has no device by which it can stave off associations of vacuity, dreariness, and desolation, from these temples, in which the service of the living voice, the open ear, and the soul that craves no earthly medium of devotion, formed no part of the builder's purpose. Thus, while there is not a Protestant city in which I did not see, as I saw most emphatically in Lausanne, ample evidence of the elevating power of a simpler, and, in my apprehension, a more genuine faith and worship, — in the cathedrals I always found my taste at variance with my profoundest convictions.

In the Lausanne Cathedral, the chancel has been converted into a cemetery, and one large division of it is filled with monuments to English residents, who have died in the city. Among these is, perhaps, the most tasteless structure of the kind in Europe, erected by Sir Stratford Canning, then British minister to Switzerland, in memory of his wife, who died shortly after her marriage. It is admirably well executed; but it introduces Hermes and quite a numerous troop of Grecian divinities, as in attendance on the dead bride.

From Lausanne I took the railway to Martigny. The route for many miles skirts the lake, and then passes into the Valley of the Rhone. At one point there is just room for the railway to turn the shoulder of a mountain, on rounding which, we came in view of the marvellously beautiful Fall of the Sallenche, which flows from the glacier of the Dent-du-Midi, a grotesque, tooth-shaped mountain, and falls into the Rhone, a broad sheet of foam. Martigny owes its prosperity chiefly to its being the usual starting-point for the mule or foot journey to Chamouny. It is charmingly situated, in a triangular valley on the Rhone, surrounded by mountains. On the brow of a hill near the town is an old Roman fortress, so solidly built that, though dismantled and roofless, it can hardly be termed a ruin.

From Martigny I made an excursion to the Baths of Saxon, — one of the principal Swiss watering-places, — in dissipation, a humble copy of Baden-Baden. The waters are regarded as a specific for cutaneous and rheumatic diseases; but the gamblers far outnumber the invalids.[1] It lies at the foot of a mountain which I ascended. Half-way to the summit I found a hamlet, which lives in my memory for the perfectness of a contrast which may be witnessed, in a good measure, in almost every Swiss village. It was, without exception, the filthiest place I ever saw; while several of the richest fountains of pure water were running entirely to waste, except that at one of them a woman was washing some hopelessly dirty linen. Is it that this, like so many other good gifts of Providence, fails of appreciation because of its unstinted abundance?

Pursuing my way still farther up this mountain, I found a very curious mediæval tower, circular, not less than eighty feet high, with no door, with no entrance except a single window some twenty feet from the ground, and with no other opening, except slits a few inches wide, for the discharge of arrows and missiles, — a strong hold that must

---

[1] The canton of Valais, in which this watering-place is situated, is the only one of the cantons of Switzerland in which public gambling is not prohibited by severe penal laws.

have been absolutely impregnable before the invention of gunpowder. The walls are at least four feet thick, and show no symptoms of decay or dilapidation. Near this tower is a deserted chapel of equally massive architecture, with a huge pile of human skulls and bones in the cellar.

One of the great delights of European travel consists in the thick-sown memorials of early and unfamiliar ages. Hardly a spot which nature has designated as of peculiar interest, fails of some such added prestige. Swiss scenery, indeed, needs no increment of its charms; but, in other parts of Europe, there are not a few of the most picturesque routes and goals of fashionable pilgrimage, that owe full as much of their special attractiveness to the glamour of legend and tradition hanging about castle, chapel, or ruin, as to the unaided work of nature. One may often find the history of thousands of years within the range of his vision, — rude and scattered remains of pristine barbaric masonry; types of Roman occupancy as indestructible as the impress of the Roman mind on the laws and politics of its subject races; vast piles that were the seat of feudal luxury, tyranny, and warfare; and edifices with all the appliances of modern art, taste, and elegance.

Moreover, there is an obvious reason for the frequent coincidence of the picturesque in nature, and in ancient and mediæval art. In early warfare mountains and hills were more easy of defence than lowland sites; and when every noble was either a freebooter, or a semi-independent military chieftain, the very spots which now seem accessible only to the mountain goat, were chosen for human habitation, and are therefore now fraught with historical reminiscences, crowned with monuments of old renown, of iron rule, of knightly prowess, and of savage butchery.

CHAPTER VI.

CHAMOUNY AND NORTHERN ITALY.

Routes to Chamouny. — The Valley. — The Flégère. — The Montanvert. — The Mer de Glace. — The Glacier des Bossons. — Sunrise at Chamouny. — The Simplon. — First Views of Italy. — Domo d' Ossola. — Lake Maggiore. — Lake Lugano. — Lugano. — Lake of Como. — Como. — Market-scene. — Milan. — The Last Supper. — Church of St. Ambrose. — Golden Altar. — Ambrosian Library.

That I should have written a chapter on Switzerland without a word about Chamouny and Mont Blanc, might seem like the omission, which has grown into a proverb, of the part of Hamlet from the tragedy that bears his name. But Chamouny, though æsthetically in Switzerland, is politically in France, — the line between the two countries crossing the summit of the Col de Balme, between two adjacent hovels that do service as hotels.

There is a diligence route from Geneva to Chamouny; but I know of it only from guide-books. For mules and pedestrians, there are two routes from Martigny, both over mountains seven or eight thousand feet high, but differing as widely in their complexion as if they belonged to opposite hemispheres. The Col de Balme path is over heights of awful grandeur, stern, rugged, desolate. On the summit, whence is obtained the first near view of Mont Blanc, there are always eddying winds; the cold, even on a summer noon, pierces to the bones; sudden snow-squalls drive across the mountain; and unmelting snow lies wherever it can escape the sun's direct radiance. The passage over the neighboring height, the Tête Noir, is as charming as it is grand, — on the brink, indeed, of ravines that seem sunless and bottomless; but in the face of bright and merry cascades, over and under cliffs heavily clothed with verdure and bloom, through rich pastures enlivened by the bell-note from vast herds of cows, at the foot of thinner and higher pastures, so precipitous that it seems a marvel that the goats that throng their sides can cling and eat at the same moment, by clefts that open deep, glowing vistas of valley, glen, and river, across brooks and torrents wild and fierce, but full of light and gladness.

The Valley of Chamouny can hardly be surpassed in loveliness during its short and rapid summer. About fifteen miles long, and less than a mile in width, fertile, and of the richest green; with mountains of immense altitude on either side, and closed in at the extremities by mountains of a lower grade, yet lofty anywhere but here; with several little villages, picturesque in their general aspect, though not in detail, and numerous farm-houses to which the same discrimination must be applied, — it seems a place to be admired and rejoiced in. The valley has an elevation of three thousand feet, yet is kept warm by the sheltering mountains. During my sojourn there I felt but one want. The atmosphere was too persistently and intensely clear to give me those constantly varying and boundlessly variable effects of cloud and mist, which are among the great charms of mountain scenery. Mont Blanc was not veiled for one moment, by day or night, nor was there any play of mists or cloud-shadows on the mountain-sides. Just after sunset, however, each evening, wreaths of mist rose from the valley, and were gloriously tinged by the rays that shot up from the western twilight.

My first excursion was the ascent of the Flégère, six thousand feet high, directly opposite Mont Blanc, and resting against the highest of the Aiguilles Rouges, a series of needle-shaped, ferruginous peaks. The path up the mountain crosses numerous cascades and torrents. The summit affords a view unsurpassed in grandeur, presenting all the mountains in their separate and widely varying contours, with the glaciers that lie between them and slope down into the valley.

After descending the Flégère, I crossed the valley to the Glacier des Bois (which is the lower part of the Mer de Glace), and entered the ice-cavern whence the Arveiron issues, — a cavern several hundred feet deep, the walls and roof looking as if built of pure rock crystal, with numberless pendent stalactites. Here torches light the visitor's slippery path. The pure brilliancy of the interior transcends all power of description; for imagery that shall give the faintest conception of it, one must refer to the Apocalyptic vision of the walls and gates of the New Jerusalem.

My next ascent was of the Montanvert, on the same side of the valley with Mont Blanc. I witnessed here one of the most stupendously grand phenomena of my mountain experience, perhaps not rare to Alpine tourists, though to me unique. I was toiling up a very high mountain-shoulder east of the valley, over which, though it was between nine and ten o'clock, the sun had not yet climbed. The mountain is covered with pines to the very top, except in the scars of the avalanches. I came to one of these scars, and looked up, when I was instantly reminded of the miracle of the burning bush, which gave the name of Sinai (*the bush*) to one of the peaks of Horeb. I saw a pine-tree burning, but unconsumed. Could it have been possible, I should have thought it actually on fire. As I looked, the next tree caught the flame, and then the next, till there were scores of these burning trees kindled into an intensely luminous blaze, and shooting up waves of flame into the sky. At length the fire-king showed his countenance above the trees, and they subsided into ordinary sunshine before his transcending lustre.

A slight descent from the Montanvert brought

me to the Mer de Glace, — an immense glacier which stretches down for thousands of feet into the valley. I crossed this, passing crevasses deeper than the eye could reach, and immense circular pits, down which torrents of water, as the surface melts, are sucked as into whirlpools. From the side of the Mer de Glace opposite the Montanvert is a very steep descent to the Chapeau, — part of the way, over the Mauvais Pas, which are narrow steps cut in the ice on the brink of a fearful precipice; and the whole of the route, under precipitous cliffs, from which pour cascades, in every form of beauty that falling water can assume, sometimes in sheets of crystal transparency, then in sheets of foam, then in showers of feathery spray. The Chapeau is a little rocky covert, with a small inn, still at a great height above the valley, whence the downward path — fearful no longer — lies by cultivated ground, by farm-houses, and among populous herds with their multitudinous tinkling; for no member of the herd is without her own bell.

I spent the next day on the Glacier des Bossons, the purest and most beautiful, and one of the largest of the glaciers. It is, in fact, a mountain of ice, which has accumulated between two other mountains higher than itself, and stretches down from an elevation of several thousand feet almost into the valley, sending out from the lower part of its surface singing rivulets and roaring torrents. I climbed its steeps, looked down into its crevasses, threw stones and fragments of ice into its whirlpools, and heard them striking against their sides, and falling into water a thousand feet below me. I leaped from crest to crest of the frozen billows, as I used to leap from rock to rock on the seashore in my boyhood. All the while, the grandeur of the ice-sea grew upon me. It seemed unutterably great and glorious, and was unspeakably splendid in its pure heights, with its unnumbered needles and pinnacles glittering in the sunlight, and hardly less so, when I descended to its lower altitudes, and saw the acres upon acres of huge rocks, gravel, and soil, which had rolled over it into the valley.

Coleridge's " Hymn " made me solicitous to see a sunrise in the Vale of Chamouny. I rose with the bell for early mass. The day-star had disappeared; but the waning moon was hanging directly over Mont Blanc, bright at first, and growing gradually pale with the increase of daylight. The air was clear; the mountains cloudless; the temperature just chilly enough to make a brisk walk pleasant and inspiriting. In a few minutes the great snow-dome of Mont Blanc was kindled with the first ray of the sun; then it was caught by its companion domes a little lower; then successively by lower and lower peaks and needles. And as each mountain caught the blaze, the light spilled over the summit, like water from an over-full vessel, and trickled gradually down the sides, till all the mountain tops and sides, except the Aiguilles from which the sun was to rise upon the valley, were aglow. All this while the sun itself was invisible. It was full two hours from the first illumination, before the sun had climbed the high mountain-shoulder, from which it looked into the valley.

The Arvé and Arveiron " raved ceaselessly ; " their voice would have been a roar, were it not so sweet. Numerous torrents and waterfalls were in sight, "and they too had a voice;" but it was almost drowned by the louder melody of the rivers. Sweet strains from Alpine horns, nearer and more distant, added to the charm. The immense glaciers sloped down from their fearful heights in full view,— as they approached the valley, surrounded by, and almost lost in vast boulders, splinters of rock, pebbles, and débris, that had been swept by them and over them from the mountains. There too was " the silent sea of pines ; " for up to the line of perennial snow, the mountains of this range, except where scored by avalanches, are all pine-clad. And the pine of Chamouny is solemn and sombre, very dark in its tint, straight in growth, slender, conical, forming one of the peculiar features of this whole region.

Glorious as the scene was, I enjoyed it alone. Of the hundreds of strangers in the village, I saw not one, though I responded to the invariable and courteous *bon matin* of a large number of residents of the valley, who were coming to mass, to market, or to their places as porters, waiters, or laundresses at the hotels.

While I was at Chamouny, a party ascended Mont Blanc, under as favorable circumstances, perhaps, as could, by any possibility, concur. A friend of mine, who was of the party, represented the ascent as involving such toil and hardship as could be endured only by a man in the fulness of his strength, and perils, not inevitable, but demanding, in order to evade them, both prudence and agility. The result was such a view from the summit as, according to the guides, is hardly to be obtained twice, sometimes not once in a season, and a showy diploma — for which a very heavy fee is always charged — attesting the fact of the ascent. I came to the conclusion that the enterprise is at once too hazardous and too doubtful as to its satisfactory issue, to be wisely undertaken, unless in the cause of science, and with all the precautionary arrangements which would connect themselves only with a carefully organized expedition. Fatal accidents occur on the mountain every season, and it seems arrant fool-hardiness to imperil life for the mere chance of a transcendently glorious sunrise on the ascent, and a sublime prospect from the summit. The other excursions from the valley — reasonably safe, and not overtasking the strength of a vigorous constitution — will give one memories that will be a life-long privilege and joy.

I went from Switzerland to Italy over the Simplon. At Sion I exchanged the railway for the diligence. A large portion of the road from Sion to Brieg ascends the Valley of the Rhone, crossing many of its smaller tributaries. For about half the way, the country is fertile, and the acclivities are all terraced for the cultivation of the vine, which here, as on the Rhine, is planted in hills, and trained on poles to a height at which the topmost tendrils can be reached by the hand. After leaving the vine-region, I found myself in what seemed to be the most sterile portion of Switzerland. There are still on this route many traces of Roman occupancy, especially of Roman military architecture, which has, in several cases, been converted to ecclesiastical uses. At Sion, a very spacious seminary for the education of Roman Catholic priests is built on the site, and from the materials of a Roman fortress. Tourtemagne (a corruption of *turris magna*) has a church, constructed by merely making the requisite alterations in the great tower — likely to stand for several centuries — from which the place derives its name.

The Simplon road commences at Brieg, and terminates at Domo d'Ossola. It was built, as my readers know, by Napoleon I., and was designed to be the chief among the unifying bonds that were to hold together his vast European empire. The conception and execution are well worthy of his surpassing genius, foresight, and energy. It is one of the most magnificent of human achievements; and for many years, until the completion of some of the more difficult railway routes, it stood alone and unapproached among the triumphs of the art and science of the engineer. It winds so gradually up the mountain, that there are no very steep grades in the ascent of between seven and eight thousand feet; and, though it is almost wholly a shelf-road, with precipices above and beneath, it is as safe, in summer, as if it were on level ground.

We passed, after the first hour, into a region of cloud, and often had no view of any object below us. Then we would get a momentary glimpse of the whiter or more dazzling features of the scenery beneath, such as the rivers and waterfalls. The road is carried through several long galleries, — some hewn through limestone, and garnished with stalactites formed by the melting of lime in the percolating water; some cut through ledges of mica-slate; some built over places where there is special danger of avalanches. One of these galleries is a long covered bridge under a river, which, issuing from a glacier above, tumbles over this structure into an abyss many hundred feet below. Wide lateral openings permit the traveller to enjoy in full the grandeur of this waterfall, and to wash his hands in its spray. It would be idle to enumerate the glaciers, cataracts, ravines, surprises of the grand, the terrific, and the beautiful, by, through, over, or under which, one passes on this road.

Suffice it to say, that the Swiss portion of it seems a close clustering, in intensified forms, of all the wilder types of Swiss scenery.

At the summit of the pass is a broad, sterile valley, flanked by mountains covered with perennial snow, with glaciers overlapping the margin of the valley. As a deep fall of snow renders the upper portions of the road exceedingly difficult and perilous, and a snow-slide may make sections of it for a time impassable, nine houses of refuge have been built by the government, and are kept constantly furnished with necessaries for man and beast. Besides these, there is, near the summit, the Hospice, a very spacious edifice, large enough to house an army of travellers, owned by the St. Bernard brotherhood, and occupied by a colony of the brethren, who furnish meat, drink, and lodging, gratuitously, though guests who can afford it, of course, leave their contributions in the charity-box. The apartments in the hospice are large and faultlessly neat, but damp, chilly, musty, and cheerless. A more dreary residence the world can hardly offer, there being nine months of pure and three of mixed winter. The monks seem the impersonation of benevolence; yet they evidently pay the price of their seclusion and their desolate abode, in the etiolation of their mental faculties. They seem stupid, dull, and impassive. Not so their huge and noble St. Bernard dogs, whose whole mien is that of human intelligence, and more than human sagacity and skill. They gave our party a most hospitable welcome, with the frank and genial air of courtly hosts receiving honored guests, and I could not but read in their speaking eyes, a consciousness of their humane mission. They and their masters hold sinecure places during the season of pleasure-travel; but for the rest of the year, the large amount of freight and traffic that passes over the Simplon tasks all their energies and all the resources of their skilled benevolence, — exposed travellers being frequently indebted to them for rescue from imminent death, and large parties being sometimes detained, for several days, by obstructions on the road.

A few miles below the summit, we passed the column which marks the boundary between Switzerland and Italy, and then rapidly descended into a most verdant and lovely plain, with types of scenery and architecture to me entirely new. The vines here are sometimes made to climb on trellises, sometimes trained from tree to tree; but they generally run over frames from three to seven feet high. The villas are charmingly picturesque, white or in bright colors, often with historical or sacred subjects, armorial bearings, or quaint devices, elaborately painted on the front wall, — beautifully embowered, — generally with square towers five or six stories high. The churches and chapels have similar towers, either at one corner, or detached, with an intervening space of a few feet.

Domo d'Ossola is surrounded by gentle acclivities, all of which are studded with such villas as I have described, while a panorama of lofty mountains bounds the horizon. I lodged here at an hotel of a construction of which I found many other specimens in Italy. It is built round the four sides of a court-yard, with no entrance from the street except an arched carriage-way, and with no interior staircases, but with roofed and railed galleries round each story, outside staircases leading from story to story, and the apartments opening on the galleries. My room was sumptuously furnished, but with a stone floor; and in Northern Italy, I found stone, brick, tiled, or marble floors, uncarpeted, the prevailing fashion. So far as my own experience is concerned, I would much rather dream of marble halls than live in them. Not only does an American crave the warmth of a carpet; his unaccustomed feet slide on the smooth surface, and he feels less safe in perambulating his own room, than in any other mode or on any other medium of locomotion.

I went from Domo d'Ossola, over a smooth road, through a succession of verdant and fertile valleys, and with rich and ever varying mountain-views, to Baveno, on Lake Maggiore. This lake is surrounded by gently sloping hills, with vineyards and locust and chestnut groves to their very summits, and dotted all over with white farm-houses, villas, and chapels. Here lie the Borromean Islands, almost tropical in their capacity of culture, teeming with the most gorgeous vegetation, and looking like the very Islands of the Blessed. The coast of the lake is sinuous, with many deep indentations and capacious coves; its waters limpid and bright; its little ports having an almost festive aspect.

I took passage on a steamer for Luino, which is an antique-looking place, with narrow, precipitous streets leading up from the lake, with many large dwellings and other buildings that have an air of effete grandeur, and with a not very large intermingling of dwellings that are both old and mean.

From Luino, a drive of two hours brought me to Lugano, on the lake of the same name, which is connected with Lake Maggiore by the river Tosa and three smaller lakes, along which my road lay. Lake Lugano is less frequented than Maggiore and Como, but is certainly not the least beautiful of the three, — lying like a crater, with a rim of irregular contour, varying in height from a few hundred to four or five thousand feet; overhung by vine terraces, olive and chestnut groves, gardens that seem suspended directly over the water, and numerous hill-side hamlets and isolated villas.

Half-way between the two lakes I had recrossed the Swiss frontier. Lugano is the capital of a Swiss canton, though in population, language, architecture, and habits, it is entirely an Italian city. The houses on the principal streets are built on arcades, which serve as an awning and shelter to the sidewalks; and not only almost all trades, but many of the occupations which *we* call domestic, are conducted on the outer margin of the sidewalks. There are several churches, only one of which, that of St. Lorenzo, is of superior architectural merit. In one of the smaller and poorer churches are three fine frescos by the elder Luini, — one originally painted where it is now seen, the others cut out from the walls for which they were designed. The hotel where I lodged, which is palatial in extent, and almost so in magnificence, is a secularized convent. Directly opposite to it is a beautiful fountain, surmounted by a colossal statue of William Tell. Near this, and most appropriately so, under an open dome supported by a circular colonnade, is a bronze bust of Washington, with the inscription, *Magnum seculorum decus.* This was erected by the Italian proprietor of a neighboring villa, who amassed an affluent fortune by commerce in the United States.

Close by the city is Mount St. Salvador, having on its summit a chapel, which, on certain feast-days, is a shrine of pilgrimage for the people, whose devotion, if measured by the toil of the ascent, must be sincere and fervent. This mountain commands, perhaps, as extensive a scope of grand and lovely scenery as any mountain in Switzerland. It lies directly opposite to the snow-covered range of Monte Rosa, fitly so termed, from the roseate hue in which the principal peak reflects the sunlight at all hours of the day, — a tint due, no doubt, to the peculiar angle which it makes with the horizon. With this mountain range, the whole of Lake Lugano, a large part of Maggiore, and the chain of intervening lakes, lie in clear view from the summit.

I crossed Lake Lugano in a steamer, and, after a pleasant drive of two hours, reached the Lake of Como, whose beauty — the theme, as it has been, of elaborate panegyric and poetic enthusiasm for more than two thousand years — cannot be so pictured to the inward eye, that the sight shall not transcend the imagination. Virgil, in one of the Georgics, erroneously names it as the greatest of the larger lakes (*tantos lacus*), and gives it the first place among these gems of Italy, in his enumeration of the points in which Italy excels all other lands. It is not, like the Lake of Brienz, a *Himmelsee*. The associations with it are Sybaritic rather than Paradisiacal. Everything in its aspect is in harmony with the evidences of taste and luxury that crowd its shores. It seems to belong to a heaven on earth, but to a very earthly heaven. A row across it on a fine summer afternoon, was the most delicious aquatic experience of my life. The water so smooth and pellucid, as blue as the sky above; the still air; the genially tempered sun-heat; the soft, thin haze on the shores and the mountains; peals of silver-sounding bells (for it was a feast-day) from the villages nearer and more remote; the slow and lazy plash of the oars (for I so far belied the proverbial fastness of Americans as **to** bid my boatman make no haste); the fleet of boats that thronged the lake, with awnings of divers tints, gay streamers, and merry parties in their holiday attire, — all have left on my memory an impression which can hardly be repeated or approached.

My boat left me at Bellaggio, perhaps the most charming place on the lake, and a favorite summer residence for English families. The principal street skirts the margin of the lake, with houses and shops on one side only, and pleasure grounds sloping rapidly upward in the rear. But a few feet from this most lovely of promenades, I was reminded how little Nature can do toward infusing her own genial spirit, fraught with the Divine love and mercy, into the soul of man. I had hardly ever seen a more revolting spectacle than on the outside of the principal church, — a spectacle, however, which was repeated to my eye several times afterward. It was a chapel — roofed over, but on the four sides protected only by a railing — surmounted with a death's head and cross bones; and within, so placed as to force itself on the sight of every one who entered the church, an immense pile of human skulls, with a charity box, and an inscription begging alms for the eternal repose of the souls to whom those skulls belonged.

At Bellaggio, I took a steamer for Como, and had, on the passage, a more extended view of the lake. It is narrow and sinuous. It sometimes so contracts and embays itself that but a small portion of it can be seen; then it spreads into a broader sheet, and permits an extended vista on every side. It is completely locked in by hills and mountains, which preclude all distant views, except that, at one point, a somewhat lower ridge permits a prospect of far off Alps. The hills are generally cultivated to a considerable height, and wooded to their summits, with only a few bare crags and a few spots abraded by avalanches. But, wooded as they are, they are seamed and corrugated like the barren hill-sides of Scotland. The villages on the shore are very numerous, and the villas numberless, often exquisitely beautiful; always showy, picturesquely situated, and making striking points in the landscape; often painted in fanciful patterns, really grotesque, yet having a fine effect as they peer out from the dense masses of foliage in which they are uniformly embosomed.

I am aware that there may seem a sameness in my description of these lakes, and it ought so to be; for they have very much the same characteristics. They might, perhaps, be best represented by the three degrees of comparison, were it not that he who saw Maggiore first would want to use superlatives, and yet would feel the need of intensifying them as to Lugano, and still more as to Como.

At the city of Como I slept under the guardian sign of the Angel, within a stone's throw of the lake, and the wash of the water over the pebbly beach gave its rhythm to my dreams. Before sunrise, I was awakened by a multitude of concurrent, but not concordant voices, bass and treble, strained to the highest pitch, and, on looking out from my window, I found what had been at nightfall a naked beach, covered with at least a hundred boats hauled on shore, which men and women were unloading of provisions of all kinds for the market, and of what I at first supposed to be rudely manufactured brooms, and marvelled that there should be so great a demand for them; but I soon found that they were fagots for culinary use, — mere brush, which we should not deem worth the space it would occupy, being almost the only wood ever brought to market there.

Attracted by this anticipative view, after breakfast I went to the principal market, and the spectacle was such a comedy as could be seen nowhere but in Italy, where childhood lingers into old age, and no experience — however stern or sad — can so overlie the mirthful element, that it will not be perpetually cropping out. The people go to market as if they were going to a play, all of which they were to see, and a part to be. On this occasion, hurdy-gurdies and volunteer-singers gathered numerous little circles of not silent admirers. News-boys were chanting, in the monotone peculiar to their tribe, the names and contents of their respective sheets. Men, and especially women, at their stands of traffic, in loud voice, were alternately lauding their own wares, and exchanging depreciatory comments on one another's merchandise,[1] — in good humor, for the most part, though the joke that went an inch too far, called out the flashing eye and the clenched fist. Fowls of every feather, alive, and imprisoned in circular coops, kept up an incessant shriek of weariness, pain, and terror. How hard it was to bring it to my clear consciousness that I was witnessing that operation — only a little less solemn than church-going — which, in our idiom, we term "going to market!"

But two objects in the city impressed themselves deeply on my memory. One is a monument to Volta, of scientific fame, consisting of a large pedestal, bearing in relief devices representing his various electrical discoveries, with appropriate inscriptions, surmounted by his full length statue. The other is the Cathedral, built wholly of white marble, with numerous statuettes and figures in alto relievo on the exterior, with an immense dome, and a ceiling which would be very grand, were it not for its gaudy and meaningless painting.

From Como I went by rail to Milan. I drove from the station to the Hotel Cavour, on the *piazza* (or square) Cavour, and the first object that ar-

---

[1] This kind of talk, half-playful, half-malicious, called, if we mistake not, in our vernacular vulgarism, "chaffing," seems to make up a large part of the conversation of Italians in the humbler departments of life. It appears to have been a characteristic of the same race in Horace's time.

" Tum pueri nautis, pueris *convicia* nautæ
    Ingerere."

rested my attention was a magnificent monument to that potential guardian genius of Italy, who, no doubt, was slain professionally by the learned Sangrados, whose chief instrument, all over the kingdom, is still the barber's lancet; for the Italian barbers all practice phlebotomy, and blazon their sanguinary art by signs too disgusting for description. The monument to this most illustrious of their late victims bears a colossal bronze statue of Cavour, with his name inscribed on the pedestal, and Italy, a draped and sandalled figure, also in bronze, with a gilt star over her head, and a stylus in her hand, represented as having just finished writing her statesman's name, her hand poised over the final stroke.

The streets of Milan are very beautiful. The hotels and all the large houses are entered by gateways opening into court-yards, which exhibit fountains, gardens, and richly ornamented grounds, frequently with frescos on the inner wall representing, so skillfully as to deceive one who does not look closely, lengthened vistas of verdure.

Leonardo da Vinci's Last Supper naturally held in my interest a place second only to the Cathedral which I described in a former chapter. The picture was painted so as to cover entirely one wall of the refectory formerly belonging to the convent of Santa Maria della Grazie. The convent church is still a church, and retains the old name, and some valuable pictures; but the other buildings are secularized, and used as military barracks. The refectory, however, is now reserved from all occupancy, except that of artists, several of whom I found employed in copying the master-work. The picture has suffered in every way, — first by smoke from the neighboring kitchen, then by an inundation and the consequent dampness, then by the use of the room as a stable in the time of Napoleon 1., also by the cutting of a door through the lower part of the table. In some places the paint has peeled off. But still the original surpasses its best copies, though there is one in a church in Vienna, painted from a copy made before the wall had sustained any essential injury, which preserves some of the details that are now obscured. It is remarkable that, while other parts are defaced, there is not one of the thirteen countenances which does not retain its expression, and not one of the thirteen figures whose attitude and action may not be traced throughout.

The most venerable church in Milan is that of St. Ambrose, built in the ninth century on the spot where, it is believed, stood the church in which St. Ambrose himself officiated. Here is a great rude stone pulpit, also an episcopal chair of solid stone. The ceiling rests on low, round arches, like those of a brick-kiln; and the strangest nooks and vaults open in every part of the edifice, which has neither symmetry, order, nor unity of design, but was evidently built at a time when architecture was a lost art. The most wonderful object in it, truly a miracle of art, and nearly as old as the church itself, is its golden altar, — ordinarily kept covered by heavy oaken slabs, secured by clamps and locks, but exhibited for a valuable consideration to others than the faithful. The front consists of plates of gold, plentifully garnished with diamonds, rubies, topazes, and other precious stones. In the centre are eight compartments, in which are figures of our Saviour and several apostles, with the traditional symbols of the evangelists, while in the lateral panels are wrought the principal events of the Saviour's life from his nativity to his crucifixion. The sides and back of the altar are of silver, enamelled, gilt, and decked with precious stones. On the sides are figures of the Apocalyptic angels with the seven vials, and of several martyrs with appropriate insignia. On the back are represented the leading events in the life of St. Ambrose. It is believed that the bodies of St. Ambrose and of two other saints lie beneath this altar.

Next to this in interest is the Ambrosian Library, which has one of the best collections of ancient books and manuscripts in Europe. The second story is a gallery of art, containing a few originals and master-works by the greatest mediæval painters, and what gratified me fully as much, large collections of pencil-sketches and studies for pictures, not designed to be preserved, by Michael Angelo, Raphael, Leonardo da Vinci, and other artists of kindred fame. Among these are a large number of grotesque caricatures of the human face by Leonardo da Vinci, evidently drawn for his own amusement, or for the amusement of children, yet showing in every line the master's genius.

But I must leave Milan, with much of what I saw there untold. I have grouped these sketches of Northern Italy with Switzerland and Chamouny, partly because I have in my plan no other room for them, but especially because this whole region is intimately associated with Switzerland, the Alps being nowhere out of sight; and the putative terminus of the Simplon road, in the purpose of Napoleon, being at Milan, and there commemorated by a magnificent triumphal arch, to which Austria added new bass-reliefs after her recovery of the city, and to which the government of Italy has added yet more recent devices and inscriptions, celebrating the inauguration of her career as an independent kingdom.

CHAPTER VII.

PARIS.

Manysidedness of Paris. — Its Exterior. — Industry. — Manufactures. — Holidays. — Charities. — Education. — Paternal Government. — The Boulevards. — The Madeleine — The Pantheon. — Notre Dame. — Chapelle Expiatoire. — Chapel of St. Ferdinand. — Père la Chaise. — Tomb of Napoleon. — The Louvre. — Jardin des Plantes. — Jardin d'Acclimatation.

The one attribute of Paris most emphatically impressed on the mind of the transient sojourner, and hardly less so, one would think, on that of the permanent dweller, is what the Germans call "many-sidedness" (*Vielseitigkeit*). It is in itself a microcosm, offering attractions for every taste, facilities for every pursuit, congenial society for every order of intellect and style of character. It might be the paradise equally of the fool and the philosopher. The most frivolous being on earth need there be in no fear of ennui; while the student can there devote himself to his books, or to self-communion, with as few distractions as in the cloisters of a university. The eye can feast itself to repletion on a walk in almost any quarter, or, better, from the roof of an omnibus; the æsthetic nature need not, as elsewhere, resort for its gratification to galleries and museums ; the philanthropist is satisfied, as in no other great city, at least by the surface-view of society ; the hospitable ear can find entertainment and instruction, copious, artistic, eloquent, learned, in drama, concert, or orchestra, in lecture, homily, or sermon, in all the tongues of the civilized world.

Paris is the cleanest city I have ever seen. The streets are daily and thoroughly swept by a regiment of women, before the earliest conventional morning hour, and though, under the long, drizzling rains of winter, mud is inevitable, it lacks both depth and tenacity.

Paris is the safest and most orderly of cities. If one contemplated living wholly for this world and its lower interests, and indulging his egotism and selfishness with the least possible interference from the equally narrow egotism and selfishness of others, Paris would be the home of his choice. But his moral nature might find little to stimulate or feed it. The great mass of the people have no other purpose than comfortable living, and there is, probably, no other city in Christendom, where the ideal and the maxims of life are so essentially atheistic as here. At the same time, in no other great city is crime so vigilantly suppressed, social tranquillity so faithfully guarded, government so like an unseen omnipresence. Vice undoubtedly abounds, and the numbers that inwardly own no restraints of moral principle, must be fearfully large ; but theft, robbery, and crimes of violence are exceedingly rare, and the persons and property of well-behaving people, both by day, and all through the brilliantly lighted night, are more secure in this great metropolis than in one of our New England rural villages.

The whole city has a bright and festive aspect. Though in winter there is less of sunshine than there is believed to be in the upper heavens over London, Paris cannot look gloomy. The principal building-stone is a limestone — almost a marble — of a very light tint, which, though durable, is so soft that it may be carved about as easily as wood. There is, therefore, a great deal of graceful carving on the front of nearly every building, — pilasters, mouldings, heads, busts, figures in bass-relief. This material retains its purity. Bituminous coal is hardly used. Wood is the chief fuel, and that is bought by the kilogram, and too sparingly consumed to load the air with its smoke.

Nowhere else is life so much like an infinitely complicated machine, in perfect order, all the springs freshly oiled, all the wheels moving without jar. The streams of pedestrians of every description meet and pass without jostling or confusion. The unceasing lines of carriages of every grade thread their way with wonderful rapidity, without collision, and, instead of the reciprocal swearing of coachmen to which an American ear becomes painfully accustomed, there is a more or less familiar exchange of salutations between the Jehus, who courteously make room for each other. Many branches of traffic are conducted on the sidewalks, or in barrows just outside of them; but they are so neatly arranged, and so quietly managed as to annoy none, and to minister to the convenience of multitudes of purchasers.

The shop-windows are an exhaustless study, for the exquisite taste, nay, the high grade of artistical skill, manifested in the choice and arrangement of show-goods. The shops are by no means so sumptuously fitted up as in our American cities. There is little expended in abnormally large window-panes, or even in plate-glass, though, in the best streets, there is more of it than of crown glass. Nor is it costly wares alone that attract admiration. However humble the department of business, its insignia are so ordered as to show and satisfy the national instinct for the beautiful.

There are no visible tokens of poverty in Paris, — not only no mendicancy (for that would be precluded by the incessant vigilance of the police), but no regions of the city that look like the nestling places of utter and hopeless pauperism, and exceedingly few persons, young or old, that are not decently dressed. This is owing, in great part, to the industrious habits of the people. There is very little strength that is not utilized. Men who could wield a sledge-hammer are not, as in the United States, found measuring tape or selling bonbons. The lighter kinds of traffic are left almost entirely to women, and they, instead of idly watching for customers, keep their hands employed in knitting, needle-work, or embroidery, even while answering questions, or awaiting a purchaser's decision.

The manufactures of Paris, too, are a source of general prosperity. About half a million, or nearly a third of the population, are officially reckoned as workmen (*ouvriers*), or workwomen (*ouvrières*), and the gold value of the annual products of their industry is estimated at not less than seven hundred millions of dollars. This estimate, of course, includes many articles consumed in the city almost as soon as produced, as in the case of the bakers and confectioners, who number several thousand. But it must be remembered that a very large portion, even of such products, is consumed by transient residents, who leave their gold to pay for it, and whose purchases are virtually foreign commerce, with no charge for freight or insurance. The manufactures are so varied as to employ every grade of strength, skill, and culture. There are heavy manufactures in brass and iron; and of the lighter and more costly products of handicraft, not textile, there is scarcely any one that enters largely into commerce which is not fabricated here. There are some manufactures of which Paris has the monopoly, such as the *articles de Paris* (so-called), under which name are included numerous articles of furniture, ornament, jewelry, and *vertu*. There are also some descriptions of scientific instruments and apparatus, particularly such as are made wholly or in part of platinum, of which Paris is almost the only source of supply.

While the Parisian is a thrifty producer of wealth, he is a frugal consumer. His skill stands to him in the stead of cost. The refuse and waste of an American family of moderate means, would feed a French family of equal number in a style of much greater luxury. The Parisian housewife buys, each day, just what she needs for the day, and no more; and the market will supply the purchaser's least demand, even to the half of a pigeon, or a chicken's wing.

As regards actual want, when it occurs, the mode of relief is so organized as to furnish the requisite supplies without cherishing pauperism. Though resort may always be had, in case of need, to the public chest, the only recognized guardians of the poor are the religious fraternities and sisterhoods specially devoted to this work, and bringing to it the discretion derived from constant experience; and whatever alms are bestowed are expended under their supervision.

The Parisian workmen have numerous holidays. The greater part of Sunday is so used, those who attend mass crowding the early services, and devoting the residue of the day to recreation. A pretty large proportion of the shops are closed on Sunday, and many handicrafts are suspended. I, indeed, cling to my faith in the Sabbath as a Divine institution for worship no less than for rest; yet I cannot but acknowledge that, to a people not addicted to intemperance or disorder, the rest alone is an infinite benefit. Then too, though there is by no means the conscientious recognition of church holidays in which Italian indolence takes so much comfort, the principal ecclesiastical festivals are observed by even a more general abstinence from labor than takes place on Sunday. And a Parisian holiday is an edifying spectacle. I was in Paris on All Saints' Day, and spent several hours of the day on the Champs-Elysées, the immense promenade and playground for the public. Thousands upon thousands of people were there in the afternoon and the early evening, — a large part of them in family groups, fathers, mothers, children, babies. All kinds of amusements were going on, — puppet-shows, fandangos, exhibitions of waxwork, of monkeys, of mountebanks, of jugglers. Many of the families were seated at little tables, with a plate of cakes, and a bottle of wine, or glasses of *eau sucré*. Others were clustered under the trees, on the elastic iron chairs, of which there are thousands in the public grounds. There was no drunkenness, no riot, no loud talking, nothing that could offend the most fastidious eye or ear, not even a rude boy; for there are no boys in Paris, — only babies, and precocious men. This immense crowd dispersed quietly and rapidly as night came on, so that at eight o'clock there remained hardly a trace of the afternoon's festivity. This, be it borne in mind, is the gathering place, not of the aristocracy, hardly of the middle class, but chiefly of what would be called, by way of distinction, the lower classes; yet there were very few whose appearance was not perfectly decent and respectable. How broad a contrast to our popular holidays!

The philanthropic institutions of the city are numerous, and munificently sustained, and there is no class of the unfortunate for which the most liberal provision is not made; but these institutions, being under government control, and managed by the red-tape system, advance less rapidly than they might, and often cling to the old methods because the formalities requisite for the introduction of the new are so long and tedious. The Parisian hospitals, as is well known, are frequented by students from the whole civilized world; but it is acknowledged that they are conducted primarily in the interest of science, incidentally in that of the patient. The first aim is to make a scientific diagnosis and statement of a case, and an accurate record, from day to day, of the varying symptoms. Experiments are tried with the utmost freedom. If the patient recovers, it is well; if he dies, the attending physicians or surgeons deem it equally well, if they have made a thorough study of the malady, and crowned their labors by a successful *post mortem* examination.

In the elementary schools of Paris, so far as I could learn, there is a close adherence to old methods. For instance, history is studied by beginning with the creation, and cramming the memory with ancient names, dates, and isolated events. The learner thus reaches the history of his own nation and of recent periods, about the time when he might commence the study of ancient history with interest and profit. But nowhere else are there superior opportunities for the higher departments of education, or equal opportunities for the pursuit of mathematics and the natural sciences. In the Academy of Paris, a university which has grown up around the old ecclesiastical institution of the Sorbonne as a nucleus, there are Faculties of the Sciences, Letters, Theology, Law, and Medicine; the professors are more numerous than those in all our New England colleges; lectures are delivered gratuitously, in every department; and the number of students ranges from eight to ten thousand, — those that have not their domicile in Paris generally occupying lodgings in the neighborhood of the University, and giving name and character to the *Latin Quarter* on the left bank of the Seine.

In Paris, one is reminded, at every step, of the minute oversight of the government, which, in this aspect, is truly paternal, treating its subjects as infants, utterly ignorant, and incapable of taking care of themselves, and prescribing by strict law transactions which elsewhere are left to common sense and individual discretion. Nothing is sold or bought in the market which has not passed under governmental inspection. Every tub of butter is tasted; every fish and fowl scrutinized. On hiring a carriage, one has the legal tariff of prices put into his hands, and the coachman who asks more than the prescribed fare, on complaint, loses his license. At a railway station, a functionary selects a carriage for the arriving passenger, superintends the transfer of his luggage, inquires his destination, and gives him a paper stating the precise sum to be paid for his fare. In all places of public resort and exhibition, gens d'armes are stationed to show visitors how and where they shall go, and they are seldom permitted to come out by the same door by which they entered. Every keeper of a hotel or lodging-house must make an immediate return to the police of the name, age, nationality, profession, last point of departure, and destination of each new guest; and the police are believed to acquire personal knowledge of the haunts and habits of every stranger. There was current, when I was in Paris, a story — probably authentic, for a well-known name was attached to it — of an American, who had taken private lodgings, lost himself on his first walk in Paris, and could remember neither the name of his host, nor that of the street in which he lived. He applied to one of the gens d'armes, who took him to the station-house, showed him the record of his name and lodging, and then led him home.

The principal streets of Paris bear the name of *Boulevards*. The oldest of these streets surround what was the city in the time of Louis XIV., and occupy the site of the fortifications that inclosed it, which were then demolished. Thence the name. The long and broad streets that have since been laid out on both sides of the Seine, have the same name, though not for the same reason. The principal of these Boulevards — continuous, though with no less than twelve local designations — is a street four miles in length, with double rows of shade-trees, with broad sidewalks of asphaltum, and a carriage-way of the most generous width. For a great part of its extent, it is lined by sumptuous hotels, fashionable coffee-houses, gay and brilliant shops. It is splendid by day; by night magnificent. It seems the exchange of all nations, and is probably thronged by as great multitudes as surge through the chief thoroughfare of London, though its superior width and the flexibility of movement characteristic of the French, render it always safe and easy to make one's way in the crowd. In front of the coffee-houses on the Boulevards, loungers of both sexes occupy chairs which are let at a small price, and often take their coffee or wine at little round tables so arranged as not to interfere with the comfort of foot passengers. On the Boulevard des Capuchins is the Grand Hotel, probably the largest and best hotel in the world, a city in itself, with seventy parlors and more than seven hundred lodging-rooms, — divided into several wards, each with its separate bureau of administration, and so conducted that each guest receives as prompt and faithful attendance as if he were master or sole occupant of the premises.

At the western extremity of this series of Boulevards stands the Church of the Madeleine, in some respects the most remarkable church in Christendom, inasmuch as it is wholly unchurchlike in its architecture, being as veritable a Grecian temple as the Parthenon. It was begun, and barely begun before the first Revolution, was partly constructed as a Temple of Glory under Napoleon I., then was made a church by the restored Bourbon dynasty, and was completed under Louis Philippe, having cost more than fifteen million francs. It is wholly of marble, without and within. It is surrounded by a Corinthian colonnade, with a magnificent frieze and cornice, and in the spaces between the columns are niches with colossal figures of saints. It has no windows, but receives light through four skylights which surmount gorgeously gilded cupolas. It has, of course, no tower or spire. The roof has a very slight pitch, with triangular pediments, in one of which is an immense group in alto-relievo, one hundred and twenty-six feet by twenty-four, representing the Saviour with the Magdalen kneeling at his feet; on the right, figures designating the virtues and graces of the redeemed, and on the left, figures of the vices that condemn the reprobate to perdition. The doors are of bronze, with eight compartments, containing groups from sacred history, each illustrating a precept of the Decalogue. There are, in the interior, several groups of statuary, among which the most striking are, in the marriage-chapel, the marriage of Joseph and the Holy Virgin, and, in the Baptistery, the Baptism of the Saviour,— John being represented as pouring water from a shell upon the head of Jesus.

The building is one which commands the highest admiration, yet not the religious awe which belongs to a temple of worship. It made me feel, more than ever before, the humanitarian, non-devotional character of Grecian architecture; for here every possible endeavor has been employed to Christianize a Grecian temple, and employed in vain.

Another building which refuses to be Christianized is the Pantheon, which, indeed, in its cruciform shape and with its immense dome, might claim a churchly status, yet is Corinthian throughout in its proportions and columns. It was the Church of St. Genevieve, and was secularized in the first Revolution under its present heathen name, which it retains, though now again made a church. The pediment over the portal contains a group in relief by David, representing France as dispensing honors among a numerous throng of artists, philosophers, statesmen, and soldiers. The interior is elegant, but bare and desolate, and it has the air of a great city hall rather than that of a church.

Far different is the impression left on my mind by the church of Notre Dame, the Cathedral of Paris. This stands on the island in the Seine, which was the original city, and still bears the name, *par eminence*, of *la cité*. It has now only the most squalid surroundings, — sheds, workshops, and waste ground, with the dismal Morgue in the rear. Its portals are of almost unequalled grandeur. In the vault of each of the three portals is a bass-relief, one representing the Last Judgment, the others, scenes in the life of the Virgin Mary and her mother, St. Anna; and all the residue of the deep arches is filled with figures, allegorical, angelic, and human, — lowest of all, rows of almost detached figures of angels and saints, conspicuous among which is that of St. Denis with his head in his hands, and above, tier upon tier of sculptured forms in alto-relievo, each wrought with exquisite skill, — reminding one, in this holy throng about the gates of the earthly sanctuary, of the "great multitude which no man could number" in the heavenly temple. This church has the three largest and most beautiful rose-windows in Europe. The interior has been greatly injured in its effect by the recent painting of the entire ceiling in veritable room-paper patterns.

I was taken into the sacristy, where there is a

marvellously rich collection of ecclesiastical vessels and utensils in gold, profusely decked with precious stones, and of sacerdotal and royal robes, especially those worn at the coronation of Napoleon I., and at that of the present Emperor. Here are also treasured, as peculiarly sacred and precious, numerous relics and memorials of the venerable Archbishop Affre, who was killed in endeavoring to suppress the insurrection of 1848.

The most striking feature of this church is the two huge and lofty square towers, fully as massive, grand, curious, and grotesque as they are represented in Victor Hugo's well known romance. The bases of these towers are surrounded by figures of various beasts, real and fabulous, in all sorts of comical attitudes, as if the purpose had been to furnish inexhaustible materials of merriment for all coming generations. These great stone images glare at the visitor with so funny an expression, that it is almost impossible not to laugh in their faces. From the tops of the towers, similar heads look down from long crane-like mouldings, projecting several feet from the cornices. The bell hung in one of these towers, is the largest bell I have ever seen, and as tolling on all the numerous great crises of alarm, tumult, and revolution, it has acquired an historical interest full of the most tragic associations. The view from the roof of the Notre Dame enables one to appreciate the greatness of the city, whose limits are almost coextensive with the visible horizon.

I have spoken of some of the grotesque details of this edifice. It is a peculiarity of Gothic architecture that it absorbs and assimilates all incongruities, as the ocean does the impurities of a river, or the atmosphere the smoke of a cottage chimney. Why such odd things were wrought, it is hard to say, — whether with a comic purpose, or with an occult allegorical design, or, like discords in music, as members of a more comprehensive harmony. Whatever theory we adopt, there are few mediæval churches in which something of this kind may not be found.

The churches that I have described are so well known by name that they seemed to crave special notice. I must pass in silence many others that might equally claim attention, were it not that they lack literary and historical associations. But there are two religious edifices of the most melancholy interest, which no one can visit without profound emotion. One is the Chapelle Expiatoire, built on the spot where the remains of Louis XVI. and Marie Antoinette were deposited after their decapitation, and preserved till the restoration of the Bourbons. The chapel is small and simple, with a modest cupola. On the right of the entrance is a marble group representing the queen as sustained by Religion; and beneath it is inscribed, in gold on black marble, the whole of her exquisitely touching letter to the king's sister, in anticipation of her own imminent death. On the left is the king, with an angel at his side addressing him in the words uttered by his confessor at the moment of his execution, *"Fils de Saint Louis, montez au ciel;"* and beneath is inscribed his will, which, as he had almost nothing to bequeath, consists chiefly of words of tenderness to his wife, counsel to his children, love to his kindred, forgiveness to his enemies, and Christian resignation and hope, — this and the queen's letter being both so redolent of the very spirit of the cross, that, as one reads them on that long dishonored, now hallowed burial-site, he cannot but take the royal pair into his heart with all the honors of sainthood. Over the portal is a bass-relief, in marble, of the transfer of the royal remains to St. Denis. In the long, covered vestibule by which the chapel is entered from the street, are two rows of cenotaphs, in honor of the members of the Swiss guard who fell in defence of the king.[1]

The other building to which I refer, is the Chapel of St. Ferdinand, erected by Louis Philippe on the site of the petty suburban grocery, into which his son Ferdinand, Duke of Orleans, was

---

[1] These same defenders of royalty — on the one hand mere mercenary troops, on the other hand religiously true to their military obligation and oath — are commemorated on their native soil by the celebrated Lion of Lucerne, hewn from the natural rock after a model by Thorwaldsen. On the rock are the names of the officers with the inscription, " *Helvetiorum fidei ac virtuti. Die* 10 *Aug.,* 2 *et* 3 *Sept.* 1792. *Hæc sunt nomina eorum, qui ne sacramenti fidem fallerent, fortissime pugnantes ceciderunt. Duces XXVI. Solerti amicorum cura cladi superfuerunt Duces XVI.*"

taken to die after he had been thrown from his carriage. This little cruciform chapel is simple, chaste, and beautiful. The very narrow lancet windows are painted with figures of Faith, Hope, Charity, and the patron saints of different members of the royal family. On the right hand of the entrance is a marble group, representing Ferdinand on his death-bed, with an angel in the attitude of prayer kneeling at his head, — the latter figure having been the work of a princess who died before her brother. In a crypt behind the altar is a picture of the death-scene, — a very poor picture as it seemed to me, yet of great interest, at once as commemorating the scene, and as giving what are said to be authentic portraits of the royal family and other distinguished persons present.

These memorials of the dead suggest, by an obvious association, the Parisian cemetery of Père la Chaise. The beauty of this cemetery is an obsolete tradition handed down from the time when every American graveyard was fearfully repulsive. As compared with our present burial-places, it is by no means beautiful. It has nothing rural about it, but is literally a *city* of the dead. Except the portion devoted to cheap and gratuitous interment,— where a grave is guaranteed for five years, and the same spot may be occupied by an indefinite succession of tenants, — the whole surface not needed for paths is covered with monumental structures, each inclosure being just large enough for a single monument, with a tomb beneath it, but without any room for flowers or shrubbery. While many of the monuments are costly and splendid, there are none equal in sumptuousness to the most costly, and few equal in beauty to the most beautiful, in Greenwood and Mount Auburn. There are many, however, that are made illustrious by the names they bear. Most venerable of all is the tomb of Abelard and Heloisa, in which the sarcophagus containing their full-length figures was constructed under his direction before he died, while the canopy beneath which it rests was built from the ruins of the Abbey of the Paraclete, of which he was abbot.

I noticed here, what has been often observed before, the almost entire absence of Christian sentiment in the inscriptions, unless the words *De Profundis*, which occur very frequently, be deemed Christian. In one inclosure, I saw a beautiful marble figure of the risen Saviour, with appropriate emblems; but in very few instances could I discern any word or sign of hope. The memory of the departed, however, is kept green. The street by which the cemetery is approached, is lined, for two or three furlongs, with stalls for the sale of memorial wreaths, generally made of amaranths, the colors so distributed as to shape the words of an inscription in the circumference of the wreath. The inscriptions are of assorted patterns, adapted to every shade of relationship, and of affinity by marriage, even to remote degrees; to every type of grief, from the intensest agony to very mild regret; and to every order of taste not too refined to purchase its words of loving sorrow. On All Saints' Day these wreaths are, indeed, in special requisition, but they are in demand all of the time. Nor are they placed on new tombs only, but on many that belong not even to the present generation. I saw rich garlands and fresh flowers on the tombs of La Fontaine and Molière.

In further describing Paris, I hardly know what to select from the unnumbered objects of admiration that crowd upon the stranger's view. I might speak of the monumental pillars and arches, among which the Arc de l'Étoile transcends in magnificence all other structures of the kind, and in magnitude and costliness surpasses even the triumphal arches of ancient Rome. Or I might describe the Tuileries, were it not that, when I was in Paris, a large portion of this immense palace was undergoing reconstruction, and while many of the old portals and façades were to remain unchanged, as they ought for their architectural symmetry and their artistical beauty, the general aspect of the building — which is more than a thousand feet in length and incloses two spacious squares — is now entirely different from that in which I saw it. Or I might enlarge on the magnificent, luxurious, *quasi*-regal appointments of the Hotel de Ville, the palace of the municipal government, whose festivities, under the auspices of the Prefect of the Seine, are on a scale of elegance and grandeur which might safely defy the competition of the whole extra-Parisian world. But I ought not to multiply descriptions of buildings, than which few things can, by excess, grow more wearisome.

Yet there is one edifice which I ought not to leave unmentioned, the Tomb of Napoleon, — to a large proportion of the French people the most august and venerable structure in the world, commanding, in many of its visitors, a reverence of look and mien which they show for nothing else in heaven or on earth. The tomb is a large and lofty chapel in the rear of the Church of the Hotel des Invalides, surmounted by a huge dome, — the most conspicuous object on the left bank of the Seine. The sarcophagus, which is of red granite, lies in a circular well directly beneath the dome, and five or six feet below the floor, with a rich mosaic pavement around it, and under a canopy of marble, supported by twelve colossal figures, allegorically representing so many epochs of the emperor's glory. The walls of the crypt behind the high altar are covered with bass-reliefs in marble, portraying the great moments of Napoleon's career. Over the altar is a wonderfully beautiful figure of the Saviour, in white marble, with a bronze cross. The entire architecture and ornamentation are massive, in faultless taste, and by no means inadequate as an expression of the prevailing sentiment of reverence and gratitude with which the French people at large cherish the memory of the first Emperor, — equally the reconstructive genius of renovated France and the scourge of Europe.

I spoke, at the commencement of this chapter, of the facilities afforded in Paris for every pursuit, and the abundance of models for every art. It would require a volume to describe all that I saw under this head; but the recapitulation of a small part may form a fitting close for this chapter. The Louvre is an immense palace, connected with the Tuileries, formerly a royal residence, but now wholly devoted to collections of works of art and curious objects of every kind, and open freely to the public every day except Monday. There are here, it is said, no less than seven miles of pictures, many of them a mere waste of canvas, yet with a moderately good proportion of master-works, and of works of high merit. Of ancient, mediæval, and modern sculpture the collection is very large, yet, as to the ancient, immeasurably inferior to those of Rome and Naples. There are here, too, halls upon halls of Assyrian and Egyptian remains, and mediæval relics; specimens of the porcelain and pottery of all nations and ages; unnumbered models of ships and objects of marine interest; furniture and utensils, rare, splendid, antique, historical; costumes of all times and lands; personal memorials of almost all the long line of French monarchs : in fine, materials for a complete history of not a few of the ornamental and useful arts, — as to the useful arts, however, surpassed by the South Kensington collection described in a former chapter.

Next in importance is the Jardin des Plantes, which comprises all classes of objects belonging to every department of Natural History, with lecture-rooms, where lectures, which may be attended gratuitously, are delivered on every province of the kingdom of Nature. The garden itself is less tastefully laid out and less carefully kept than the Royal Gardens at Kew, near London; but it is immeasurably better stocked with exotics from every zone and climate. In the garden is a menagerie nowhere surpassed in the number and variety of birds and quadrupeds. In the buildings that surround the garden are immense cabinets of botany, mineralogy, zoölogy, and comparative anatomy. The zoölogical cabinet is by far the largest in the world; yet there are some particulars in which the illustrious naturalist, whom imperial munificence has failed to win from his adopted soil, has made our infant museum at Cambridge undoubtedly its superior. There is a higher art, a more perfect system, a clearer evidence of organizing genius, in our museum than in the Parisian cabinet. It is also the richer of the two in corals, shells, and fishes, in duplicates available for exchange, in specimens and materials for the study of embryology, and in fresh materials for future investigation with a view to the advancement of science. At the same time, there is nothing in Paris to be compared with the admirable diagrams and paintings, and the wonderfully delicate sections of shells, that have been prepared under Mr. Agassiz's direction. I was most impressed, in this French cabinet, by the multitude and variety of the birds. Were they alive and on the wing, they would people thousands of acres of forest. There are humming-birds alone, to the number of several thousands. The building is larger than the projected dimensions of our Cambridge Museum, of which the present edifice is but half of one wing; yet in many parts it is crowded, in all well filled.

Hardly inferior to the Jardin des Plantes in interest, is the Jardin d'Acclimatation, devoted to the naturalization of such foreign plants as it is deemed desirable to have cultivated in France, and the acclimation of such animals of all kinds as it is supposed may become useful or ornamental citizens of the empire. Of course, the fiercer beasts have no place here, and there are few carnivorous animals. There is hardly an animal on the ground that is not tame enough to feed from the hand. There are innumerable strange and grotesque varieties of the species with which we are the most familiar, as of the goat, the sheep, the horse, the ox, the swine, together with various species of the yak, the llama, and the zebra. The varieties of the deer are very numerous, from the gazelle that can be fondled like a kitten, to forest giants with horns like trees. There are camels, too, of several races, that all seem the meekest of beings; and as they bow their tall heads to browse on the grass or twigs the visitor offers them, and ask for more with such tenderly beseeching eyes, they would melt even the functionaries of an English poor-house. There are dogs, also, of every size, hue, and use, — the only discontented members of the great family, evidently yearning for human society, and always ready to desist from worrying one another for the privilege of licking a visitor's hand through their prison-bars. There are here, too, fowls and feathered bipeds of every description, from ostriches to which a man six feet high has to look up, yet which behave like the very silliest of all flesh, to the smallest birds that are capable of being raised, and not unworthy of being eaten. There is also a vast aquarium, with an extensive school for the education of fishes, whether shell or scale, — an immense apiary, too, and a nursery for the various species of silkworms, and for the kinds of food on which they respectively are nourished. Under the regulations of the government, seeds, plants, and animals are here sold to citizens from all parts of France; so that the empire is to be made cosmopolitan in its fauna and its flora, as far as the laws and limitations of nature will permit.

In preparing this chapter, I have felt oppressed

by the affluence of my materials. Perhaps I have not selected wisely; but I have chosen the aspects and objects of Paris, which seemed to me most truly distinctive and characteristic. No one can sojourn in Paris without owning its preëminent claims, as, in the material arts, in all that ministers to the culture of the æsthetic nature, and in the sciences that belong wholly to the realm of things seen and temporal, the capital of the civilized world.

CHAPTER VIII.

NAPLES AND ITS VICINITY.

Naples. — Views. — People. — Modes of Living. — Vesuvius. — The Solfatara. — Monte Nuovo. — Lake of Agnano. — Stufa di Nerone. — Virgilian Sites. — Avernus. — The Acherusia Palus. — The Elysian Fields. — Cave of the Cumæan Sibyl. — Road to Sorrento. — Sorrento. — The Blue Grotto. — Capri. — Palace of Tiberius. — Road to Amalfi. — Amalfi. — Salerno. — Peasants' costume. — Present Condition of Italy. — Protestantism in Naples and Florence.

THERE is, probably, no other city in Europe, around which cluster so many charming associations as hang about Naples, — not for its own sake alone or chiefly, but on account of its position as the metropolis of a region in itself gloriously beautiful, full of sites of transcendent mythological and historical interest, and rich in memorials of ancient wealth, luxury, and art.

The Bay of Naples, on which the city lies, cannot be surpassed in loveliness, nor can the broad streets and the long, narrow park that run along its shore; and from the height on which the Castle of St. Elmo stands, with the intervening streets, as they lie beneath, almost lost to sight, the water view, becoming much more extensive, grows upon the admiration; while, landward, the eye ranges over scenes that cease to be intensely beautiful only where they rise into sublimity.

The streets of the city, except those that skirt the bay, are narrow; even the Toledo — the Broadway of Naples — is of quite moderate width; and the few public squares are not large or very attractive. The lower strata of society are densely peopled, — too densely for the hope of their rapid elevation. But there has been already a marked progress. Beggary, as a profession, has declined; and while filth and squalidness are still prevalent, there are numerous tokens of the growth of mechanical art and of the smaller manufactures. Yet the patient, provident industry of more northern climates is hardly to be found anywhere in Southern Italy, where work in its intensity and duration is measured by the stress of need. The poorer people live almost wholly out-of-doors. They have no domestic life worthy of the name. They cook generally on the sidewalks, in little brass pans, over fires of brushwood or charcoal; and if they eat under a roof, it is just within the threshold of an open door. Where they sleep at night, I know not; but in the day large numbers of them sleep in the sun, wherever they can find a nook or angle to lie in, — those who use baskets for the carriage of tools or goods, often emptying them of their contents to curl themselves up in them for the afternoon nap. This out-of-door life lasts all through the winter; for it is drier and warmer outside of the house than within, — the poorer houses seldom having windows on the lower story, and the floors being either earthen or of brick. Fire for other than culinary purposes is a luxury enjoyed by the very rich alone. The principal heating apparatus is the *scaldino*, a small earthen pot filled with embers. This is used throughout Italy, is carried about in the streets by all sorts of persons, and in one instance, at least, was put by a mediæval painter into the hand of an angel, about to start, it may be supposed, on some hyperborean mission.

I was in and near Naples for twelve days, close upon the winter solstice, and during that time, there were two or three days that reminded me of our mid-summer, and but one day which seemed suggestive of winter. No vegetation, except the foliage of the vine, was withered. Orange and lemon trees were laden with ripe fruit, and at the same time snowy with the blossoms of the next crop, — the air replete with their delicious fragrance. One evening I bought on the street, for half a franc, a huge nosegay of camellias and orange blossoms, large enough to have furnished all the official personages at a New England wedding with more sumptuous bouquets than are recognized in traffic by our florists. All this is, no doubt, due in a great measure to the subterranean fires, whose fearful proximity is attested by many phenomena besides those of the ever open chimneys, and especially by earthquakes, whose frequency has led, in that entire region, to the building of vaulted roofs, which, on obvious mathematical principles, can resist a severer shock than either flat or angular roofs could sustain.

My volcanic experiences — not to say "perils by fire" — may not unfittingly form the first section of my story of adventures in the vicinity of Naples. It was my misfortune to visit Vesuvius a year too soon. The mountain was so quiet that, by night, to the distant observer, it gave no sign, and by day, sent up only a very thin pillar of smoke. In ascending Vesuvius we exchanged our carriages for horses and guides in one of the suburbs of Naples. For about an hour and a half, our upward way was through cultivated grounds, and through vineyards whose grapes alone produce the luscious wine known as *Lachrimæ Christi*, — then over vast fields of lava and of volcanic scoriæ. The lava here had cooled in the most fantastic shapes, so that one could trace in it the contour of almost every beast or object that could be named, and a great deal of it lay in folds or ridges, such as, on a small scale, hot hasty-pudding assumes when poured into a plate. It cools very slowly, except upon the surface. From an aperture not more than three or four feet deep, our guide took out for us pieces so hot that we could hardly hold them in our gloved hands; yet this was lava that had been discharged in an eruption eight years before. These lava fields — black as ink — extend for several miles on each side of the bridle-path. In a brief oasis on this dreary ascent, are a hermitage with its chapel, and a royal astronomical observatory. Here we halted for a few minutes, and then went on again over lava fields, in what was the crater of an older volcano, of which the present Mount Vesuvius was the core, or centre.

At the foot of the present cone, we left our horses, and commenced what seemed to us an almost perpendicular ascent — each person being pulled up by two guides in front, and pushed by one behind — over huge scoriæ that would have been loose, were they not too heavy to be easily dislodged. This extraneous help is not, I think, necessary for an able-bodied man; but it would require a Briareus, with as many clubs as hands, to stave off the guides, who seem to spring up out of the very stones, are wild, fierce, and bandit-like, and make themselves intolerably annoying to the traveller who will not employ a full complement of their number. Indeed, had I not wielded with some little vigor a staff which I had retained, my three would not have been less than six; and every man who can, by any possibility, come in contact with a traveller, claims *backshish* of him.

Under this convoy we reached the rim of the Vesuvius which then was, and looked down into the still reeking and smoking crater, taking into our nostrils the fumes of chloride of sulphur which steamed up from the seething cauldron below.

We found the interior of the crater richly variegated with rocks and lava, containing larger or smaller proportions of sulphur, and not a few perfectly formed crystals of sulphur. We descended into the crater, which was then entirely crusted over, and walked with conscious security, except to our boots — they were badly blistered — over places where we could not lay our hands without burning them, over apertures in which an egg could be boiled in three minutes, over chasms in which paper thrust down with a cane was instantly ignited.

The prospect from the summit of Vesuvius is enchanting. Among mountain-views it appears to me as preëminent as Niagara among cataracts. Seemingly close at the foot of the mountain spreads the bay, with Capri, Ischia, and numerous smaller islands studding its surface, and with unnumbered fishing-boats lying or floating like mere specks on its bosom. The city of Naples and several picturesque towns, with gayly painted villas and white farm-houses interspersed along the valleys and hillsides, form a vivid contrast to the desolation immediately around and below; and the city so lies that, seen from this point, it has a more than earthly grandeur of aspect, — all that is mean and squalid being lost or glorified in the distance, while the more salient and massive features are thrown into a perspective that magnifies and exalts them. On all sides but that looking toward the bay, mountains — lying as in a billowy sea — of every type, conical, abrupt, craggy, jagged, verdant, shut in the horizon, while to the north rises a range of the Apennines, always crested with glittering snow. On the day of my ascent, the sun shone without a cloud, and the shadows of the mountains formed the only 'scuro in all the glorious landscape. The sea was so still that it looked, not like molten silver, but like a boundless sheet of burnished silver.

Our descent was very rapid. A guide took each of us by the arm, and rushed down with us over a side of the mountain which consisted wholly of ashes, lying so loosely that we sank ankle-deep at every step.

At a short distance from Naples is the Solfatara, — a volcanic opening, at which there are always tokens of peculiar activity when Vesuvius is in repose. The fires are always audible and visible, through an oven-like aperture about a hundred feet wide, in the side of a hill not more than three or four hundred feet high. The noise is as of the roaring of a thousand forge-fires; while from the cavern and from many breathing-holes in the surrounding arid plain, issue pungent vapors of sulphuretted hydrogen and muriate of ammonia. The soil, for a great distance around, is so hot that one cannot hold a handful of it with impunity; and it is evidently but a thin crust over an old volcanic pit; for it sounds hollow under the foot, and responds in a deep, sepulchral tone to a heavy tread.

A still more remarkable monument, though not now to the eye a memento of volcanic forces, is the Monte Nuovo, or New Mountain, — a hill more than a mile in circumference, and nearly five hundred feet high, which was thrown up by a series of volcanic eruptions, more than three centuries ago, and remained a mere heap of scoriæ for more than two centuries. The tufa has, in the lapse of years, crumbled sufficiently to afford soil for quite luxuriant vegetation.

Two or three miles from Naples, is the Lake of Agnano, from which a dense cloud of steam is always ascending, so rapid is the evaporation induced by the heat of subterranean fires. Hard by the lake is the Stufa (or Stove) di San Germano, — a house built over a vent-hole whence issues a stream of sulphureous gas and vapor at a temperature of a hundred and eighty degrees. Here are rooms for vapor-baths, where the patient receives this exhalation in its untempered heat, and other apartments, fitted as bed-rooms, where the heat is somewhat diminished by distance from its source. This hospital — a mere hovel, barren of all the comforts of civilized existence — is regarded with great favor by gouty and rheumatic patients, — many chronic and stubborn cases having yielded to the curative virtue of the stove, or, as is currently believed, to the intercession of the saint whose name it bears.

A few steps from this stove is the Grotta del

Cane (Grotto of the Dog), known to Pliny, who speaks of it as one of " Charon's breathing-holes." [1] Here there are constantly exhaled from the bottom of the cave, puffs of vapor saturated with carbonic acid gas, which, of course, seeks the lowest level, so that a man can live there while a dog would die. The entertainment of the place consists in the asphyxia of an unfortunate dog, who, in the travelling season, thus dies several times a day, and is reanimated by exposure to the external air.

One more fiery trial, — the Stufa di Nerone (Nero's Stove), a narrow subterranean passage several hundred feet long and a hundred and eighty degrees hot, with several hot wells, or springs, boiling up beneath it. I trust I may never again be brought into so close physical sympathy with John Rogers, as when I was persuaded to travel this burning road. The remote remembrance is terrible. Yet there are several men and boys, capable of working, who get their living by boiling eggs in this Tophet. How Nero's name came to be appropriated here we know not, unless it were given as his *quantum meruit*. But for whatever reason bestowed, the name of the stove must be nearly as old as that of the emperor; for Martial, in three different places, alludes to these wells, in one of them referring to their curative efficacy. "What is worse than Nero? What better than his wells?" [2]

---

[1] "*Spiracula Charonea* scrobis mortiferum spiritum exhalantis."

[2] "Quid Nerone pejus? Quid *thermis* melius *Neronianis* ?"

It is in the near vicinity of this horrible place that Virgil, whose favorite residence was Naples, has laid the successive scenes of the descent of Æneas into the infernal regions. This was undoubtedly in accordance with the current, though not generally credited mythology of his own time, and with the confident belief of earlier ages; and what was more natural than to connect these terrific prodigies with a fearful underworld, — a prison-house and place of torture for ill-deserving souls, — the kingdom of Pluto, the fire-god, and the seat of his lurid court?

I found no little pleasure in following the steps of Æneas, like him a living man in the realm of the dead. But how things have changed! Avernus is a charming little gem of a lake, about half a mile in diameter, with a very *facilis descensus*, but one as inviting as it is easy. It is almost circular, and walled all round by gently sloping hills; and its waters are pure and bright. Its name denotes *birdless;* for it was said that no bird could fly over it, and still live; but the birds certainly do not shun it now. There is now no forest-growth in its neighborhood. It is not improbable that, when it was surrounded by a dense and frowning forest, it was, because of its very littleness, dark and gloomy; and in that region of foul smells, mephitic exhalations that have since found some other vent, may have risen from its banks.

The Acherusia Palus, a salt-water lake, notwithstanding its ill name, can never have had anything infernal about it, unless, perchance, the epithet may have been applied by irreverent lips to its oysters, on which I lunched at Baiæ, and found them not only coppery, but charged with various flavors suggestive of a sulphureous underworld. The Lucrine Lake is hard by, and that, it is well known, had unequalled fame for its oysters, which now are of the same quality with the Acherusian. Have tastes changed? Or have the *mollusca* shared in the degeneracy of their human consumers? Both of these lakes are bright and beautiful, with gently undulating shores, and with tokens of no little activity in the oyster business.

Bordering on the Palus Acherusia, are the Elysian Fields, the only uninviting spot in that whole region. The inhabitants are the poorest and most beggarly of the peasantry about Naples. The only crop raised here is cotton, which, though it may minister largely to the social regeneration of Italy, is far from being ornamental, after the harvest is gathered and the plants are left dry and black. The Elysian Fields are the site of numerous ancient *columbaria*, each consisting of several tiers of receptacles, of about the shape and size of *dove-cotes* (whence the name), for urns containing the ashes of the dead.

Among the most interesting of my Virgilian researches was my visit to the cave of the Cumæan Sibyl. I walked by torch-light through a circuitous underground passage several hundred feet long, then mounted a man's back, was carried through a subterranean lake more than knee-deep, and deposited on a rocky platform, on which are shown the Sibyl's bed-place, bath, and seat, as also the outer opening through which her votaries sought, and the orifice through which she gave her oracles. I was taken also into several other little chambers in the rock, and saw, radiating from them, passages which have become filled up, but which, probably, once led to the upper air.[1] The situation of this cavern, close by Avernus, and its interior topography, make me believe that it is the very cavern of Virgil's Sibyl. Moreover, the Sibyl was no doubt a real personage. Nothing is more probable than that this cave was inhabited by a crazy woman, whose insane but high-flown words were regarded as tokens of inspiration, attached associations of sacred awe to her dwelling, and brought multitudes to her lair to make such meaning as they could from her fragmentary and oracle-like utterances.

These several Virgilian sites are in close proximity to one another, are but a few miles from Naples, and would be a very fascinating study for a prolonged residence. My visit to them was necessarily brief and rapid.

There are, to the west of Naples, two or three other places of no little interest. Nearest to Naples is Pozzuoli, — the Puteoli at which Paul found

---

[1] "Aditus centum, ostia centum."

friends, and stayed seven days on his way to Rome. The road to it leaves Naples through the Grotta di Pozzuoli, a tunnel half a mile long, and in some places eighty feet high, which was constructed before the time of Nero, and is a splendid monument of the masonry of that age. Near this tunnel is the so-called tomb of Virgil, the genuineness of which is a subject of dispute among antiquaries. The most interesting object in Pozzuoli is the ruins of the celebrated amphitheatre, in which Nero degraded the imperial majesty by fighting with beasts, probably less brutal than himself, for the amusement of the king of Armenia. This is the most perfect ruin of the kind that I have seen, with the single exception of the amphitheatre of Verona, in which all the seats remain entire, so that performances still take place in it. In the amphitheatre of Pozzuoli we can trace the entrances and vomitories, the portions of the building occupied by each class of spectators, the subterranean cells where the beasts were kept, the wells through which they were drawn up by machinery to the arena, and the robing and refreshment rooms of performers of various kinds. St. Januarius and his companions are said to have fought with beasts here, without injury, before their martyrdom; and his reputed prison has been converted into a chapel to his honor. There is here a white stone, which is said to turn red annually at the very moment when his blood is liquefied in Naples, — probably not without the semblance of truth; for nothing can be easier than to perform, before two sets of equally credulous spectators, two simultaneous pieces of jugglery.

There are also, in Pozzuoli, the remains of what is commonly called the Temple of Jupiter Serapis, whose colossal statue was found within its walls. I am inclined to think that it was a splendid bathhouse; for, on that hypothesis, it is perfectly easy to trace the several bath-rooms, and the conduits by which the hot springs in the neighborhood were led into them. Moreover, Puteoli was, for several centuries, one of the most fashionable of watering-places, remarkable for its hot baths.

There is a similar open question as to three imposing ruins at Baiæ. One of these, called the Temple of Venus — an octagonal building — is in excellent preservation, and has, at the several angles, pilasters containing water-pipes. It is well known that Baiæ was second, in the sumptuousness of its baths, to no place in the Roman Empire; but if these so-called temples did not serve that purpose, the bath-houses, which must have been spacious and magnificent, have perished without a sign. Of the numerous villas of illustrious Romans which once adorned this luxurious city there are few vestiges, and the village that now occupies its site is squalid in the extreme.

South, a little to the east of Naples, on the Bay of Naples, lies Sorrento. In going thither, I took the railway as far as Castellamare, so called from a most picturesque castle of historical renown — now partly in ruins — covering the whole of a little island a few rods from the shore. The railway skirts the bay, and offers a series of magnificent views. From Castellamare, I took a carriage to Sorrento, — still by the bay, — under rocks and immense crags completely honeycombed by time and water; by and over ravines where vast cliffs had been torn asunder by earthquakes, and the chasms on both sides terraced, and filled with orange and lemon groves; on shelf-roads, between beetling precipices overhanging the sea and terraced hills planted to their summits; through tracts of the most delicious verdure and fruitage; under large towns crowning the hill-tops and clinging to the hill-sides.

Sorrento is a port of considerable commerce, and one of the chief *entrepots* for the exportation of oranges and lemons; and on the way thither and in the streets, we encountered hundreds of women and girls from the whole neighboring country, with large flat baskets of fruit on their heads. The town is a busy place, celebrated for the exquisite fineness and delicacy of its wood-carving, and carrying on quite an extensive traffic in ornaments of this class. Its situation is beautiful beyond description. There is not a landward view that is not Eden-like, and the sea is overhung with orange groves that extend to its very margin. The contour of the sea-line is so curved as to break the impetus of the waves, which reach the shore **in lam-**

bent curls of silvery spray and with the softest murmur. Directly over the sea, stands the house in which Tasso was born, — now an inn. It is a house dilapidated by time and water; the chamber in which the poet saw the light has disappeared; and the entire edifice, projecting over its foundation-walls, with a strong inclination seaward, needs but a slight shock of earthquake to cant it over.

From Sorrento my friends and I took donkeys to Massa, over a mountain commanding a series of magnificent sea-views, and at Massa we embarked for Capri, in a neat and roomy boat, fitted with both sails and oars, with a weather-beaten old skipper of seventy-seven, and six stalwart, brown, barefooted boatmen, in physique and in temper as fine a boat's crew as I ever saw. Capri is a nearly circular island, about three miles in diameter, and consists of two closely contiguous mountains, with a very deep valley between them. Its coast is so precipitous as to furnish but two landing-places. The acclivities of the shore abound in the honey-combed rocks of which I have already spoken; and though, to my experience, the sea within the arms of the Bay of Naples was as smooth as a lake under the summer sun, I have nowhere else seen more decisive tokens of its mordant rage, and that for from one to two hundred feet above its surface. The island is wholly of volcanic formation, and the rocks, being of tufa, offer but feeble resistance, and are eaten into by the very spray.[1]

The waves have hollowed out numerous caverns, whose mouths are covered when the sea is high, and are entered with difficulty in smooth water. The most remarkable of these is the Blue Grotto. The mouth of this is so low that it can be entered only in a small skiff, — the passengers lying prostrate in the bottom of the boat. Within, we found an apartment about a hundred feet square and forty feet high. The light is so reflected through the opening, and refracted by the luminiferous upper strata of the outside water, as to make the water within look like a sheet of lambent blue flame. A normal part of the entertainment is for the white-headed boatman, in his shirt and drawers, to swim round the boat, in which operation he loses all semblance of humanity, and seems a veritable demon sporting in a lake of fire.

The valleys and ravines of the island are richly cultivated. The Capri wine has a world-wide fame. Besides the vineyards, there are large olive plantations, and extensive lemon and orange groves. The variety of cactus known as the prickly pear, here reaches an enormous size. It grows wild, is cultivated in hedges, and is much prized by the natives

[1] The rocks on the margin of the Bay of Naples, perpetually recalled to me the participle *exesus*, so frequently applied to mountains and cliffs by writers who must have been familiar with these same scenes. *Eaten out* would be the very epithet which one would apply to them spontaneously.

for its fruit. This is nearly as large as a Bartlett pear, has a sweet but insipid pulp, and, together with the seeds of the stone pine and fish from the sea, forms the chief diet of the poorer inhabitants, — some of whom told us, as designating the depth of their penury, that they could not procure macaroni oftener than once a week.

After leaving the grotto, we landed on the beach, and ascended, by what seemed a staircase rather than a road, to the principal hotel, the Tiberio, near the town of Capri. Thence we took donkeys, each pushed and pulled by two or more black-eyed, olive-colored, bare-headed, and bare-footed women or girls, and mounted to the summit of the highest cliff. Here, seven hundred feet above the sea, are the ruins of the principal among the twelve palaces which Tiberius built on the island, and which were all demolished, by order of the Senate, after his death. There are few vestiges of the other eleven. Of the one which I visited, there remain vast foundations and substructures. Parts of the walls of the immense bath-rooms are still standing, as is much of the wall of the great reservoir constructed, filled, and stocked as a fish-pond, in which the fish are said to have been fattened on human flesh. Many of the apartments of the palace can be distinctly traced, and some of the very beautiful mosaic floors are almost entire. We stood on the spot from which the tyrant used to have the victims of his cruelty and jealousy thrown, over an almost perpendicular precipice, into the sea.

We were called from our meditation on the many gloomy themes which the very name of Tiberius suggests, to an exhibition which the kindness of some of our party had pre-arranged for the common benefit. In a little hostelry near the palace and the precipice, several of our donkey women and a few swains loitering about the premises, performed for us, to the music of cymbals and castanets, the national dance called the Tarantella, — a wild, fantastic dance, conducted with so much energy, and with so much of what looked even like fanatical fervor, that I could not help thinking it came down by tradition from the ritual of some Pagan festival.

On our sunset passage back to Massa, the promise of a macaroni supper bribed our boatmen to sing; and once launched on the current of their boat-songs, they ceased not till we reached the beach, where our donkeys awaited us. Their voices were both sweet and strong, and it may have been happy for us that they were strong; for we passed very near the rocks of the Sirens, and if those maidens have not deserted their old dwelling-place, we needed a powerful counterspell to drown their seducing melody.

The next day we drove from Vietri to Amalfi, over a road said to be the most beautiful in the world. It lies along the Bay of Salerno, which is hardly inferior to the Bay of Naples. It follows, as closely as possible, the line of the coast. To call it serpentine would be to describe it inadequately; for no serpent ever had so many and so deeply involved sinuosities. Thus the view — always grand — varies from moment to moment. The road is generally many feet above the sea, finely built, sustained by a very massive wall, and drained by frequent sluice-ways. It has, towering above it, rocks, cliffs, and crags of every conceivable style of grandeur and beauty, with not a few of fantastic form and poise, — rocks vermiculated by the rain, — cliffs perforated by deep caverns, once the retreat of brigands, now occupied by charcoal and lime burners, and sending jets of smoke and flame from their mouths, — crags over which swollen torrents leap in feathery cascades. But the main feature of this road, and the most charming, is the almost tropical vegetation that drapes all, from the water's edge to the summit of the cliffs. From every crevice in the rocks, hang long streamers of maidenhair, or of some other equally delicate fern. Gigantic growths of cactus shoot out from the seemingly soilless surface of the precipices. Above and below the road, is a seldom broken series of terraced gardens, — sometimes not less than thirty or forty terraces, one above another, — planted with orange and lemon trees, interspersed with the olive and the stone pine. The orange-trees are often trained on trellises and over horizontal frames, as grape-vines are, and thus cultivated, they seem even to surpass themselves in beauty, as the eye glances up and down into a succession of penthouses completely roofed with ripe fruit and festooned with white flowers.

Amalfi stands on a very bold and high promontory, which forms one of the arms of the Bay of Salerno. It was, in the Middle Ages, the seat of a principality, had fifty thousand inhabitants and great political importance, and was rendered memorable by the reputed discovery within its walls of the lost manuscript of Justinian's Pandects. It has not now more than one fifth of its former population, and probably has not a church or a dwelling-house that is less than three centuries old. It is an entirely unique place, — the most perfect extant type of the union of magnificence and squalor, ostentation and discomfort, high walls and narrow spaces, which characterizes the mediæval cities of Italy. They are commonly built, for purposes of defence, on the top or brow of a hill. The streets are so narrow as almost never to admit a sunbeam. The houses are so dark that they are unfit for occupancy in the daytime. The churches are generally magnificent, and, in number and space, far exceed the needs of the present population; and to these the women resort at all hours of the day, — undoubtedly with a sincerely devotional purpose, but also, as it seems to me, impelled in part by the unacknowledged yearning of the æsthetic nature —

chastened, but not killed — for light, cleanness, and beauty.

The site of Amalfi is a declivity so steep that its streets are rude and irregular flights of stairs, over many of which a carriage could not be drawn, nor a well-nurtured horse induced to climb. Through the middle of the city tumbles a fierce torrent, which is arrested, on its downward way, to feed magnificent fountains, and which somehow succeeds in the creation of a great deal of mud, and does not make the town or the people seem less than the dirtiest south of Switzerland. This torrent is the chief wealth of the place, furnishing water for numerous manufactories of macaroni, paper, and soap, — the former having a cosmopolitan reputation.

The principal building is the Cathedral, which is very rich in beautiful mosaics and precious marbles, is almost Saracenic in its style, and has bronze gates of exquisite workmanship, which are known to be nearly nine hundred years old, and were probably of Byzantine origin; for Italy could not then have produced them. The crypt, which is itself a large church, contains a splendid monument to St. Andrew, with a colossal statue of him in bronze, and his reputed coffin, lighted by a perpetual lamp, and inclosed in a most richly wrought and gilded tomb. This church was, for many years, enriched by the dampness of the crypt. The moisture and mould that gathered rapidly upon the coffin, were sold under the name of "manna of St. Andrew;'

and not only was this manna deemed a specific in disease, but on one occasion, it was successfully employed in scattering a Turkish fleet.

Returning from Amalfi, we made Salerno our next resting-place. Salerno is beautifully situated on a crescent-shaped beach, to which the principal streets run parallel, and from which the town slopes gently upward about half-way to the summit of a hill of moderate height, whence it is overlooked by the ancient castle of Robert Guiscard. The Salerno Cathedral has bronze gates as old as those at Amalfi. Besides these, its chief wealth consists in the spoils of Paganism. The inclosed quadrangle on which the Cathedral stands is entirely surrounded by columns stolen from Pæstum, and there are several more within the building. In the quadrangle are no less than fourteen Pagan sarcophagi, covered with mythological devices, and there are three within the church, adorned with some of the most scandalous scenes from classic fable, all of which have been appropriated for Christian sepulture.

After breakfast, our landlord courteously invited us to walk in his garden, and, oddly enough, led the way up-stairs, through the attic and scuttle, out upon the almost flat roof, and thence into a garden on its level, the lowest of ten or twelve similar gardens on successive terraces. Here, just before Christmas, the first object on which my eye rested was an immense palm-tree, full of ripening dates. There were also flowers in profusion, especially roses, camellias, and laurestinas, — green peas, too, and lettuce ready for the table, and an abundance of ripe fruit.

On the south of Naples, one seldom marks any striking peculiarities of costume, though sometimes the attire of the peasant-women arrests attention. But to the northwest of Naples, the peasantry (who are often seen in the city) retain the national costume, probably with no change for several centuries. The women wear a head-dress that looks like a folded white napkin, a stiff scarlet bodice, white sleeves, and a white or blue skirt. They are almost always seen with loaded baskets on their heads, walking erect as pines, with their hands at their sides, and with a majestic gait that would have done no discredit to Juno. The men are less picturesque, and are often ragged and dirty. But they all wear breeches, long woollen stockings in numerous plaits or folds, and instead of shoes, pieces of untanned leather fastened to the feet by a complicated set of rope-yarn ligatures passing several times round the leg. Some old women wear this same foot-covering; but most of the women wear sandals and stockings.

I will say a few words here, simply because I have no room for them elsewhere, on the present condition of Italy, — a subject which might well deserve a separate chapter or even a volume, but the adequate discussion of which demands more than the cursory observation of a traveller. I might fill many pages with conjectures and speculations I can tell all that I know in two or three pages.

That in an industrial point of view, the Kingdom of Italy is rapidly improving, there can be no doubt. Agriculture is more skillfully conducted than formerly, and with largely augmented returns. In the whole of Southern Italy, cotton is extensively and profitably cultivated. Manufactures, both on a small and a large scale, by hand and by steam and water power, have increased, throughout the kingdom, with very great rapidity. The chief drawback to prosperity is the immense national debt, swollen enormously by the last war, with the oppressive taxation thus made necessary. This burden must be increased, in order to evade national bankruptcy; for the present tax is inadequate to pay the expenses of the government and the interest on the debt. An insanely and ruinously large standing army at once enhances the imposts, and drains the industrial force of the kingdom. In 1866-67 the rate of taxation in Italy bore to that in the States of the Pope the ratio of seven to two; for, as the Papal church and government own about one third of the territory of those States, the income thence derived of course lightens the burden on the independent proprietors. This condition of things is among the chief hinderances to the amalgamation of the Papal States with Italy, — the large tax-payers being almost unanimously opposed to annexation.

In Italy there is now universal religious toleration. The monasteries were suppressed and secularized at the beginning of the last year, with suitable provision for the army of cenobites unfit for secular callings. Protestantism is active at all the principal centres of influence, especially in Naples and Florence. In Naples I found two very well stocked Protestant bookstores, in one of which I saw stacks of several thousands of a next year's almanac, anti-papal in its text and its numerous wood-cuts, skillfully compiled, and for sale at about four cents of our money. There are at Naples, under Protestant auspices, ragged schools, and schools of a higher grade, at which several hundreds of children are receiving the rudiments of education, most of the pupils being from nominally Roman Catholic families.

At Florence, the American, English, Scotch, and Waldensian clergymen are very assiduous in the work of evangelization. The Waldensian clergyman told me that he had held in surrounding villages frequent public discussions with Romish priests, in every case with decided advantage to what he deemed the cause of truth. In and about Florence there are many persons who, without formally forsaking Romanism, never attend church or go to the confessional, but hold on Sundays neighborhood meetings, at which they read the Scriptures in the vernacular. There are no less than five hundred of these Scripture-readers in the city alone. As Protestants, we certainly have reason to rejoice in every such movement; but in Florence there is special ground for congratulation, as the progress of Protestantism is not the subversion of an established faith, however erroneous it may be by our standard, but an aggression on a prevalent skepticism, which, especially among men of average intelligence, had become the prominent phasis of religious thought, and than which there can be no force more perilous to private virtue and to public tranquillity and order.

CHAPTER IX.

POMPEII, PISA, PERUGIA, AND BOLOGNA.

<small>Destruction of Pompeii. — Its Streets, Shops, Houses, and Temples. — National Museum at Naples. — Unrolling of Manuscripts. — Relics of the Buried Cities. — Pompeii a Commentary on the Classics. — Pisa. — The Cathedral. — The Baptistery. — The Leaning Tower. — The Campo Santo. — Perugia. — The Staffa Madonna. — Pietro Perugino. — Bologna. — Raphael's St. Cecilia. — Guido's Madonna della Pieta. — The Campo Santo.</small>

On my way from Salerno to Naples, I spent a day at Pompeii, alighting from the railway carriage at the (so-called) Pompeii station, about two minutes' walk from the buried city. How strange this close juxtaposition of the railway, the type of the highest civilization of the nineteenth century, with the arrested and embalmed civilization of the first!

Pompeii was but a second-rate provincial town, yet a place of great private wealth, splendor, and luxury, — probably an abode of elegant leisure for many persons of high social consideration, and, like other towns in the neighborhood of Naples, a seaside residence for citizens of Rome. Previously shaken and severely injured by two successive earthquakes, it was finally overwhelmed by discharges of ashes and pumice-stone from Mount Vesuvius, which fell, it would seem, mingled with rain, — the steam from the mountain being condensed into rain over the doomed city. These moist showers of course precluded conflagration, though many objects were charred by the intensity of the heat. The roofs of the buildings, being generally of wood, were broken down by the superincumbent mass, which the walls of brick sustained uninjured. The air-tight covering over all the city has preserved entire many otherwise perishable objects, — in some instances in their original colors or but slightly faded, in others blackened or discolored.

Horrible as was the catastrophe, there is reason to believe that it was attended with less loss of life than is commonly imagined. The city was buried, not at once, but by several successive showers; and between the earliest of the series there may have been sufficient intervals for escape, and even for the removal of goods. That this was the case, is rendered probable by the fact that a very small number of skeletons have been found, and still more, by the scantiness of the amount of plate, jewelry, and coined money that has been disinterred, as compared with the known wealth of the city.

The surface of the whole region was essentially changed during that most eventful year in the history of Vesuvius; and the site of Pompeii had passed away from the knowledge of man, when it was accidentally discovered a century and a half ago. Excavations were commenced about a century ago, and are still prosecuted by the Italian government, though with a slowness and languor quite characteristic of Southern Italy.

Pompeii may be studied in detail, either on its own site, or in Naples. On its own site remain the streets, temples, theatres, houses, shops, with many beautiful mosaic pavements, and many exquisite frescos on the walls. But such mosaics and pictures as could be cut out from the floors and walls without injury, and all movable objects have been transported to the National Museum at Naples, where they are well arranged, sedulously guarded, and kept open for the inspection of the curious, the pencils of copyists, and the critical investigation of antiquaries.

The streets of Pompeii are very narrow, generally with room for but one carriage-track. Were it not for deep marks of wheels in the pavements, we might imagine that wheeled carriages were not used there; for it is not easy to say by what system the frequent collision of vehicles moving in opposite directions, could have been prevented. Two long steps will suffice to cross the carriage-way; the sidewalks are considerably raised; and there are elevated stepping-stones in the middle of the street, on each side of which one wheel of every pair must have passed. The pavements are of blocks of lava, doubtless quarried in the suburbs of the city, which was built on the lava of some pre-historic eruption.

Where the poor, if there were any, lived, it is hard to imagine; for, though some of the houses that have been disinterred are small, there are few which, in their materials, structure, and ornaments, do not indicate the wealth or competence of the occupants. Perhaps the laborers and proletaries lived in the suburbs, under shelters so frail as to have mingled long since with the stone and ashes that destroyed them.

The buildings preserved are generally of brick, covered with a stucco which is, of course, broken and defaced. The shops may be distinguished by their marble counters and their painted signs. An eating-house — for such it must have been — has, on its walls, pictures of men in the act of dining, and of bottles and foaming beakers. There is an apothecary's shop, with a serpent for its sign, and with an inscription still clearly legible, indicating that such shops were, in the old time, as now, favorite lounging-places, — "*Otiosis non est locus; discede, morator;*" "There is no room for idlers; loafer, begone." The buildings — both shops and houses — seem to have been in blocks, and the only gardens, except those attached to suburban dwellings, were within the walls of houses, of necessity all of them small, most of them very small.

I will endeavor to explain the usual interior arrangement of the houses, and it is believed that the houses in Rome were built on essentially the same plan.

The street-door opens upon the *vestibule*, which consists of one or more not very commodious apartments. Opposite the street-door, a door opens into the *atrium*, or court, which is the chief living-room, and generally contains more, and more sumptuous articles of ornament than any other apartment, having, in the better houses, a mosaic pavement and painted walls. The atrium is roofed, with an opening in the centre, toward which the roof is inclined on all sides. Under the opening is a tank for the reception of water from the sky, and here there is often a fountain fed by water-pipes from the public aqueduct. Behind the atrium is the *tablinum*, designed as a repository for the family archives, statues, portraits, and ancestral relics. Opening on either side of the atrium are smaller apartments. Behind the tablinum is the *peristyle*, surrounded by porticos that rest on rows of equidistant columns, and generally ornamented by statues, vases, and other works of art. The peristyle, like the atrium, has an opening in the roof, with a tank, or, it may be, a fountain beneath it; and this is the garden of the house, planted with trees, shrubbery, and flowers. From the peristyle open the lodging-rooms, and the eating-room, or *triclinium*, so called from the three couches which were placed on three sides of the low table, the fourth side being left open for the removal of the dishes. The lodging-rooms are mere kennels, just large enough for a couch, with no space for any other furniture, and with no light except from the peristyle, — an arrangement which indicates that the toilette must have been made elsewhere, — by the men, probably at the public baths. The triclinium is spacious, and in the richer houses, very highly ornamented. In addition to these apartments, there are various store-rooms, bath-rooms, sometimes a library, sometimes a chapel for the Lares and the Penates, sometimes saloons designed for festive or other purposes. In the less sumptuous houses, the atrium serves as the kitchen, the cooking being performed over braziers or stoves. In houses of a better sort, the kitchen is a separate apartment, in the rear of all the others. In very large houses, there is a second peristyle, with guest-chambers opening from it.

Such is the general construction of the Pompeian house, of course with many deviations from the plan, and, in the richer dwellings, with additional apartments for various purposes of convenience or luxury.

Most of the houses give evidence of but one story, though in some of them there are traces of staircases, both within and without the walls of the house. Moreover, we have reason to believe that in Rome the second story was always of wood, and if this was the case in Pompeii, there may have been an indefinite number of second stories that have left no vestige of their existence. As most of the light for the house was received from above, it is probable that the second story, where it existed, did not wholly cover the first. There were often gardens occupying a part of the roof. On the lower story there were seldom, if ever, windows opening upon the street; but there is ground for supposing that there were outside windows in the walls of second-story apartments. Panes of glass, even framed windows, have been found in Pompeii; but it is hardly probable that they were in general use. Chimneys are seen in connection with bath-rooms and bake-houses, but none in private dwellings. There are traces, in a few instances, of the conducting of heat by pipes from the bath-room to the triclinium and other private apartments; but probably, braziers were used for the most part on the few days in the year when artificial heat was needed for comfort. The smoke from the culinary apparatus, if in the atrium, had its easy escape into the open air; or, if in a separate apartment, it was suffered to find its own way through doors and windows. The chimney furnishes by no means the only instance, in which an invention of extended capacity of usefulness has been, for a long time, limited to the specific purpose to which it chanced to be first applied.

The Pompeian house enables us to attain, in

many respects, a clear comprehension of the life of its inmates. The ideas embodied in that most complex and blessed of words, *home*, can have had no place in such dwellings. There was nothing that could have served the purpose of a family apartment. The atrium made the nearest approach to it, but that was public, — a common passageway, and the place for a great deal of the household work. Moreover, the rain-water cistern in the centre must have been a dissociating institution, and the smoke, when the cooking took place there, still more so. Life must have been passed chiefly out of doors; and the places of public amusement that have been already discovered, would have seated the whole population twice over. Retirement must have been as alien from the habits of the people as domesticity; and we can hardly conceive of the more delicate tracery of character and the amenities of life as existing without the opportunity for both.

While we find in Pompeii numerous tokens of the refinements of self-indulgent luxury, the moral character of the inhabitants must have been coarse and sensual. There were discovered not a few works of high art, especially in carving and statuary, — the subjects being generally the commonplaces of the Greek and Roman mythology; but the paintings on the walls are, for the most part, voluptuous scenes, and some, which must have been perpetually before the eyes of whole families, are such as would be now tolerated only in the acknowledged haunts of profligacy.

There have been excavated two theatres, and an amphitheatre almost entire, large enough to seat ten thousand spectators. Several temples have been laid open to daylight, all of them, I think, of the Corinthian order, and of very elaborate workmanship.

As I have intimated, but few remains, or vestiges of human bodies have been found. There are some skeletons, and some moulds of human forms, in the moistened and then hardened ashes in which they had their age-long sepulchre. In the house in the outskirts of the city, to which the name of Diomede has been attached, several skeletons were found, — that, no doubt, of the proprietor of the house, who perished in a passage leading to what may have been his garden, with the key of the garden-door in one hand and a purse of gold in the other, and those of eighteen members of the household who had taken refuge in the wine-cellar. Two of these were children. Most of the others were probably females, as they had gold necklaces and bracelets. It is supposed that they stayed to take care of their goods till the doors were hopelessly obstructed. This is one of the largest of the houses, and must have been a suburban villa. Between it and the city is the Street of the Tombs, — evidently a public cemetery, or at least one in use by families of wealth and distinction. The sepulchres that have been opened here, are not unlike those that have been found in the neighborhood of Rome.

In the Museum at Naples, I saw even more of Pompeii than among the roofless walls. There I was interested in nothing more than in the rolls of charred papyrus,[1] of which there are hundreds, all more or less legible, though, to an unpractised eye, they might seem utterly worthless. Those that remain as they were found, look like cylindrical lumps of charcoal. The fragments of those that have been unrolled, which are all carefully preserved, look like layers of cinders of burnt paper. The process of unrolling is, perhaps, the most delicate mechanical operation ever undertaken. A narrow strip of goldbeater's skin is pasted upon two or three inches of the manuscript. This is attached by fine silken threads to a micrometer screw, which, being turned, slowly raises the portion of the manuscript in gearing at the time. This is read, copied, detached from the roll, and laid aside, and then the process is repeated for the next portion. I saw several of these machines in operation, and there is evidently work enough in hand to occupy many years.

While these shrivelled scrolls seemed to bring me very near their writers, I was even more vividly impressed by articles that spoke of the hurry and

[1] Most of these rolls are from Herculaneum. In the Museum, the relics of both cities are placed side by side, though so much the greater part of the articles, other than manuscripts, are from **Pompeii** **as** to make the collection preëminently Pompeian.

dismay of the victims of this calamity, such as specimens of uneaten food, all ready for the table, and as well preserved as yesterday's dinner might be. There are uncut loaves of bread, some of them in precisely the shape known to us by the name of *Sally-lunn*; fowls trussed, and probably roasted; a dish of the nuts which we call English walnuts, cracked for the table, together with smaller articles of diet, all easily recognized, the charring having been the only change wrought upon them.

In the culinary department, in which very numerous utensils are preserved, it is astonishing how little alteration has been made. The gridirons, stewpans, ladles, graters, skimmers, kettles (oftener of bronze than of iron), in shape closely resemble like vessels and instruments of to-day. There are jelly-moulds and formers for pastry, which might be used for a modern table without exciting any surprise. I saw moulds that represented chickens, hares, pigs, and hams, and a former evidently designed for the making of heart-shaped cakes like those which we have always been accustomed to see. The Pompeian gentleman boiled his eggs on his breakfast-table as we do; only, in the largest boiler that has been found, he could cook twenty-four at a time. Several quite elaborate cooking-stoves, — one with two openings for boilers, — have been discovered. It seems that careful housewives were then, as now, afraid of copper in certain branches of their art; for they had bronze stew-pans plated with silver on the inside.

To pass from the kitchen to the shop, we have not only the common balance (*bi-lanx*, the double scale), but steelyards of a considerable variety of style, all evidently adjusted with great accuracy, and some graduated with a nicety which could hardly be needed except in weighing the precious metals. Then there are compasses like those now in use, plumb-lines, weights, measures of length, measures of liquids, and dry measures. The measures are not, like ours, plain cylinders, but neat and pretty vases, and the weights are commonly busts of gods or emperors, figures of animals, or the form of some not unattractive object in nature. Some of the weights have their number of pounds stamped upon them. Among these is one in the form of a swine — the largest of the whole — with the letters P. C. (*pondo centum*, a hundred pounds). One of the weights has EME (buy) on one side, and HABEBIS (you shall have) on the other. In this department, enough has been discovered to reproduce, were it lost, the entire metrical system of Southern Italy, which was probably identical with that of Rome.

In no respect are the spoils of Pompeii richer than in lamps, lustres, and candelabra. Columns of the most graceful design, statues, figures in relief, forms of gods, men, and beasts, are employed to sustain the one, two, three, or at most, four burners; while the lamps themselves are made to assume fanciful shapes, among which the likeness of the sandalled foot is not infrequent. The simplest Pompeian lamp is graceful and beautiful, — a piece of coarse pottery, it may be, yet made as if an artist had sat at the wheel. But as for the light these lamps gave, the best that can be said of it is that it was fed by inodorous olive-oil. It would have been physically impossible to bring together as many of the ancient lamps as would shed, on any one square foot of surface, the quantity of light now given by a single argand or carcel burner. There is not a vestige of anything like the numerous contrivances by which, before gas came into general use, we had learned to enhance the illuminating power of oil.

Of sacred utensils the Museum contains a large and curious collection, embracing not only altars, censers, tripods, vases, and *aspergeoires*, but also various instruments used for the butchery of victims, and others of a more elaborate structure, for the examination of their entrails, — articles known to have been in the service, not of the shambles, but of the gods, from their having been found within sacred precincts. Withal there have been discovered not a few idols, or statues so situated that they must have been objects of worship, as also several of the magnificent couches on which the divinities were borne in public processions. In the Pompeian temples, we may find the origin of a custom which still prevails in most of the Roman Catholic countries of Europe, — the votive offering and suspension near the altar, of the form of any part of the body which was the seat of disease, and was subsequently restored to soundness. The ancients commemorated such cures in bronze and marble; the less costly gratitude of our century employs wax instead; but it is extended to almost all portions of the human frame, and I saw in the Strasburg Cathedral, miniature waxen faces, necks, backs, and windpipes, as well as hands and feet.

Armor, both of defence and assault, is to be seen in the Museum. The Pompeians themselves were probably men of peace; but there was, undoubtedly, some military garrison or guard within the city.

Various articles of harness and horse-furniture present both resemblances and contrasts to the modern style of equipment.

There is a large collection of surgical instruments, which throw much light on ancient surgery, and prove the antiquity of some of the most important, critical, and delicate operations of the present day, as well as the possession of an amply adequate apparatus, — in some cases, I am assured, not inferior to instruments now in use. Indeed, there was shown to me one instrument, — I forget for what purpose, — which has been adopted from Pompeian into the best modern practice.

There are numerous specimens from Pompeii of articles of the bath and the toilette, — bathing tubs (like our own), mirrors (of polished steel), combs, dressing-cases, hair-pins, crochet-needles, — also specimens of the stylus, the pen, the inkstand,— also fish-hooks, musical instruments, dice,— all denoting conveniences, habitudes, employments, recreations, closely corresponding to those appertaining to the most advanced luxury and refinement of the present time. There are locks and keys, not unlike ours, but more rude and clumsy,— hinges, house and table bells, knockers. There are open carriages, that seem to have been light, airy, and elegant. Then there are axes, hatchets, chisels, trowels, pincers, saws, vices, hammers, garden-tools, which show that the more common mechanical and industrial arts — skillfully exercised, as we know — had implements little, if at all inferior to those employed by our own artisans and laborers.

The workmanship of such articles of jewelry and personal ornament as have been found, is of the most elaborate kind, and the fashions are such as would not seem grotesque or inappropriate now.

The mosaics and frescos from Pompeii, preserved in the Museum, as to their style of execution, are of the very highest character, indicating the most perfect command of the resources and methods of those arts respectively; and of the magnificent collection of ancient statues, some of the choicest gems were dug up from the buried city.

Not to pursue an enumeration which might become wearisome, it may suffice to say that the city itself and the Museum, together furnish the data for a hardly less adequate conception of life in Pompeii, than were we carried back in retrospective vision to its palmy days. Moreover, it is mainly through the discoveries thus made that we are able to interpret many Latin words, to understand many of the allusions in the Latin classics, and to enter fully into the meaning and spirit of the lyric and epigrammatic poets, and the satirists, who furnish indeed the most copious commentary on the life of their times, but who sorely need on themselves precisely such a commentary as was preserved by the mud-showers from Vesuvius.

I propose to devote the residue of this chapter to some of the smaller Italian cities, among which Pisa may fitly claim our first regard. Pisa was, rather than is. In its venerable and not wholly decayed magnificence, it has an air of architectural stateliness, majesty, and amplitude, beyond all proportion to the numbers, wealth, business, and social importance of its present inhabitants. Therefore its palaces look sombre, less because they are gloomy, than because we get stray hints of sunken fortunes and plebeian occupancy; and the city seems deserted, though there is no lack of people, certainly none of beggars, because we look in vain for the kind of people that belong there. The city lies on both sides of the Arno, which is here very rapid and very yellow, and is crossed by a ferry and three bridges. The most busy and cheerful streets are those on each side of the river. The University of Pisa long had a world-wide celebrity. It lingers now in a sort of "death in life," and its buildings look more like the sepulchre than the cradle of learning.

But were all the rest of the city burned or buried, Pisa would still invite reverent and loving pilgrimage for its Cathedral, Baptistery, Bell-tower, and Campo Santo, — the four constituting an allied group, — the last three owing their existence and locality to the Cathedral.

The Cathedral is one of the largest edifices of its kind, being more than three hundred feet long, and nearly two hundred and fifty feet in height to the top of the cross that surmounts it. It was built before the Gothic style was fully formed, and represents a transition era, — being half or more than half Byzantine or Greco-byzantine, yet with many Gothic features, and especially showing the change that took place during the fifty years occupied in its erection by becoming more and more Gothic as it rises, the lower arches being round, the upper pointed, and corresponding differences being clearly traceable between other details of the lower and those of the upper parts of the edifice. This apparent welding of the two styles — to be seen in all the remaining parts of the original building — is rendered more striking by the fact that, nearly three centuries ago, the cupola and the upper portions of the nave were destroyed by fire, and rebuilt more purely Gothic than before.

What is worthy of emphatic mention is, that one feels no sense of unfitness in this mingling of styles here; nor is it always easy to define the precise point at which the one ceases, and the other begins. It is as if the Gothic had grown naturally out of the Byzantine in the architect's own mind and work.

The exterior is remarkable equally for the grandeur of its proportions and the inequality of its finish, — there being some parts constructed of mosaic work and the most rare and costly stones, while in others, the builders availed themselves of any materials on which they could lay their hands. Blocks of stone, of unequal size or of unlike tint, are laid side by side, or over one another. In some places stones from edifices of the classic ages, with Latin inscriptions, and even with idolatrous devices, are wrought into the structure, thus preserving not a few valuable antiquities. The front façade is unsurpassed in magnificence, having five successive stories of massive arches supported by rows of Corinthian columns. The bronze gates are most richly wrought with scenes from the life of the Saviour and that of the Virgin Mother. These, however, were made after the fire. One of their predecessors which escaped the fire, is preserved in one of the transepts, and is probably the earliest extant specimen of Italian bronze-work, this side of the classic ages. It presents scenes from the Gospel history, with no reference to perspective, in the rudest taste and the coarsest workmanship. It is no doubt between seven and eight hundred years old.

The interior is finished throughout, and the details are such as to enhance the visitor's sense of the vastness of the structure, though the effect is somewhat impaired by the glitter of the profusely gilded ceiling. There are no less than twelve altars, said to have been constructed from designs by Michael Angelo, and certainly, in their simplicity, massiveness, and grandeur, worthy of his genius. There are also, in a profusion of pictures and statuary, many works of art that have an extended celebrity. But, while I enjoyed these, I was yet more gratified to see, still swinging from the same point in the ceiling, the bronze lamp whose oscillations are said to have suggested to Galileo the theory of the pendulum.

Detached from the Cathedral, as is always the case in Italy, but very near it, is the Baptistery, which seems to me, though less grand than many others, the most faultlessly and exquisitely beautiful building I ever saw. It looks small by the side of the Cathedral; yet it is about a hundred feet in diameter, and a hundred and eighty feet in height. It is circular, and surmounted by a dome. In the centre is an octagonal white marble font designed for immersion, with four smaller fonts, adapted to the present usage of the Romish church, at alternate angles of the larger. From the centre of the larger rises a shaft on which stands a statue of John the Baptist. The pulpit in this building is deemed superior in design and execution to any other structure of the kind in existence. It is hexagonal, and stands on seven columns of as many different kinds of stone. These columns rest alternately on crouching human figures and on figures of beasts. On five sides of the pulpit (the sixth being used for the staircase and door), are carved scenes representing the Nativity, the Worship of the Magi, the Presentation in the Temple, the Crucifixion, and the Last Judgment.

The Campanile, or bell-tower, of the Cathedral, also detached, as is customary in Italy, is the celebrated Leaning Tower. I think there can be no doubt that this was intended to be perpendicular, and that it began to settle unequally while it was in building; for, above a certain height, the columns on one side are longer than on the other, — with the design to make the upper part deflect from a perpendicular as little as possible. The ground in the neighborhood is porous, and almost marshy; and the Cathedral itself has suffered so much from this cause that there is not a single vertical line in it, and all the nicer architectural correspondences are disarranged. The tower looks in as falling a condition in its own form as in photograph, and in ascending it or standing on its top, it is impossible for one to feel as perfectly secure as he knows himself to be. A plumb-line let down from the depressed side of the roof, would reach the ground thirteen feet outside of the base; but this inclination, great as it is, might be doubled, and still the centre of gravity would remain within the base. The tower is about a hundred and eighty feet high, and has eight stories, each story consisting of a circular colonnade, with rounded arches between the columns, thus constituting a series of open galleries. It has little ornament except these columns and arches; but they are wonderfully beautiful in their proportions and details. It is by far the most sumptuous, tasteful, elegant, and impressive structure of its kind in Southern Europe. In the upper story are seven bells, the largest — placed on the least depressed side of the tower — weighing more than twelve thousand pounds. Two of the larger bells were rung for vespers while I was on the bell-deck, and I found that not the slightest vibration or jar was communicated to the tower. The view from the top is very extensive, but flat and tame.

The Campo Santo — the remaining building in this group — is an inclosed gallery running along the four sides of an oblong court more than four hundred feet long, and a third as wide. It was built in the twelfth century for the reception of earth brought from the Holy Land for use in burial. Into it have been removed numerous monuments from the Cathedral; old Roman tombs and sarcophagi have been adopted in large numbers; curious mortuary inscriptions and memorials of various kinds, classic and mediæval, have been deposited there; and there are modern monuments of wonderful beauty by the best artists of the last and the present century. The history of sepulture, and the various phases of art connected with it in Italy for two thousand years and more, might be pretty thoroughly studied within those walls. While the Campo Santo yields to Westminster Abbey as to personal associations, it very greatly surpasses it as to the diversity, and the artistical beauty and interest of its contents. The walls were frescoed by artists of renown; and, though they have suffered excessively from dampness, and in many places the outer pellicle of plaster has peeled off, the paintings may still be traced without difficulty. Among them is an invaluable and most expressive series of scenes from the Book of Job, by Giotto.

Besides this group, the most remarkable building in Pisa is a little chapel on the river-side, dedicated to Santa Maria della Spina, which is a perfect gem of its kind, and entirely unique. It has the proportions of a Grecian temple, is perhaps forty feet by twenty, of white marble; and its entire exterior surface is so covered with statuary and figures in alto-relievo, that hardly an inch of naked wall can be seen, so that it looks, not like a building, but like a solid mass of white-robed saints and angels.

Perugia is one of the most charming places in Italy. Its site is more than beautiful, — it is glorious. It lies on an uneven and rugged eminence, with sweet valleys below, a glimpse of the Tiber in the distance, a splendid range of nearer hills, and beyond them some of the higher snow-crowned peaks of the Apennines. In ascending to the city, the horses of our diligence were reinforced by a pair of the magnificent snow-white oxen of the country, of the breed of which we have read so much — and not too much — about their majestic mien and gait in the sacrificial pomp of the Romans, in which they went to the slaughter with gilded horns, and crowned with festal garlands.

The city is wholly mediæval, quaint, strange, dilapidated, with vestiges of former grandeur everywhere, yet evidently with little remaining wealth, except of art. Most of the streets are too narrow for carriage-ways, and are frequently darkened by arches thrown across them from house to house. The city is surrounded by very old walls, with massive arches over the portals. Some of the portals are Etruscan, and probably bear a date prior to the building of Rome. One of them has an inscription, indicating that it was placed in its present site under the auspices of Augustus Cæsar.

The churches are very magnificent, and full of memorable works of art. The Cathedral, externally, is very spacious, but in no other way remarkable; within, it has a vast wealth of frescos, pictures, and carved work. It has a singularly beautiful pulpit on the outside, opening from within, — designed for preaching to out-of-door congregations. In the Church of St. Peter are some of the finest paintings in the world. In the town-hall are frescos hardly surpassed in beauty. In a private palace is the Staffa Madonna of Raphael, the earliest of his celebrated Madonnas. It is a small cabinet picture, representing the Virgin with a book, and the child looking into it as she reads. The expression both of mother and child is heavenly; and had not Raphael afterwards often surpassed himself on the same theme, this would, I cannot but believe, have been peerless among the Madonnas.

In the University is a very rich collection of pictures, and there and in the churches are to be seen the master-works (and they are very many) of Pietro Perugino, a native of this place, and the preceptor of Raphael. His paintings are marvellously soft and sweet. His saints and angels have countenances full of love and worship. His Madonnas have the presage of the blended majesty and grace, which his greater pupil no doubt caught from him, and carried to perfection.

There is, in the University, a very rich museum of Etruscan antiquities, comprising sarcophagi and sepulchral urns, together with pottery, some of it in forms which the finest art of our day can approach only by copying them, some of it in forms closely resembling our homeliest earthen ware, and offering even the precise prototypes of our bread-pans and bean-pots.

I saw at Perugia the most beautiful of Italian sunsets, — the clouds so luminous that they seemed condensed rainbows, and the whole firmament bathed in the purest azure.

Bologna has less of the aspect of decay than most of the other smaller Italian cities, not because it contains many new buildings, but because most of the buildings look as if they were fully occupied, and because in every street there are tokens of industry and enterprise. The streets are wider than in the Italian cities generally. In the greater part of the streets the second stories of the houses project over arcades which form a covered sidewalk. There are many splendid palaces within the walls; on the hills in the rear of the city are beautiful villas; and from these hills the view is charming, embracing numerous villages, and between them farmhouses, lying so near together as to indicate a minute subdivision of the land, and a densely peopled country. This is one of the particulars in which Tuscany has the advantage of Southern Italy, where the land is held in large estates, and so occupied and cultivated as to yield profitable returns with a minimum of labor.

There are in Bologna more than a hundred churches. The largest of these, but little smaller than St. Peter's, is consecrated to St. Petronius, — a name which had for me no saintly associations, the only person of the name with whom I was acquainted being Petronius Arbiter, whose works breathe any odor but that of sanctity.

The chief attraction of Bologna is the gallery of the Academy of Fine Arts. It is full of master-works, and contains more of Guido's pictures than are to be found anywhere else. The greatest picture there is Raphael's St. Cecilia. St. Cecilia, the central figure, is the very impersonation of sainthood; radiantly beautiful, but with the beauty of holiness; young, but with the maturity of profound experience, equally of earthly trial and of heaven-breathed peace. She is surrounded by a group, in which are St. Peter, St. Paul, St. Augustine, and Mary Magdalene, all so subordinated to her in the action of the picture, that she stands forth as the one queenly presence. She is holding her lyre, but as if she knew not that it was in her hand, and her face is turned upward in rapt devotion. Above the group is a clear blue sky, in the midst of which, surrounded by softly luminous rays, is a choir of angels, their lips parted as if in singing. They hold before them an open music-book, which is not angelic; yet it is so gracefully disposed, that, instead of marring, it enhances the beauty of the picture, as it helps to give concentration to the eyes, and to define the parted lips of the angels.

Hardly inferior, and among the few great works, the seeing of which is an epoch in one's life, is the **Madonna della Pièta of Guido**. It is a very large picture, and more vividly colored than any other of the works of the old masters. In the upper part of the canvas the dead body of the Saviour is laid at full length on a table, and the Holy Mother is bending over it, with a weeping angel on either side. Never have I seen the representation of so profound grief: yet the angels, with whom it is hard to associate the thought of sorrow, seem none the less angels; for their countenances and attitudes are expressive, not of earthly weakness, but of heavenly pity and sympathy. Below are the four patron saints of Bologna, all exquisitely painted, yet not so as to draw off attention from the group above, but rather by the contrast — if such a contrast can be — of lesser with greater majesty, to add to the solemn beauty and grandeur of the principal figures.

About a mile from one of the gates of the city, is the Campo Santo cemetery. A covered way under arcades leads to it, — some of the arcades having buildings behind them, but the range continuing without a break where there are no buildings. Behind some of the arcades nearest to the cemetery are shops for the sale of wine and confectionery, — one of which bears the name of the Orphan's Tavern, suggesting a source of consolation not strictly canonical. The cemetery consists of the cloisters of an immense old Carthusian convent, extended and modernized. Within is a series of arcades built round a hollow square, which is crossed by other series in various directions. The walls of these arcades, which are, perhaps, ten or twelve feet thick, are pierced with oven-shaped niches for the reception of coffins, and when a deposit is made the niche is closed. The monuments are either slabs let into the walls, frescos upon them, sculpture in relief upon them, or structures built close against them. A few only of the more illustrious dead have monuments that stand out in the centre of a cloister. The most conspicuous among these is the monument of Joachim Murat, Napoleon Bonaparte's king of Naples, whose statue does ample justice to his soldierlike countenance and bearing. Connected with the cloisters is a church, whose architecture is fully worthy of its surroundings. This cemetery is by far the most beautiful I have ever seen; and its method is to be preferred, I think, to that of our rural cemeteries, as it may be visited without exposure at all times; while, in our country, funerals and visits to burial-places are not infrequent causes of fatal disease.

CHAPTER X.

ANCIENT ROME.

First Impressions. — The Seven Hills. — The Capitol. — The Forum Romanum. — Trajan's Forum and Column. — Baths of Caracalla. — The Colosseum. — The Pantheon. — Aqueducts. — The Tarpeian Rock. — The Mamertine Prison. — The Cloaca Maxima. — Ancient Sculpture. — Inscriptions. — Church of St. Clement. — The Catacombs. — Hadrian's Villa. — Tivoli. — The Campagna. — The Tiber. — Vestiges of the ancient Roman Race. — Saturnalia on the Eve of the Epiphany.

ROME is, of all cities, the most difficult to be described. It is three cities in one, — the ancient, which has indeed its own waste regions densely peopled by tradition and memory, but of which there are not a few monuments amidst the life of to-day; the mediæval, with its churches, palaces, and ecclesiastical pomp; the modern, with its filth, squalidness, and beggary. The mediæval is, in numerous instances, built over the ancient, and constructed from its spoils; the modern has defaced and desecrated both the ancient and the mediæval in pretending to utilize them.

The first view of Rome is not attractive. The **Piazza** di Spagna, the principal square, is indeed bright and beautiful; the Corso, though too narrow, is a showy, stately street; the Pincian Hill, in trees, shrubbery, and magnificent views, is unsurpassed among the drives and promenades of Europe; the vast inclosure of St. Peter's is worthy of the world's capital; and there are many other spots in which we feel profoundly the indestructible grandeur of the Eternal City; but degeneracy, dilapidation, and decay are the initial expression of Rome as a whole. Yet, as the traveller lingers there, the old glory revives; its tokens multiply; its spell takes an ever stronger hold on sense, and thought, and emotion; and he who remains there a week, feels as if months and years would not suffice for objects which crowd perpetually on his curiosity, when seen, crave to be studied, and when studied, seem worthy only of being seen the more.

As regards ancient Rome, I was, at the outset, disappointed in the Seven Hills, which, though they all are marked elevations, are by no means so high as I had imagined, — not much higher, indeed, than the three hills on which Boston stands have been within my remembrance. But they, probably, were higher. There can be no doubt that of the earth and gravel which have buried much of the old city to the depth of several feet, while a part came from the river, a part is the débris of the hills, whose soil ceased to be held in its place by the masonry that once covered it. But the elevations grew daily to my eye, till the Capitoline Hill at length became to the sight, no less than to the thought, the august and solemn height which it was when it enshrined the insignia of the Republic and the Empire.

The Capitoline Hill is approached by a steep ascent, and its summit is now occupied by three palaces designed by Michael Angelo, making three sides of a quadrangle. On the fourth side is a broad flight of steps, guarded at the foot by two Egyptian lions placed there by one of the Popes, and at the top by colossal statues of Castor and Pollux standing by their horses, — works undoubtedly of high antiquity, recovered from the Ghetto, where very many of the choicest relics of the classic ages were long buried. In the centre of the quadrangle, — its third position, — is a colossal statue in bronze of Marcus Aurelius. There are various remains of ancient art in the open square and the surrounding palaces, — almost all of them brought thither from other parts of the city. The Dying Gladiator, which I described in a former chapter, is here. The Venus of the Capitol is peerless in beauty, combining with consummate symmetry, grace, and loveliness, the freedom and energy which belonged to the ideal of woman not yet limited and enfeebled by the restraints of artificial life. Here too, is the Faun, with which all have been made familiar by Hawthorne's Marble Faun, and which fully justifies his description of rare human beauty, conjoined with an expression of blended simplicity and cunning which somehow bears the beastly mark, though it is impossible to say to what beast it belongs. Here are also series of busts of emperors and of distinguished men, — many of them so characteristic as to attest their own genuineness. Here too is a mosaic of four doves drinking, found in Hadrian's Villa, which seems to be the very one described with admiration by Pliny,[1] — one of the finest specimens of workmanship in any age, and formed, not, as the Roman mosaics now are, of bits of porcelain manufactured for the purpose, but of actual stones so small that a hundred and sixty of them may be counted in a square inch.

Directly below the Capitoline Hill, between it and the Palatine, is the Roman Forum. Here the arch of Septimius Severus stands almost entire, and there are portions of the colonnades of three temples, with large masses of substructures and fragments. The geography of the Forum can be distinctly traced, and the ruins that remain are still magnificent in their dismantled and desolate condition, indicating what an immense wealth of genius and art must have been grouped around the assembled multitudes that thronged this vast area. In standing there, one wants to reperuse on the spot all Roman history, and still more the orations of Cicero, and in reconstructive fancy, to restore as he may, the

---

[1] "Mirabilis ibi columba bibens et aquam umbra capitis infuscans; apricantur aliæ scabentes sese in canthari labro." Pliny calls works in mosaic *lithostrata*.

objects of the nation's pride to which the great orator so often pointed, and from which so many of his most forceful illustrations were drawn.

On the Palatine Hill, the Palace of the Cæsars has left wide-spread but shapeless ruins, with only here and there a fragment, from which possibly a scientific architect might construct a pillar or an edifice, as our great naturalist builds up a fish from a single scale, but which to me — however impressive — gave but a faint idea of buildings, in extent, splendor, and beauty as far transcending the most sumptuous palaces now existing, as did the Empire thence governed surpass its individual provinces, — themselves now empires. On this hill are shown the various sites connected with the history of Romulus and Remus, and the cradle of the Roman Republic, — of course without any warrant or strong probability in favor of their genuineness. Not so, however, with the sites of the houses of Cicero and Clodius, which vividly recalled the passage in one of Cicero's orations, in which he says to Clodius, " I will build my house higher, not that I may look down on you, but that I may intercept your view of the city which you have sought to ruin." [1]

The Forum of Trajan is several feet below the present level of the surrounding streets. The whole space has been excavated, and while the upper

---

[1] " Tollam altius tectum, non ut ego te despiciam, sed ne tu aspicias urbem eam, quam delere voluisti."

portions of the columns were destroyed or worked up many centuries ago, the portions that were underground remain, so that the forum is now studded all over with the bases and stumps of marble and granite pillars, which must have been of unsurpassed beauty. In the centre of this truncated stone grove stands, where it has stood for seventeen centuries and a half, Trajan's Column, of white marble, somewhat discolored, but otherwise in perfect preservation. It is a hundred feet high, and from the base to the capital there is a spiral arrangement of figures in relief, as if on a scroll wound around the column. Here are not far from twenty-five hundred human figures, besides fortresses and military objects of various kinds, — the whole constituting a sculptured history of Trajan's successful and triumphant campaigns on the Danube. The column, though combining several orders, is graceful in its proportions, and the carved work could not be more skillfully executed. It was originally surmounted by the colossal statue of Trajan, with a globe in his hand. The globe remains, and is deposited in the Museum of the Capitol; and instead of the Emperor is a colossal St. Peter, in bronze heavily gilded. Not unlike this in style, with a similar scroll-like record of military achievements, is the Column of Marcus Antoninus, which is now crowned with a colossal statue of St. Paul.

These are the most nearly perfect of all the

monuments of antiquity. There are many single columns of temples, and clusters of two or three columns, remaining detached from all other buildings, looking as if ready to fall, yet as beautiful as they ever were, and evincing a purer taste than can be found in any of the structures of mediæval or modern Rome. There are also many remains of ancient buildings, which have been made parts of modern buildings, — pillars, cornices, large portions of houses and temples, built into public edifices, private dwellings, even bakers' shops; columns of Pagan temples transplanted into churches; fragments of old walls incorporated into new walls; portions of imperial baths utilized for various purposes of the present day.

The baths of ancient Rome are among the most majestic ruins in and about the city. Luxury had, in the days of the emperors, reached such a height, that bathing, and the amusements, relaxations, and personal indulgences connected with it were among the chief occupations of life. Several of the emperors built baths more extensive than their palaces, and covering many acres. The ruins of the Baths of Caracalla are nearly a mile in circuit. This vast establishment included halls for every kind of game and recreation, a large theatre, a temple, a picture-gallery, together with arrangements on the most extensive scale for hot and cold bathing, and for all the luxurious accompaniments of the bath, which were introduced as Rome became more and more like the cities of the East. There was room here for sixteen hundred bathers at a time. Enough of the foundations, walls, and partitions of the various apartments remains, for the identification of their several styles and uses, and many of the mosaics are so nearly perfect, that the contour of the figures on the floor can be distinctly traced. Some of the choicest statues now in the galleries were found here. Nothing excites so much admiration of the wealth and grandeur of the ancient city as this forest of brick and mortar. Such structures as these were undoubtedly meant by the emperors who built them, as the purchase of their lives. By throwing open these costly and sumptuous places of resort to the people, they procured an amnesty which would not otherwise have been granted them for tyranny, ferocity, and licentiousness; staved off for a season the inevitable massacre which commonly put a period to their reigns; and even gained a certain popularity among those of their subjects who were not near enough to the throne to be its expectant victims.

My first view of the Colosseum was by the light of the full moon, and I am sure that in the face of no work of man can the solemn grandeur of that occasion ever be repeated in my experience. The Colosseum stands apart from the city, as such a ruin should; and Rome is so very dimly lighted, and so still by night, that there was only a faint glimmer from the streets, and hardly a sound of voice or wheel to remind us of the living world. And then such deep arches, such heavy shadows, such dreary vaults and passages, such sudden flashes of moonlight as one emerges from them, such weird, ghostlike forms as visitors, guides, and sentinels appear to one another, such sombre memories of the night-side of humanity as haunt the scene, and seem to project themselves visibly on that once bloody arena, — all conspire to make the first night-visit a most noteworthy epoch.

The Colosseum was so built as to seat nearly a hundred thousand spectators. It is an elliptical amphitheatre, nearly circular, with tiers of seats rising rapidly one above another, to the number of sixty or eighty, — each tier so elevated as to permit its occupants to look over the heads of those next below them. The seats surrounded an arena large enough for the conflicts of a little army of wild beasts or the manœuvres of several hundred gladiators. The building had no roof; but the spectators were protected by awnings. Externally more than a hundred and fifty feet high, it consisted of four stories, the piers or pilasters in the lower story being of the Doric order; those in the next, of the Ionic; those in the two upper, of the Corinthian. This was doubtless designed with a view to the adaptation of the Doric to the sustaining of heavy weights, the lightness and airiness of the Corinthian, and the position of the Ionic as midway between the two and partaking of the properties of both. Several of the palaces of Rome have been built from the pillage of this structure; but the spoiler's hand has now been arrested. Rome lives by its ruins, and cannot afford to have them further tampered with. The Colosseum shows, by daylight, patches of modern masonry, which have been inserted to hold the old together; and the Pope, partly in order to make its dilapidation an act of sacrilege, about a century ago consecrated the entire edifice as a church, in memory of the numerous martyrs — St. Ignatius among the rest — who, from this arena, passed through a bloody death to heaven. There is now a rude pulpit in the centre, with stations for worship in various parts of the arena; and I never was there in the day-time without seeing some suppliant kneeling at these specially sacred spots in their order.

The flora of the Colosseum is said to be gorgeous in summer, and the species that may be found there amount to several hundred. I saw a few hardy species in full bloom in mid-winter.

Among the ancient edifices of Rome, the only one that can be said to approach complete preservation, is the Pantheon, which was, as its name implies, the house of Roman hospitality for the gods of all nations, was saved, no doubt, by its consecration as a Christian church early in the seventh century, and has sustained no essential change. It is a rotunda, with a very much flattened dome, of a height from the floor about equal to the diameter of the building. It has seven deep recesses, containing altars, and most of them, tombs, the tomb of Raphael being of the number. It is lighted wholly through an opening in the dome, and is abundantly watered through it, the floor, which is of porphyry and other precious stones arranged in patterns of great beauty, being as wet on a rainy day as the pavement outside. It is also liable to be overflowed whenever the Tiber rises above its banks, — a habit to which it is as much addicted as it was in the days of Horace. The portico of the Pantheon is second only to the Parthenon, among the extant specimens of temple architecture. It consists of sixteen Corinthian columns of granite, with marble capitals and bases, eight of them in front, and the other eight filling in the sides.

Ancient Rome was supplied with water by several aqueducts, from sources the most remote of which was nearly fifty miles distant. Among the most picturesque ruins are these structures, one of which has remained entire, and furnishes the best water the city has; and others have, in some places, long lines of arches still tight and strong, needing only the rebuilding of short connecting portions to make them again serviceable. The Roman aqueducts were carried as nearly on a level as was possible; for the ancients knew not that water conducted under ground would rise to the same level with its source. Accordingly, the elevation of these works above the low, marshy ground of the Campagna makes them often by far the most conspicuous objects in the landscape, and constantly deepens our admiration of a building power whose structures seem hardly less enduring, and have probably been less impaired by eighteen or twenty centuries, than the Alban Hills.

The Tarpeian Rock still faces the Forum, and presents a precipice not less than seventy feet in height; though, with gardens above and below, it has lost much of the terrific aspect which it bore, no doubt, when it was the place of execution for traitors.

A church is now built over the Mamertine Prison, and the descent to this horrible dungeon is from the porch of the church. The prison was constructed by Ancus Martius, and is in the heaviest style of Etruscan architecture. It consists of two subterranean cells, one above the other. It is believed that St. Paul and St. Peter were confined there, and the upper cell is now dedicated as a chapel to St. Peter. From beneath the earthen floor of the lower cell bubbles up a limpid spring of living water, which is referred to in Roman history as having existed at an earlier date, but which, according to the church tradition, welled up miraculously to supply St. Peter with the means of baptizing his converted jailors. On the staircase leading into the dungeon is a deep indentation in the rock, which is believed, on the authority of the church, to have been occasioned by St. Peter's striking his head against the wall as he descended in the dark.

Another relic of the kings of Rome is the Cloaca Maxima, which must have approached in magnitude the present Parisian sewers; for there were parts of it through which a wagon of the ordinary size could be drawn. The masonry at its outlet, composed of huge blocks of peperino, is still entire, and from its mouth on the bank of the Tiber issues a spring, at which women may daily be seen washing their clothes. Of course its utility as a sewer has ceased, else even Roman housewives — regardless as they are of decency — could hardly employ it as a lavatory.

Among the most beautiful remains of ancient art there stand on the summit of the Quirinal Hill bronze statues of Castor and Pollux, each holding his prancing horse by the bridle. The horses are as spirited as life could make them. You almost hear their breathing, and expect them to break loose from their masters. They were taken from the Baths of Constantine, and are currently believed to have been the works of Phidias and Praxiteles. Certain it is that horses of higher artistical merit can never have been moulded or cast.

These four figures are entire, and almost uninjured. It is, however, a very common thing to see a statue truncated of some feature or limb, sometimes of head, feet, or hands, very often of the nose, — yet in what remains a master-work, and the study and joy of modern sculptors and connoisseurs. In the Museum of the Capitol are preserved several colossal hands and feet of surpassing perfectness and beauty, belonging to works of the residue of which no vestige remains. Some of the statues have been restored by modern sculptors, and not always so skillfully as to conceal even from an unpractised eye the decline of plastic art. Sometimes in the putting together of the members of ancient statues there is an evident discrepancy between the parts, reminding one of the legendary miracle of St. Spiridion, who, when on his way with several of his brethren to the Council of Nicæa, finding that the Arians who lodged at the same caravansary had cut off the heads of all the horses of his party, replaced the heads in the dark, and started on his journey before dawn, but saw in the morning twilight that he had attached black heads to white horses, and white heads to black horses.

The Gallery of the Vatican is richer in ancient sculpture than all the world beside. By far the most impressive of these works, in my estimation, is the Laocoön, of which no copy can give more than a faint idea. The victims seem almost to shriek audibly, so intense and vivid are the lines of terror and agony in their faces and limbs. It is often said that sculpture should represent repose, not action; and I think that I have never seen action represented by a modern sculptor, without feeling that his work was a failure, — often grotesque where it was intended to be grand or pathetic. But not so the Laocoön. Not so the Athletes in the Vatican. Not so the Apollo Sauroktonos, with his bent bow, every muscle of his beautiful face strained to its utmost tension to give his arrow death-dealing power.

Among the objects of curious interest to me were the ancient inscriptions to be found almost everywhere in Rome, and of which there is an immense collection occupying two very long halls of the Vatican. In these halls the pieces of marble or stucco containing the inscriptions are fastened into the walls, and classified under appropriate titles, the Pagan on one side, the early Christian on the other. I was much impressed by the contrast between the two classes of mortuary inscriptions, — the Pagan expressing hopeless grief, often despair; the Christian uniformly indicating the power of the Resurrection, and the hope full of immortality. The Christian epitaphs are short and simple, yet frequently containing some touching expression of undying love no less than of religious faith. The words *In pace*, "In peace," are found in many of them, as if, in those times of persecution, the first thought concerning the dead had reference to the profound repose of the grave, or rather, of heaven, as a refuge from a life of perpetual disturbance and harassment in this world. Many of these inscriptions have emblems carved in connection with them. The dove, with or without an olive branch, occurs more frequently than any other; the sheep, not unfrequently; the fish, often. The fish is probably the earliest of Christian symbols, comprising at once reference to the original calling of the apostles, and to their spiritual office as "fishers of men," but employed chiefly because the Greek word for *fish*, $ἰχθύς$, is composed of the initials of the words Ἰησοῦς Χριστός, Θεοῦ Υἱός, Σωτήρ, "Jesus Christ, the Son of God, the Saviour."

Among Christian antiquities there are few that inspire a more vivid interest than the buried church of St. Clement, which was discovered only about ten years ago. It was known that there was an early church called by the name of Clemens Romanus, St. Paul's friend, perhaps built even in his lifetime. On the spot where it was believed to have stood there have been for many centuries a now very ancient church and convent bearing the same name. In 1858, in repairing the convent, the workmen found an old wall, and on pursuing their investigations, they disinterred, directly under the present church, and coextensive with it, an entire edifice, with marble and granite columns, and beautifully frescoed walls. The frescos are not so perfectly preserved as those at Pompeii; yet I could determine some of the subjects without difficulty, even by flickering torch-light. From the absence of the *nimbus* about the heads of the saints, it has been inferred that these paintings are of a very early age. There are inscriptions found within the walls, which contain the names of men known to have been consuls under Constantine.

There are similar indications of buried churches under other churches now standing. They were probably built in part under ground, either to avoid attracting the attention of the enemies of Christianity to the worship of its disciples, or to facilitate concealment or escape in case of a descent of the imperial police. Then, in more prosperous and ambitious times, churches were built over them; they were no longer needed or desirable for worship, and were left unused; the passages leading to them were in the course of years floored over, or blocked up by new walls, or obstructed by rubbish; the grade of the streets was raised; and generations came forward that knew not the history, and preserved not the sacred traditions of the spot.

Among the memorials of Christian antiquity least of all should the Catacombs be overlooked. The country around Rome, outside of the walls, is completely honey-combed with them. They were, no doubt, of Christian origin. In Pagan Rome the bodies of the dead were burned, and their ashes collected in urns, and placed in sepulchres which were generally above ground, or in *columbaria* which always were. But whether Christians aerived the practice of burial or entombment from the Jews, were led to it by belief in the literal resurrection of the body, or — what is most probable of all — saw in it the likeness of the Saviour's death-slumber, and thence the presage of an awakening like His, they very early, in all parts of the civilized world, began to inter or entomb their dead; and the Catacombs were here their places of sepulture. As Christianity gained ascendency, the use of these cemeteries became general, and probably continued so till the capture of Rome by the Goths, and perhaps longer. Their connection with the persecutions of the Christians is only incidental. They probably were not dug in times of persecution, or for the purpose of concealment; for such labor could have been very easily detected. But, having been prepared in seasons of tranquillity, they were resorted to for concealment and for worship during the paroxysms of persecution, as the Christians had there the threefold safeguard, of a retirement from which no sound could reach the upper air; of intricate, labyrinthal passages in which they might easily baffle pursuit; and of the superstitious fears which made a Pagan Roman very unwilling to meddle with a burial-place. It seems almost incredible, yet on careful inquiry I find no reason to doubt that there are at least sixty of these cemeteries within a few miles of Rome, and that the interments in them cannot have been less than six million.

I visited the Catacombs of St. Callixtus, in which several of the Popes, or, rather, early bishops of Rome, were interred. This cemetery consists of five stories or tiers of narrow galleries, with frequent angles and branches, seemingly arranged without definite plan, — passages having been dug, as it would appear, in one direction or another, horizontally or with a steep declivity, as the convenience or fancy of the moment dictated. All along the galleries are openings six feet, more or less, in length, and just broad and deep enough to receive a human body. At short intervals there are circular chambers containing several of these openings. In many of the chambers there is one of the apertures (in some of them more than one), vaulted above, and with a flat stone bench, altar-shaped, beneath. These last are believed to be the resting-places of martyrs, as are also some of the ordinary grave-places. The martyrs are distinguished by various emblematic devices, such as the palm, and especially by bottles containing their blood, which were generally entombed with them, and in some of which the congealed blood has been clearly identified. Many of the inscriptions over the grave-places are as easily read as if they had been cut yesterday. There are also sculptures and frescos, some of them very beautiful, with Christian devices, the most common of which is that of the Good Shepherd followed by his sheep, or carrying one of them on his shoulder. Over a very short grave-place, where a child had evidently been laid, I saw the Shepherd with a lamb in his bosom. The most elaborate fresco that met my eye was the Adoration of the Magi. The reputed burial-place of St. Cecilia, who was a Roman matron in an elevated social station, is shown. In a circular recess hard by the niche where the body lay is a picture of the Saviour; near it is that of an elegantly dressed female figure, below which is that of a man, with the name Urbanus, traced upon the painting. Now Urbanus, the Bishop of Rome, St. Cecilia's intimate friend and spiritual counsellor, is known to have deposited her body here after her martyrdom. The body was subsequently removed to a church dedicated to her on the other side of the Tiber.

The use of the larger apartments in the Catacombs as places of worship is indicated by sockets evidently designed for lamps. Preference would naturally have been given to the chamber where a martyr lay. Hence the shelf, altar, or communion-table, so often found directly in front of such grave-places. As for the marks of elaborate ornamentation in these cells of the martyrs, it is out of the question that such work should have been accomplished while a persecution raged; but in peaceful times the living would have wrought lovingly in honor of the holy dead, and after Christianity became the established religion of the empire, adorning the sepulchres of those who had laid down their lives for the faith, would have seemed a preëminently pious work.

I have spoken of the immense extent of the Baths of Caracalla. Some twelve or fourteen miles from Rome are the still more extensive ruins of the Villa of Hadrian. That such an imperial residence could have been built in a reign of twenty years, from the revenues of an empire, however strongly reinforced by extortion and pillage, would be inconceivable, were it not true. This rural residence of the emperor covered a space not less than eight miles in circuit, and was itself a not inconsiderable city, containing not only the largest of imperial palaces, but two amphitheatres, several temples, barracks for some thousands of troops, houses for the great officers of state, quarters for hundreds of domestics, and ranges of small cells, in three stories, for the lodging of many hundreds of slaves. There are still on the ground materials enough to build a town that should contain eight or ten thousand inhabitants. Very little of the ornamental work remains; but there are some frescos not obliterated, and some patches of mosaic floor. There is one portico six hundred feet long, of which the arches and a great part of the wall are standing.

This villa is near Tivoli, the ancient Tibur, which is so closely connected with ancient Rome as the nearest favorite rural resort and residence, that some notice of it may not be inappropriate here. A more beautiful spot there can hardly be. It is situated on the Anio (now called the Teverone), which here falls more than three hundred feet into a vast circular gorge, that from almost every point looks like a crater with no outlet. Some parts of the gorge are lined by huge cliffs that have been carved by the freshets of successive centuries into the most fantastic shapes; while in others the most luxuriant vegetation extends to the water's edge. The river is turbid, and almost of a milky whiteness. There are foot and donkey paths leading down to the gorge, by zigzags that present new and varying views from moment to moment. Then, from the heights that rise above the river, the prospect extends in some directions over the Campagna, till in the far distance, as the expanse melts into the blue heavens, it is hard to believe that the horizon is not bounded by an undulating sea; while in other directions rise the Alban Hills, almost like clouds, as they nestle in the azure of the sky. Unrivalled in its own type of beauty as *Tivoli* may now seem, *Tibur* must have been even more charming in the time of Rome's fresh glory; for, to prevent the recurrence of terrible inundations, the river has been diverted from the downward path in which it had been its own engineer, and has been led into a safer way, with little detriment indeed to its picturesque effect, yet manifestly with the loss of some very desirable points of view.

Near the falls are the ruins of two ancient temples, built of travertine, a very beautiful and durable limestone abounding in that region. One of these temples is almost entire. It must have been consecrated to Vesta; for it is circular, and her temples were generally circular, with the *focus*, or hearth for the perpetual fire, in the centre. The other, which also is well-preserved, was probably built in honor of the last of the Sibyls, Albunea, whose special seat of worship Tibur was, — she having doubtless been the Meg Merrilies of the village, with poetry enough in her madness to pass for inspiration.

These scenes are familiar to every classical scholar through the frequent references to them by Horace, the site of whose favorite Tiburtian villa is shown (but on very questionable authority), on the brow of a hill commanding the fullest view of the downward rush of the "headlong Anio." He speaks often of the genial soil and the dense shade of his beloved Tibur,[1] and in one of his Odes says, "O that Tibur may be the seat of my old age!"[2] Catullus was born and had a patrimonial estate in Tibur, and the very attractive site of his villa is shown to all visitors; but there is some reason, from one of his songs, to suppose that his farm was not where it is said to have been, but on the very outskirts of aristocratic Tibur, and near the Sabine frontier.[3] He speaks of having resorted

[1] "Domus Albuneæ resonantis,
Et *præceps Anio*, ac Tiburni lucus, et uda
Mobilibus pomaria rivis."

[2] "Tibur, Argeo positum colono,
Sit meæ sedes utinam senectæ."

[3] "O funde noster, seu Sabine, seu Tiburs.

to his Tiburtian villa to get rid of a bad cough contracted and fairly earned by a course of sumptuous suppers in Rome.[1]

We found the road to Tivoli charming, but desolate, — so much so, that there had been some recent instances of robbery, even by daylight. For a great part of the way the only buildings in sight were a few shepherds' huts. The flocks are numerous and very large. I had always supposed the line of the hymn,

> "Flocks that whiten all the plain,"

an exaggeration; but the description is literally applicable here. I saw acres of sheep huddled so closely together as hardly to leave an inch of green in sight.

Some notice of the Campagna belongs of right to ancient Rome. The name is applied to an almost uninhabited region stretching from the city in every direction. There is good reason to suppose that it was densely peopled sixteen centuries ago, and we have no evidence that it was peculiarly unhealthy then. Now it is regarded as unsafe, except in the winter, to pass so much as a single night there. The husbandmen and laborers who work on the

> Nam te esse Tiburtem autumant, quibus non est
> Cordi Catullum lædere; at quibus cordi est,
> Quovis Sabinum pignore esse contendunt."

[1] "Fui libenter in tua suburbana
Villa, malamque pectore expuli tussim;
Non immerenti quam mihi meus venter,
Dum sumptuosas appeto, dedit, cœnas."

plain have their homes on the more remote hills, and not unfrequently carry home with them fatal fever. Even close to the gates of Rome, splendid villas and grounds, which it must be the greatest sacrifice ever to leave, are occupied by their owners only for a few months in the year; to remain in them after Easter is to incur fatal risk. The problem is, Was the Campagna deserted because it was unhealthy; or is it unhealthy because it is deserted? The latter seems to me immeasurably the more probable. Occupancy and cultivation no doubt checked the over-rank growth of vegetation, led to a certain amount of drainage, and especially insured the frequent moving of the soil, and the utilization and the reproductive consumption, in dressing for the land, of decaying animal and vegetable matter, which else would have been deleterious. Were the land attainable now on reasonable terms, and open with the prospect of large returns to Anglo-Saxon colonists, this whole region would be reclaimed and made healthy in a single generation, with perhaps no greater amount of suffering from fever at the outset than has been encountered in many sections of our Middle and Western States that now enjoy a salubrious climate.

The Tiber ought not to pass unnoticed, as the least changed of all mutable features of ancient Rome. The *least* changed, I say; for it is not in all respects the same river. It was navigable in the Augustan age, and for the two or three succeeding centuries, by the largest vessels then in existence, corresponding in draught of water to our present ships of a thousand tons; though there is reason to suppose that the larger vessels were obliged to take in and discharge a part of their cargo outside of the mouth of the river. Now it is navigable only by vessels of a very light draught. It is as yellow and turbid as of old, — rapid too, though probably less so than when its affluents were fuller. Nor can it be subject to as sudden and violent alternations of level as formerly. There are parts of the city that are liable to be inundated every year; but there can hardly have been in recent centuries an overflow like that described in the second ode of Horace, in which a Temple of Vesta that had stood from the time of Numa Pompilius was destroyed.

Of the ancient Roman people, the vestiges are few and doubtful. Some of the palaces bear names suggestive of classical names, and some of the noble families profess themselves descendants of families that were distinguished under the Republic and the Empire; but there is not a single instance in which the pedigree is not vitiated by a break of several centuries. If there are genuine Romans in existence, they are much more probably the descendants of obscure than of distinguished families; for the latter would have been exterminated or driven into exile in revolutions or invasions, by which the former would not have been disturbed. If I saw any men who were Romans in mien and gait, it was the Trasteverini, dwellers beyond or on the right bank of the Tiber, who are coarse and rude in appearance, but are often possessed of a vigor of frame and a high standard of physical development, with the type of beauty thence resulting, the like of which we see nowhere else in Italy. This region of the city furnishes not a few beggars and models. The favorite models — men, women, and children — are some of the finest specimens of the human face and form that are to be found upon the earth. Among them I remember an old man, who sat to one of our American artists for the prophet Jeremiah, and who would more than fill out our ideal of the most venerable of the ancient Romans. I have seen a Trasteverine beggar wrap his tattered raiment about him, and stretch out his hand for alms, with as much majesty and grace as Cicero can have shown when he rose to address the Senate.

Whether I saw many or few of the posterity of the old Romans, I had the satisfaction of witnessing a festival, which has evidently come down in a direct line of transmission from their Saturnalia. The eve of the Epiphany is given over to the Genius of Misrule. The sport begins in the early evening, and culminates at midnight. I went with two friends toward midnight to the neighborhood of the Pantheon, which is the centre of the frolic, and probably was so when it was a *Pantheon*, and the motley population of the city resorted for their mad sport to the temple where every man could find his own god. The whole district was filled with a noisy, riotous, but perfectly good-tempered mob. The streets were barricaded so that no horse could pass, and there were stretched across the streets, at frequent intervals, rows of torches and of pans filled with oil, with pieces of cotton cloth ablaze in them, elevated on posts and poles. There were numerous booths for the sale of dolls, toys, and eatables; and the people were making purchases corresponding to our Christmas and New Year's presents. Almost every man, woman, and child was armed with a tin trumpet, or with some equally inartistic instrument of sound, not to say music; and every one who had a trumpet was blowing it with all his or her might. Every few steps we encountered little processions of trumpet-blowers, with or without torches, and generally with a huge jumping-jack, or some similar large figure, kept in perpetual motion by wires or strings, and held aloft for a banner. These parties repeatedly endeavored to draft us as conscripts for the march or dance, but readily desisted when they learned that we were strangers. There were engaged in the sport persons of all ages, and seemingly of all conditions in life. Whether the Roman nobles or gentry were there I cannot say; for I did not know them. But there were many well-dressed Roman men and women actively engaged in the crowd; and, of course, of English and American gentlemen and ladies, not a few were present as spectators. There was no drunkenness, and no personal violence, but the spirit of unrestrained fun and jollity ruled the night. It cannot be a Christian festival. It certainly has nothing to do with the Epiphany, except that it is so thoroughly gentile, so unmistakably a remnant of heathenism. I cannot be mistaken in deeming a description of it a fit close for a chapter on ancient Rome.

17

CHAPTER XI.

MODERN ROME.

St. Peter's. — The Vatican. — Sistine Chapel. — The Last Judgment. — Raphael's Creation. — Etruscan Museum. — Hall of Maps. — Vatican Library. — Manufacture of Mosaics. — Christmas at St. Peter's. — The Cardinals. — The Pope. — Christmas at the Ara Cœli. — Scala Santa. — Church of St. Stephen. — Vault of the Capuchins. — Monks in Rome. — State of the City. — Palaces. — Artists. — Houses of the Poor. — Beggars. — Chestnut Venders. — Bad Police. — Fox-hunt. — Protestant Cemetery. — Falls of Terni.

The most striking object in modern Rome is St. Peter's, which must, I suppose, fall short of every visitor's expectation, simply because it is a human and mundane work, and it is a superhuman and supramundane idea of it that we have been led to form by the superlatives in which we have seen and heard it described.

The exterior is, I think, permanently disappointing. It is impossible to obtain a good side view of it; and the front, which is immense in breadth and height, shows no large spaces, being broken up, not only by doors, but by a tier of half-length windows over the doors. These windows also belittle the portals, which are really very grand. Then, too, the dome, which is the most vast and imposing feature of the exterior, cannot be seen in full from any accessible point near the church; while, beheld from a distance, it seems to float in the air, as if poised upon the clouds, — a work beyond the highest scope of human art.

The interior, impressive from the first, grows more and more so, the longer and oftener it is seen. It has the sublimity of some great work of nature. Its proportions are as simple as they are vast. The greater part of the floor and of the aerial space within the walls, is unobstructed and void, and invites one to contemplate, simply and solely, the majesty of the dimensions, the symmetry of the design, and the exalted reverence due to the genius in which the edifice had birth. There is no painted glass, no tawdry ornament of any kind, nothing either to intercept the view, or to lower the tone of sentiment.

The floor is, in part, of marble, tessellated in large and simple figures; in part, of designs in mosaic. The statuary is mostly of marble, and all colossal. There are no paintings; but the pictures are chiefly enlarged copies in mosaic of well-known master-works, — the stones, or rather the blocks of porcelain that constitute the mosaics, being so fine and so closely set that it is very hard to believe them not oil-paintings. The monuments — principally tombs of popes — are for the most part large enough to belong to the department of architecture rather than to that of sculpture; and yet, large as they are, they are nowhere suffered to be prominent, but are placed against the walls, and seem dwarfed by the vast spaces around them. The rear wall bears, on an elevated and richly decorated structure, a splendid bronze chair, inside of which, and invisible, is the chair[1] which the Church supposes St. Peter to have occupied. The high altar, under which are the relics of St. Peter, is directly beneath the great dome, and has over it a gorgeously wrought bronze canopy supported by four spiral columns. The great dome is about four hundred and fifty feet high from the floor, and, as one looks up to it, it seems to belong to another sphere. It is as graceful and beautiful as it is grand. There are four smaller domes, themselves immense.

Among the objects which should not be forgotten is the colossal bronze statue of St. Peter, seated in a marble chair. This figure attracts more visible worship than any shrine or altar in the church. Most antiquaries, who are not Romanists, believe it to have been a statue of Jupiter Capitolinus. It is very majestic in attitude and expression; but it lacks the grace and symmetry that belong to the best days of classic art. The great toe of the right foot is nearly worn off, and the next is beginning to suffer appreciable diminution, by the incessant kissing of worshippers, and still more, perhaps, by constant

---

[1] This inclosed chair was uncovered and examined while Rome was under the sway of Napoleon Bonaparte, and there was found on it the inscription in Arabic. "There is one God, and Mahomet is His Prophet!"

wiping; for every votary that has a handkerchief wipes the toe, kisses it, and wipes it again. But this is the only form of idolatry that is witnessed at St. Peter's. The church is wholly free from the paltry shows which attract the ignorant and credulous, even in the great cathedrals, — from bedizened madonnas, and the like.

The most impressive view of the interior is from a gallery which runs round the base of the dome. Standing there, and looking alternately down from an altitude from which men on the floor were as grasshoppers, and up into the vault which stretched higher above me than I stood from the floor, I felt the grandeur of the building as I felt it nowhere else. The temple below me seemed to reach out into shadowy depths of unmeasured space, and the vast dome looked more like an horizon of colored air than like a man-made structure. It is impossible, without seeing it, to estimate the rich work of that dome. Its inner surface is composed wholly of figures and pictures in mosaic, in the most brilliant colors.

The roof of St. Peter's is adorned in front by statues of the Twelve Apostles, which look diminutive from below; but when I walked among them, I found them very roughly carved granite figures not less than twenty feet high. From the cupola that surmounts the great dome, the view of the lesser domes and the various roofs is as if not a large building, but a small city, lay beneath; while the height is so great as to overtop not only the Seven Hills, which are insignificant hillocks compared with it, but all the nearer mountains (so-called), and to command a prospect to which they can make no pretension. I climbed into the gilded ball which is the summit of the whole edifice, and which from below looks of the size of a small apple, yet is large enough to contain four or five men at a time.

The Vatican Palace, which adjoins St. Peter's, is an immense and irregular mass of buildings of various ages, some of them at least as old as Charlemagne. It has been the principal Papal residence for nearly five hundred years, and is now the present Pope's only residence; for though the Quirinal Palace is kept in readiness for his occupancy, he has not crossed its threshold since his flight from it in 1849. Into his private apartments and grounds there is, I believe, no admission for unintroduced strangers. The public apartments make the Vatican by far the richest and most magnificent palace in the civilized world.

Most noteworthy among these is the Sistine Chapel, a very plain apartment, smaller than the average of our country churches, but celebrated for its world-renowned frescos, especially those by Michael Angelo, on the ceiling and on the wall opposite the entrance. On the flat portion of the ceiling are subjects from Scripture history, and on the arched portion a series of prophets and sibyls (who were in the painter's time accounted as prophets), the majesty of whose forms and features no tongue or pen can describe, nor could the imagination conceive of them from any human figures that one has actually seen. But if we take for the basis of our conception the most majestic human beings we have ever seen, and add to them the mass of mind, soul, and character which must accrue to them from the highest inspiration, from intimate communion with the Almighty, and from the prolonged exercise of such functions as have been assigned only to the elect few among mortals, we have something like these pictures. The rear wall is covered by the Last Judgment, — sublime, terrible, reminding one of the most intensely wrought descriptions in the "Inferno," probably the most awe-inspiring picture ever painted. Even at the Saviour's right hand, horror is blended with the expression of ecstatic joy; for the martyrs are there with the symbols of the various tortures through which they passed to immortality. On his left hand, in the fall of lost spirits into the abyss of their torment, the most terrific scenes of the classic mythology are mingled with those which more properly belong to the realm of Christian art. Thus Charon is seen ferrying a full freight across the Styx, and striking down contumacious spirits with his oar. The light of the chapel at best is poor; and the Last Judgment has been greatly injured both by dampness and by the smoke of candles and incense. I could not have taken in its details with any certainty or satisfaction, had I not previously studied a copy of it on a wall in the Academy of Fine Arts in Paris.

There are, in the Vatican, several porticos and halls that were frescoed under the superintendence of Raphael, and painted in great part by his own hand. One of these frescos, the Creation, while of course lacking the element of terror, in grandeur of conception, boldness of execution, and all that indicates a master's transcending genius, falls hardly short of the Last Judgment. The first scene, the separation of light from darkness, vies in sublimity — in the representation of the formless dark of chaos startled into potential shape and order by the light-creating fiat — with the more than epic grandeur of the sentence of Holy Writ that describes it.

I referred, in a former chapter, to the Picture Gallery in the Vatican, and to its master-work, Raphael's Transfiguration. Next to this in merit is the Communion of St. Jerome, by Domenichino, — representing the dying saint as he receives the sacred emblems from Ephraem Syrus. The blending of death and of beatification accomplished, heaven begun, in the saint's countenance and mien, cannot be surpassed in the imagination, while all the details of the picture are in perfect harmony with the central figure and the sacredness of the scene.

The Sculpture Gallery of the Vatican consists of

many magnificent apartments, and one who has not seen it can form no conception of its wealth. There is an Egyptian museum, much inferior to the corresponding department in the British Museum. The Etruscan Museum is undoubtedly the richest in the world. Indeed, it contains materials for reproducing all the details of the domestic life of that wonderful people, — a nation already in decay when Rome was born. In the collection are articles of the kitchen and of the toilette, ornaments and jewelry. There are also sepulchral monuments, emblems, and urns, in great number and variety, — some of the urns with the ashes of the dead still in them. The mythology of the Etruscans seems to have had much in common with that of the Romans, who doubtless borrowed from them a large proportion of their objects of worship and their mythical stories. Their art was exquisite in beauty, and many of its forms have never been surpassed. They must have been a very highly civilized people, yet they have almost no history, except such as has been disinterred from their sepulchres.

Opening from one of the apartments of the Sculpture Gallery is the hall hung with the original tapestry, woven from the designs furnished by Raphael's cartoons. The colors are but little faded. Beyond this room is a narrow apartment, five hundred feet long, painted on both sides with a series of maps of Italy and the islands on its coast, on a very large scale, with the most minute specification of every locality that has a name, executed in a style of the highest artistical beauty, and, apart from their geographical value, as charming to the eye as a richly frescoed wall.

The Vatican Library contains the most valuable collection of manuscripts in the world, numbering nearly twenty-five thousand, together with about forty thousand printed books. Not a book of any kind is to be seen, the whole being locked up in unglazed cabinets. Portions of the walls and the entire ceilings of the magnificent suite of apartments that constitute the Library, are splendidly frescoed with appropriate subjects, and there are numerous curiosities that are open to the inspection of visitors. The manuscripts can be consulted only by special favor, and under onerous restrictions, and of the books there is not even a catalogue of any kind, so that no other library in the world is so nearly useless.

One of my most interesting visits in the Vatican was to the long suite of apartments devoted to the manufacture of mosaics for ecclesiastical uses. I saw a great deal of the finished work, and witnessed every stage of the manufacture. The ground of one of these mosaics is a composition as hard as marble. On this is spread a coating of moist, tenacious clay, on which the design is traced with a pencil, the artist having also beside him a colored copy of the picture which he is to reproduce. He removes a minute portion of the clay at a time, and replaces each portion so removed by an almost type-shaped piece of glazed porcelain of the tint required, each piece being dipped in a liquid cement to hold it in its place. The larger pieces are set by the hand, the smaller by pincers. Each workman has at his side a series of little boxes filled with pieces of various shades, arranged like the boxes for the different letters of a font of type. The tints used are reckoned by the hundred, and the varieties of size and tint, that is, the different kinds of pieces employed, are more than ten thousand.

I was at Rome during the Christmas festivities, and will now describe what I witnessed of the ecclesiastical ceremonies. Between two and three o'clock on Christmas morning, I went to St. Peter's to hear the *pastorale*. The service consisted of the intoning of a few prayers, and the singing of songs or hymns in celebration of the Nativity. It is considered the choicest musical entertainment of the week. It is in one of the chapels, or rather, open side-recesses of the church, itself large enough to contain an audience of four or five hundred, with two organs, only one of which was in use. The singing was simple, sweet, and tender. A portion of it was the supposed song of the shepherds, and it had much of the pastoral artlessness and naïveté. The singers seemed to feel their own work, either artistically or devotionally, — I trust both. I obtained a seat in front of the unused organ, and stayed there an hour. Then for another hour, I wandered up and down in the vast body of the church, enjoying the effect of the music at different distances, as also the amazing grandeur of the edifice by the dim light; for it lay in darkness, except where a broad bar of light streamed from the illuminated chapel, and a few feeble rays from the tapers always kept burning around the crypt containing the supposed relics of St. Peter.

I returned to the church early in the forenoon, to witness the great ceremonial of the day. At ten o'clock the procession entered the church. First came a splendid array of the Pope's various descriptions of soldiers, in dazzling uniforms, — his body-guard, in the picturesque and absolutely grand dress designed for them by Michael Angelo; also a company of halberdiers, in veritable mediæval steel helmets and plate-armor. Then came several hundred ecclesiastical dignitaries of various grades, — the prelates arrayed in the most showy and gaudy millinery, glittering with gold and jewels, with gilded mitres, and the cardinals in scarlet, with ermine tippets. Near the close of the procession, the Pope was carried in his chair of state, on the shoulders of twelve men, under a magnificent canopy, with two immense fans of peacocks' feathers borne behind him, — he wearing the jewelled tiara which is worth untold millions, and garments, the like of which can be seen nowhere else but in oriental fable. His bearers were in the costume of Italian nobles of the Middle Ages, with high ruffs, lace bands, silk doublets, heavy gold chains, and long swords. The chair swayed a good deal as it was carried through the aisles, and its motion reminded me of that of the cars in which I have seen children ride on the back of an elephant. It is said that the Pope dislikes the motion. It makes him seasick.

He was first set down near the relics of St. Peter, and there he received the homage of the ecclesiastics, and gave them his benediction, — they kneeling in succession before him, those of the highest grade kissing his gloved hand, those of a lower order, his slippered foot; while for others, the blessing was received by the proper functionaries in their hands, and conveyed to the hands of those entitled to it, by a process precisely like that with which all my readers must be familiar, in the game whose formula is, "Hold fast what I give you." This service of man-worship concluded, the Pope was removed to his official chair; and after many preliminary ceremonies, he advanced to the high altar, and, with several assistants, performed high mass, intoning his part of the service in a remarkably loud, clear voice, not unmusical. During the service, his tiara was exchanged for a plain gilded mitre, then for a plain white mitre; then for a time he wore only a white skullcap, like a nightcap without ruff or border, and for a little while his white head was bare. Once he needed a handkerchief, and, with great difficulty, he fished up from deep recesses in his raiment — the only time he did anything for himself — a red bandanna. I saw that some other dignitaries of exalted rank were similarly furnished. I am sorry to say that, even in the most solemn parts of the service, there was a great deal of snuff-taking among the celebrants; and I inferred that the accessory of the toilette which I have named — long obsolete with us — is of the *haut ton* in Rome. The service was in great part choral, with the aid of a fine military band; and at the elevation of the host a brief and most impressive silence was broken by two silver trumpets in the clearest, sweetest notes I ever heard from a wind instrument. The service lasted about two hours and a half; and when it was closed, the procession was re-formed, and the Pope carried out as he had been brought in. There was privileged standing-room for gentlemen in black, with dress-coats; and such ladies as were dressed in black, without bonnets, and with lace veils, were comfortably seated. The church was not full, though when the congregation moved off through the great square in front, the multitude seemed immense. According to the most trustworthy estimate, there could not have been less than ten thousand persons present.

The cardinals are among the most imposing portions of an ecclesiastical pageant in Rome. Antonelli is the only one among them who does not look either in senile or premature dotage. His countenance is that of a clear-headed, strong-minded man; but it is not a face that could possibly command confidence. The state of the members of the sacred college is more than princely. On most public occasions, they wear scarlet trains at least two yards long, which are borne by minor ecclesiastics. By the way, it takes four men to carry the Pope's train. The carriages of the cardinals vie in splendor and in profuse gilding with the coronation-coaches of kings; their horses are dressed with scarlet plumes; and each member of the college has a coachman and two or three lackeys standing on the footboard behind his carriage, in liveries so showy, and, at the same time, of such costly materials, that an unpractised eye might easily mistake them for coronation-robes.

The whole Christmas pageant was interesting, considered as a mere show; as a Christian ceremonial, it was simply disgusting. Were the enemies of Christianity to devise a farcical celebration of its Founder's birthday, designed to burlesque the spirit of his religion, they could invent nothing more appropriate than this; and nothing can be more preposterous than for that old man, bedizened with more lace, embroidery, and tinsel than would set up a dozen Parisian milliners, and requiring the services of two men to take off or put on his cap, to term himself the representative of the manger-born Saviour, with his plain, seamless garment, and the successor of the Apostles, who labored with their own hands, to supply their own wants and to help their fellow-disciples.

The Pope's face does not please me. It is a whity-brown, parboiled sort of a countenance, with a blandness that seems the result of constant study, and is not radiant enough to be benevolence, and with an expression denoting a feeble intellect, yet no lack of cunning. If I met him as a stranger in common clothes, I think that I should both feel that he was not a man to be trusted, and be sure that he would employ every possible artifice to make himself confided in.

On Christmas afternoon I attended a very different celebration, — one which attracts the common people of the city and the peasantry from the country in great numbers, and which, I confess, suited my taste better than that at St. Peter's, there seemed so much more of heart in it. It was at the Ara Cœli Church, which stands where the temple of the Capitoline Jupiter stood. On one side of the church was a very good scenic representation — with the aid of transparencies — of the manger of the Nativity, the Holy Mother and her child, the worshipping shepherds, the oxen; in the background, a hill-country with various rural and pastoral objects; and above, a luminous cloud, with the "multitude of the heavenly host" floating in the expanse. On the opposite side was erected a stage five or six feet high; and on this a series of little girls, one after another, *preached*, as they term it, that is, recited short speeches prepared for the occasion, in honor of the infant Saviour, and inviting the hearers to join the shepherds in their adoration. The speeches were well learned, and sweetly spoken; and they were listened to with rapt attention, — a murmur of admiration passing round as each child closed her performance. The whole was about on a level with some of our American Sunday-school celebrations, and because it was so, I liked and enjoyed it; for the hearers were as little children, and these rites, which might have been rejected by a fastidious taste, evidently excited their fervent gratitude, and breathed into them the true spirit of the day.

Of the churches of Rome, there are so many which might claim distinct mention, that I know not how to choose among them, and shall attempt no description of any. The Church of St. John in the Lateran has, perhaps, more objects of interest in it than any other, except St. Peter's. Hard by it is the *Scala Santa*, the twenty-eight marble steps, fabled to have been those in Pilate's house, down which Jesus passed after his examination by the Roman Governor. They are covered with stout planks, which yet are considerably worn by constant use. Penitents ascend these steps on their knees, the greater part of them manifestly in weariness and pain, though I saw among them some boys, seeming as much in earnest as their elders, yet evidently finding the task by no means difficult. There were placards defining the benefits to accrue from this penance. A certain number of years of purgatory — I forget whether ten or a hundred — were to be remitted for every step. There were several who ascended more than once while I was there. The penitents were present in crowds, and the stairs were constantly full. I know not whether it is always so. My visit was on the festival of St. John the Evangelist, which had attracted great multitudes to the adjoining church. It will be remembered that it was while Luther was toiling up this staircase on his knees, that the words of Scripture, "The just shall live by faith," flashed into his soul as by a sudden inspiration, and with them the germ — all ready for the most rapid growth — of his favorite doctrine of justification by faith.

In the chapel at the top of the staircase is shown a portrait of the Saviour in his boyhood, by St. Luke. There are a good many pictures exhibited as his in other parts of Roman Catholic Europe. I confess they do him no honor. Moreover, some of them do not look very old, and the best of them, but for the name of so illustrious an artist, would be deemed worth neither selling nor keeping.

One of the most curious churches in Rome is that of St. Stephen, supposed to have been a meat-market in the time of Nero. The inner wall is completely covered with frescos of martyrdoms, comprising all the terrible forms of death recorded in the annals of the Church, and this, too, in the coarsest style of art, and so literally as to make the representations horrid and appalling.

The crypt or vault of the Church of the Capuchins has left even a more grim and ghastly impression on my memory. In this vault is a limited quantity of earth from Jerusalem, in which all the brethren, for many generations, have wanted to be buried. Each, therefore, has his turn. When a brother dies, the senior occupant of the sacred soil is disinterred, and what remains of him is placed in a standing or sitting posture, in one of a series of cloisters devoted to this use alone. Many of the bodies retain enough of form and feature to look even more hideous than skeletons. Most horrible of all, — the bones of the bodies which, with the utmost possible care, could not be held together, have been wrought into wreaths and other fantastic patterns, some made of vertebræ, some of skull-bones, some of ribs, some of the bones of the arm or the leg.

The living monks of this establishment, and, indeed, the greater part of the monks to be seen by scores in Rome, are remarkable for nothing more than for what seems a chronic hydrophobia. They believe cleanliness to be at the opposite pole of humanity from godliness, and whatever may be their general consistency of conduct, no one can deny that, in this respect, they are true to their creed, both in person and in apparel. No active board of health would tolerate them in the streets.

In taking leave of things ecclesiastical, I am constrained to say that Romanism looks worse at Rome than anywhere else. I *heard* much that it was a joy to hear; for the music was attractive, charming, almost heavenly. I *saw* very little that I like to recollect in connection with a church, which, with all its blemishes, numbers among its members on earth and in heaven, not a few men and women, in the humblest place at whose feet we might deem it our highest privilege to sit as learners and imitators.

There are in Rome several palaces, and in its suburbs several villas, containing celebrated works of art, which are thrown open to the public at certain times during the day or week. The most beautiful grounds in the whole region are those of the Villa Borghese, — so tastefully arranged that Art is constantly kept subordinate to Nature as her satellite and exhibitor. Groves and clumps of trees are left in their native denseness; rocks are suffered to clothe themselves at their own will and in their own way; and drives and foot-paths are made so to wind and return upon themselves as to keep always close upon some prospect which the visitor feels reluctant to change even for its equal. In the house or *casino* belonging to these grounds is a large collection of works of art, especially of statuary, of which the most remarkable piece is Canova's Venus Victrix, for which the Princess Pauline Borghese, the sister of Napoleon I., sat as model. The grounds of the Pamphili Doria Villa are hardly inferior to these, and more extensive, covering several square miles.

Within the city, there are about a hundred buildings called palaces, and they are, in general, remarkable for their roominess, their massive and substantial architecture, the simplicity and elegance of their style, and the strong kindred which they bear to classic art as to their general effect, though there are very few points of detail in which a modern Roman palace resembles an ancient Roman house. I might name many master-works to be seen in these palaces; but I will content myself with the mention of Guido's remarkable fresco of Aurora, on a ceiling in the Rospigliosi Palace. This is the most deeply and vividly colored fresco I have ever seen. It has as great an affluence and diversity of the most brilliant tints as can be found in any picture on canvas. It represents the Sun's chariot drawn by four magnificent and gayly prancing horses, with seven Horæ (the " Rosy Hours ") dancing around it, and Aurora on the wing scattering flowers before it. It covers almost the entire ceiling of an apartment of, perhaps, twenty-five feet by eighteen.

I need not say that Rome is the favorite home of artists from all parts of the world, and of not a few from America. I was in the studios of several of our sculptors, and should do wrong were I to speak of some of them, as my limits will not permit me to speak of all. I was in the studios of but three American painters in Rome, — that of Mr. Ropes, who shows great fidelity, pure taste, and skilful execution in his landscapes; that of Mr. Hamilton Wild, who has been wonderfully successful in single figures and groups, both Italian and Spanish; and that of Mr. Tilton, who appears to me unsurpassed among recent painters in rendering on canvas the peculiar tints of the Italian heavens.

A few words about the general aspect of Rome. There seems to be no medium between the splendid and the squalid. Except in the region where strangers congregate, which is not extensive, there are very few houses that are intermediate in style and quality between the palaces (many of which have become lodging-houses, or are leased in single apartments or suites of rooms) and dwellings absolutely mean and utterly comfortless in their whole aspect. The interior of the poorer houses is cheerless in the extreme. The lower story is lighted only through the open door, and all the household and needle work that demands the use of the eye must be performed near the door or outside of it. In seeking some ruin in the rear of such a house, I was courteously invited to pass through it, and though it was midday, I needed to be led through apartments in which I could not see my own hand.

The streets are dirty, and most of them narrow. Beggars swarm everywhere, and a defect or deformity sufficiently painful or revolting to second the appeal for alms, seems to be considered as a God-send. Next to the beggars, the roasters and venders of chestnuts — the mammoth chestnuts sometimes seen at our street-corners — are, if not the most numerous, the most conspicuous portion of the population. They establish their furnaces at short intervals all over the city; but it seems to me that if they do not feed altogether on their own wares, they cannot make a living profit. I dare not say how cheap their chestnuts are; but I know that I could not find a copper coin small enough to buy me as few chestnuts as I needed, though, on a chilly day, I used them both for fuel and for food, warming my hands with them till they grew cold, and then eating them.

Rome is undoubtedly the worst governed city in the civilized world. It is deemed unsafe to go out alone after dark. One who does so incurs a double risk, of assault and robbery by some desperado, and of being shot by the Pope's guard; for, while the police are utterly powerless for the purposes for which they are needed, there is a most vigilant watch maintained against whatever looks like political discontent or treasonable design. There are certain localities — especially a long flight of steps leading from the Piazza di Spagna to the church La Trinità de' Monti, over which strangers are frequently passing — at which the sentinels are ordered to fire if their challenge is not instantly answered; and a foreigner thus challenged is in danger of hesitating from sheer ignorance of what he ought to say.

While the French troops occupied Rome, the city was much safer than it is now. They were an efficient police, and were not stupid enough to shoot an inoffensive stranger for his unreadiness in a foreign tongue. One of the first measures of the Papal government, after the French troops were withdrawn, was to drive beyond the walls of the city all Protestant worship. When I left Rome, the American chapel, a room in a private house, under the flag of the embassy, was the only Protestant place of worship remaining open, and that, if I am rightly informed, has since been closed.

Another measure of the Papal administration, adopted at the same time, was to restore the old right of sanctuary to the churches, so that a criminal who can find shelter in a church is free from arrest. As there is a church every few rods, he must be very lame or very foolish, who cannot elude the ministers of justice. One day, while I was in Rome, some zealous police officers had the effrontery to chase a thief up the high steps of a church. A priest came out, let the rascal in, shut the door upon him, and then took down the names of his pursuers, to be reported for censure or punishment as guilty of sacrilege. Does the Pope mean to verify what the Divine Teacher said to the Jews about their "house of prayer," "Ye have made it a den of thieves?" Under his auspices crime was assuming, in the winter of 1866–67, a degree of audacity unknown under the French régime. One morning before sunrise, on the Piazza di Spagna, the most public place in the city, a baker, serving his early customers, was knocked down, and robbed of the contents of his tray; and similar deeds of violence were reported almost daily.

There seemed to be during that winter, and I believe there are now, no serious symptoms of immediately impending revolution; but the prevalent belief was that the Pope's temporal power was fast approaching its terminus, and measures of the kind I have specified are certainly not adapted to retard that consummation.

The environs of Rome are very beautiful. One of my most pleasant excursions from the city was in the train of a fox-hunt. Arrangements are made for this sport every Monday and Thursday during the season. On the occasion on which I was present, there were, perhaps, forty mounted hunters, male and female, in picturesque costume, half as many hounds, and a hundred carriages. In one of the carriages, by invitation from a party of friends, I drove about eight miles, to the summit of Monte Mario. The Apennines were white with a fresh fall of snow. Soracte [1] stood out, alone and snow-

---

[1] "Vides, ut alta stet nive candidum
Soracte."

crowned, in the distance. In the transparent blue of the atmosphere we beheld the Campagna, with its varied green, and its slightly undulating surface, for the distance of many leagues, till it seemed gradually to melt into sea; and, though the Mediterranean was far out of sight, the horizon looked as if it were bounded by the ocean on every side.

At some distance outside of the city gates is the Protestant cemetery, filled principally with the graves of Englishmen and Americans. There are many very beautiful monuments and touching inscriptions, among them not a few names that are the world's property. The bodies of Keats and Shelley, or rather, the ashes of the latter, lie here with very plain headstones, bearing the inscriptions with which most of my readers must be familiar. The wall of this cemetery abuts upon the old Roman monument of Caius Sextus, — a pyramid more than a hundred feet high, with a very small sepulchral chamber, in which it is supposed that no one has ever been laid except the man whose name it bears. It is cased throughout with marble, once white, now black through age.

In connection with Rome, and as one of the most interesting objects in Italy, I will close this chapter by describing the Falls of Terni, about two hours by rail from Rome, on the way to Florence. The falls are artificial, and though their direction has been somewhat changed since, they are the **result** of a bold experiment in engineering more than two thousand years ago, by which the waters of the Velinus, now Velino, with those of several lakes connected with it, were poured over a descent of more than a thousand feet into the Nar, or Nera. These falls cannot be anywhere surpassed in grandeur. I saw them, indeed, under favorable circumstances, after very heavy rains; but as I saw them, Niagara does not present an aspect of greater sublimity; and, though the actual volume of water must be immeasurably less, the apparent volume is at least as great as that of Niagara. The fall is made in three successive leaps, — the first of only fifty feet; the second, of more than six hundred feet; the third, inclined at a slight angle from the perpendicular, completing the descent to the Nera.

The road from the village of Terni to the falls, ascends by a very steep grade, bringing into view an ever expanding panorama of valley, glen, and ravine, with the River Nera running quietly at a great depth below. Suddenly, as we turn a sharp angle, we come upon the Velino, at the point where it rushes over the first precipice. It is of a deep yellow, broken by the rocks over which it falls into wreaths and whirlpools of crested foam, and then into smoke-like spray, which rises in a vast cloud above the hills, and spreads for a great distance around. The main fall is as broad, if I can trust the measurement of my eye, as the broadest segment of Niagara, and there are several lesser cataracts, each with its own peculiar setting of rock and vegetation, and all so intensely yellow, as to look more like the product of some cyclopean chemical laboratory, than like sheets of water.

We descended by a winding path to the bottom of the falls, and as we looked up, the water seemed to be actually poured down from the clouds. This lower view is the most sublime view of falling water that has ever met my eye. At the same time, we had around us in that deep gorge the most superb hill and mountain scenery, — the precipices that hemmed us in rising to the height of more than a thousand feet, and above them, the white summits of the Apennines. The rocks here are very picturesque. Some of them contain wonderful petrifactions of leaves and twigs. Some of them have been carved by the water into forms in which can be traced grotesque likenesses to man, and bird, and beast. One extensive series of cliffs is composed wholly of beautiful alabaster, in alternate layers of white and red.

I would rather have lost some of the most renowned cities of Continental Europe, than not to have seen the Falls of Terni.

CHAPTER XII.

GERMANY.

Nuremberg. — Aspect of Antiquity. — Fountains and Markets. — Instruments of Torture. — Old Curiosity Shop. — Honor to Distinguished Natives. — Prague. — Hymns to the Virgin. — Cathedral of St. Vitus. — The Judenstadt. — Old Synagogue — Church-customs. — Heidelberg. — Castle. — Fair. — Market. — Baden-Baden. — Castles, Old and New. — High Play. — Hot Springs. — Freiberg. — School of Mines. — Practical Mining.

I HAVE quite full notes of what I saw in the great capitals and chief cities ordinarily embraced in a European tour; but about most of them, I fear I should say nothing new. I certainly should write a chapter about Venice, had not Mr. Howells, in his recent book, described admirably well all that I saw and felt there, and much more. I wish I could occupy new ground; but, though I travelled quite extensively, at what place could I have sojourned, where my fellow-countrymen would not have preceded or followed me, and where many of my readers would not track me, and verify my reminiscences by their own? I will, however, in my closing chapter, deviate a little from the inevitable route of a tourist, and describe, I will not say some of the seldom visited, but some of the less frequently visited cities of Germany.

I am sure that any of my readers who have been at Nuremberg, will be glad to go thither again with me. It is the most perfectly unique city in the civilized world, — hardly less a fossil city than Pompeii, yet not without a multitudinous, busy, and prosperous life of its own, and though fossil, undecayed and untarnished, — as fresh, clean, and bright as if it were no older than San Francisco or Chicago. What is very strange, it is a railway station; yet it seems rather to bend the steam-giant to its ways than to take on his. In that region, the fastest trains average hardly more than fifteen miles an hour, and the time-tables of the merchandise and slow trains might invite the rivalry of an enterprising equestrian. The stations are frequent, — many of them insignificant, indeed; but if there be no passenger to leave or take, the train stops till every functionary belonging to it has interchanged salutations and hat-liftings with all the functionaries at the station.

There is no place which it is so difficult to describe to an American as Nuremberg, — everything is so steeped in a more venerable antiquity than we know, and not only everything, but the people equally. Even the babies look antiquated, and are dressed in ancestral fashions, so as to remind one vividly of the scriptural saying about the child "a hundred years old."

The city is, and always has been rich; and the inhabitants, taking pride in antiquity, have kept up the old in its original forms, but where needed, with fresh materials, instead of demolishing and rebuilding. Thus within the walls there is nothing ruinous, and nothing new. When a part of a building becomes dilapidated, it is repaired in the pristine style, so that the portion supplied looks as if it had always been there. The population has, however, extended considerably beyond the walls; and the outside portion of the city makes no disguise of its newness, flaunts its bright colors, dispenses with superfluous gables, and has all its carpenter's work done on the plumb and square.

Nuremberg lies on both sides of the little river Pegnitz, which, within the walls, is crossed by frequent bridges. The river-banks in the suburbs present tame but attractive scenery, with frequent gardens and ornamented grounds, and with two or three public tea-gardens in admirably well chosen sites.

The two concentric walls that surround the city are high, thick, and massive, superbly mantled with ivy. Between the outer and the inner wall is a deep ditch, now dry, and for the most part occupied for gardens. There were formerly three hundred and sixty-five towers on the walls. There remain about a hundred, some of which are singularly beautiful specimens of mediæval architecture and masonry.

The city has several public fountains that are fully as ornamental as they are useful. One of them has appropriated to itself a name which, in strict justice, belongs to them all, — *Schöne Brunnen,* " Beautiful Fountain." It is an octagonal pyramid in open stone-work, more than fifty feet high, with innumerable carved figures, and twenty-four life size statues, — eight in an upper tier representing Moses and seven other prophets, and in a lower tier sixteen, embracing seven Bavarian Electors, and nine names conspicuous in the annals of heroism, and chosen in equal numbers from the Pagan, Jewish, and Christian camps. Near this is the Goose Fountain, in which a man has a goose under each arm, and the water flows from the mouths of the geese. In the vicinity of this fountain is the Goose Market, almost wholly given up to the use indicated by its name; and if I was authorized to judge by the supply I saw at the market, I should have supposed a goose predestined, that day, for every spit in Nuremberg. The geese are offered for sale alive, tethered by wisps of straw to the wicker baskets in which they are brought. Another market seemed similarly devoted to the sale of young pigs, which, being also sold alive, were equally eligible for the table and the sty. The markets, of which there are several besides these, have all a most exemplary neatness and order, and are all served chiefly by peasant women, who wear two or three different, and very peculiar and grotesque costumes, the badges of their respective races or nationalities. The prevalent head-dress is that of the Bavarian peasantry, — a very high turret-shaped structure just behind the crown, swathed with a red scarf, which is then wrapped round the whole head, and hangs over the neck.

There are several magnificent churches here, all but one Protestant, all rich in objects of art, and all adorned to a great degree by native artists, — by Albert Dürer, architect, painter, and sculptor, Adam Krafft, sculptor, and Peter Vischer, bronze-founder, who were all contemporaries; while in the same generation the city gave birth to Hans Sachs and to Melancthon (or *Schwarzerd*, " Black Earth," which was his family name, by him translated into Greek). The houses of Dürer, Vischer, and Sachs are still standing, and that of Dürer is most appropriately occupied by a society of artists. In the Church of St. Lawrence there is a very remarkable work by Krafft. It is a sanctuary (that is, a repository for the elements of the Eucharist), in form pyramidal, of stone, with numerous figures of sacred and ecclesiastical personages, some in relief, others in groups of detached statues, and with a great deal of the most delicate carved work, — the whole representing the principal scenes and events of the Saviour's Passion. This structure reaches to the ceiling, and seems to bend under it, its apex assuming the form of a bent twig. The whole is sustained on the shoulders and backs of the kneeling figures of Krafft and his two assistants, which are said to have been perfect likenesses.

I visited several of the oldest and best of the houses, and I have nowhere else seen domestic architecture so rich. I have, indeed, seen houses as costly, palaces much more so; but not even in kings' palaces have I beheld such elaboration of design and delicacy of finish in all the details of house-building as may be witnessed here. The houses are, in general, ornamented with carved work and sculpture on the outside, and in the interior, the decorations are such as could have become general only at an epoch when the love of art was the ruling passion of the people, as we know it was in Nuremberg in the age of her great men. Many of the best houses have very low eaves, roofs with a heavy pitch, and three, four, or five stories within the gable; but in this case, the gable either faces the street, or stands on a corner, and is so shaped and ornamented as to be the glory of the house.

In one of the towers on the wall are the apartments occupied by the King of Bavaria, when he visits this portion of his kingdom. They retain the original style of finishing, and are fitted up with a plain and substantial elegance, contrasting strongly with the gaudiness of his magnificent residence at Munich. Attached to the royal residence are two very old chapels, one above the other, containing interesting specimens of the best art of their times.

In another part of the same tower are preserved

the instruments of torture that were used in the Middle Ages in the (so-called) administration of justice. Beneath every depth is a lower deep. On my way from this tower, I felt as if I had sounded the lowermost abyss of cruelty, and witnessed vestiges of the most diabolical aspects of humanity. But I went thence to the dungeons of the *Heimliche Gerichte* (Secret Tribunal), which formerly extended its irresponsible despotism throughout Germany; and there I found cells much deeper and darker than those of the Mamertine Prison, trial-rooms very far beneath the ground, into which no ray of daylight ever penetrated, and instruments of torment more horrible than, had I not seen them, I should have supposed within the range of human ingenuity. Most horrible of all is the Jungfrau or Mädchen, — a figure of the Holy Virgin, which opened to receive the prisoner, closed upon him with knives that literally cut him in pieces, and re-opened to drop the victim into a well some hundreds of feet below. Is not the time coming when men will regard the mutual laceration, maiming, and slaughter of human beings in foreign and civil war, as we now regard these tortures, which, three centuries ago, were deemed, not only consistent with the Christian law of right, but absolutely requisite for the well-being of society and the defence of the true faith?

Among other odd places, I visited an old curiosity shop, from which Dickens, if he ever was in

Nuremberg, must have derived his shop so entitled; kept too, by a man as old, as weird, and as unlike other people as Little Nell's grandfather was. It occupies and fills all the stories and rooms of a very large old house, — the simple domestic concerns of the little family as to bed and board, being not fenced in by any geographical line. It contains antiquities of every conceivable kind, — furniture, armor, jewelry, watches (including several of the *Nuremberg eggs*, as the first watches made there were not inappropriately called), plate, books, costumes, pictures. There are two other similar, but less extensive establishments of the kind in the city.

Nuremberg is famous all over the world for the manufacture of toys. I went into no factory expressly designed for that purpose; but I found toys of a great many varieties and of very curious styles among the products of an immense *papier-maché* manufactory, where also I saw the most perfect imitations of all kinds of fruit. Indeed, on leaving that establishment, it seemed to me that there was no substance in the visible universe which might not have its fac-simile in *papier-maché*.

The *Rathhaus*, or City Hall, is interesting as containing some of Dürer's best pictures on canvas, and an entire wall of the great council chamber was frescoed by him. From beneath this building, subterranean passages run in almost every direction, having been constructed in turbulent times, to facilitate the escape of the magistrates in any public commotion.

The churchyard of St. John, containing the graves of Dürer and Hans Sachs, is a very curious cemetery. The monuments, which are numbered up to thirty-five hundred, and crowded very close together, are generally huge, solid blocks of stone, cut into an oblong form, with small bronze plates let into the upper surface for inscriptions. Between a house which now bears the name of " Pilate's House " and the gate of the cemetery are seven pillars, placed at regular intervals, with bass-reliefs representing scenes in the Saviour's Passion, executed by Adam Krafft. Their origin was in this wise. Ketzel, a citizen who owned and occupied what has since been termed " Pilate's House," wishing to attest his devotion by some costly gift, determined to measure out and adorn, between his then dwelling and what he supposed to be his last home, stations corresponding to those on the Via Dolorosa, the way of Jesus from the house of Pilate to Calvary. He went to Jerusalem to measure the distances, lost his memoranda on his way home, and returned to Palestine to repeat the measurement.

It was pleasant to witness the pride of the Nurembergers in the illustrious men to whom their city has given birth, whose names the visitor finds constantly recurring, and whose memory seems less like transmitted fame than a living presence.

I went from Nuremberg to Prague. This is a wonderfully picturesque place, lying on both sides of the Moldau, climbing lofty acclivities, and overlooked and commanded by the Hradschin, the vast, rambling palace of the old Bohemian kings. About half of the inhabitants are Bohemians, and speak their native language. Almost every sign is painted double, in Bohemian and German.

The Moldau is here quite broad, and a very majestic stream. It is crossed by two bridges, — one an exceedingly graceful iron suspension bridge; the other said to be the longest and the most magnificent bridge in Germany, profusely adorned on both sides by massive groups of statuary. The building of this bridge was commenced under the auspices of Charles IV. At its eastern extremity stands a monument built in 1848, to commemorate the close of the fifth century of the University. In this, the bronze statue of Charles IV. is the principal figure; in niches at the sides of the pedestal are seated allegorical figures representing the four Faculties, Arts, Theology, Law and Medicine; and at the angles are portrait-statues of four illustrious contemporaries of the Emperor.

On my first evening at Prague, I witnessed a very impressive religious service. Near the principal market is a high pillar, surmounted by a bronze statue of the Virgin Mary, with a shrine for her worship just above the pedestal. Passing in that neighborhood, I heard singing, and going to the spot, I found the shrine lighted, and some forty or fifty women in front of it, singing hymns to the

Virgin. The music was inexpressibly sweet and tender. They all seemed to be poor women, some with children in their arms, some with baskets on their backs, most of them with a handkerchief or shawl for their only head-dress; and for a part of the time they knelt on the cold pavement, though the air was even frosty. I learned that this service is commenced every first of May, — May being the month specially consecrated to the worship of the Virgin, — and is continued till the approach of winter puts an enforced period to it.

The principal church, or Cathedral, is dedicated to St. Vitus. Though smaller, it bears in its general style and aspect a striking resemblance to the Cologne Cathedral, and is, like that, unfinished, though commenced in the fourteenth century. It contains a most magnificent mausoleum, constructed wholly of marble and alabaster, in which several emperors of Germany and kings of Bohemia have been interred. One of the side chapels of this church is composed entirely of rare and precious stones, principally amethysts and jaspers, arranged in a sort of coarse mosaic, and representing scenes in the Saviour's life, and other sacred themes. In this church also is a huge and very old candelabrum, which the inhabitants believe to have been brought from Solomon's Temple. One of the chapels contains the shrine of the patron saint of Bohemia, John Nepomuk,[1] which probably is not exceeded in

[1] Canonized in the hearts of the people, several centuries before his

costliness and splendor by any similar structure in the world. It is constructed wholly of wrought silver, weighing about two tons. Within is a silver coffin, supposed to contain the saint's body, which is held poised in the air by silver angels of human size. Around the coffin are silver candelabra, in which candles are kept perpetually burning; and the whole is surmounted by four silver angels who seem to be hovering in the air.

Next to the Cathedral in interest is the Teynkirche, formerly belonging to the Hussites, though now Roman Catholic. Tycho Brahe was buried here. His monument in red marble has a bust of him in relief, and is inscribed with his favorite motto, *Esse potius quam haberi*, "To be rather than to be esteemed." In a side-chapel are two very beautiful statues of the first Christian missionaries to Bohemia, and an altar with bass-reliefs of the baptism and the first communion of the earliest Bohemian converts.

On the public square on which this church stands is the very magnificent *Rathhaus*, or City Hall, a Gothic edifice finished some twenty years ago, but retaining a façade, portal, and tower of the four-

---

sainthood was decreed at Rome. He was the confessor of the queen of King Wenceslas. The king ordered him to be drowned in the Moldau, because he would not betray the secrets of the confessional, which the monarch, in a fit of jealousy, imagined (probably without reason) would be damaging to the honor of his wife. St. John Nepomuk is, therefore, not inaptly invoked as a protector against slander and slanderers.

teenth or fifteenth century, — the tower having a clock even more remarkable than that of Bern, in which a figure of Time strikes the hour, and the Twelve Apostles come out and move in solemn procession when the hour is struck.

The Jewish population of Prague is said to be not far from ten thousand. They were formerly confined to a particular district of the city, which bears the name of Judenstadt, and most of them live there now, though the richer Israelites are fast emigrating to more airy and salubrious quarters. The Judenstadt is a labyrinth of mean, narrow, crooked, dirty streets, with large, old, dilapidated houses, as densely peopled as the most crowded sections of New York and London, but, unlike them, abounding more in haggard old women than in children. It is the only place where I have ever encountered smells more noisome than the odors of Cologne. Yet the sanitary statistics show a considerably greater average longevity among the Jews than among the Christians.

In the heart of the Judenstadt is an old Jewish burial-ground, in which the headstones stand so close together that it is difficult to tread between them. The stones are upright and very thick slabs of dark slatestone, covered all over with Hebrew inscriptions. Near this cemetery is the old synagogue, held in the most profound reverence by all the Hebrews. Three or four centuries ago, some laborers, in digging, came upon what proved to be the walls of a synagogue, of the existence of which there was neither record nor tradition. With regard to its actual age, there are opinions that range over at least ten centuries, — the Jews maintaining that it was built by the first exiles of their race who settled in Prague, not long after the destruction of Jerusalem. I could see nothing to militate against this theory; and if it were said to have been built when Noah left the ark, appearances would accord with the hypothesis. It may have been originally subterranean, and designed for a secret place of worship; or it may have been buried by the elevation of the ground around it. However this may be, the Jews cleared the ruins from rubbish, roofed it over, and made it their specially holy place. They show a tattered parchment manuscript of the Pentateuch which was found in it. Of course the building is damp and dark. It is the dirtiest place I was ever in, redolent of mould, tallow, and rancid oil, its walls absolutely greasy with lampblack, the tabernacle and reading-desk looking as if they had possessed a certain comeliness centuries ago, but could hardly hold together now. It is only a less dreary place than the dungeons at Nuremberg. It has no gallery for women; but a narrow corridor runs along one side of the building, with bull's-eyes looking into the synagogue, and there the women stand, and see what they can through the thick glass. There is a very spacious and handsome synagogue hard by; but this ancient edifice is used for all the great festivals.

I noticed in the Prague churches two customs, which, perhaps, are not peculiar; but I saw them nowhere else. One is the traffic in candles during divine service. While mass is performing, even during the elevation of the host, an old woman goes round among the kneeling worshippers, with a bunch of dipped candles. The persons whom she accosts, if devoutly disposed, buy one, two, three, or half a dozen each. She pockets the money, lights the candles, and places them in an iron frame duly pierced for their reception, with a large dripping-pan beneath, very near the altar. The other custom is this: The friends of a deceased person erect in the church a scutcheon wreathed with black, having inscribed on it his name, and a request to the faithful to pray for him, and to this is attached a socket holding a very large candle, which is lighted while mass is said for the repose of his soul.

Prague has the aspect of extensive business, great activity, and abundant wealth. The shops are very showy. There are many palatial residences, with extensive parks and gardens sumptuously and tastefully laid out. There are several promenades on very high ground, overlooking the city, and commanding an almost Swiss range and diversity of scenery, including, on the north, the nearer summits of the Saxon Alps.

We will now pass from the East to the West

of Germany, and pause at Heidelberg. Here the principal object of interest is the Castle, which is the most extensive and magnificent mediæval ruin in Continental Europe, and second only to Fountains Abbey in the civilized world. The Castle is on the brow of a high hill, which towers directly behind the city. It was commenced in the thirteenth century; it was largely added to and embellished in subsequent times; and the most magnificent portions of it were built by the unfortunate Elector Frederic V., who became king of Bohemia, and married the daughter of James I. of England, but whose wife and children were, in after years, dependent on scanty charity for the necessaries of life. A part of the castle was blown up by the French in 1689; it has been twice struck by lightning; it has been repeatedly captured and dismantled; and yet enough of it remains standing to make it one of the wonders of the world. The walls are, in some parts, seventeen feet thick. The portion that was blown up is an immense fragment of a tower, which separated from the rest entire, and still reposes unbroken, in part on the main wall of the tower, in part in the ditch below. The English Tower, so called in honor of the English princess who commenced life so brilliantly here, still shows the two most richly ornamented fronts that I have ever seen, — walls not less than sixty feet high, decked and surmounted, in every space that will admit of such occupancy, with statues and figures in relief,— a large number of them bearing tokens of a very high order of artistical merit. Many of the figures are entire, and as beautiful as when they came from the sculptor's hand. Others are mutilated, — here a nose sliced away, there a leg wanting. In one case, a head has rolled off and back, and lodged between the neck and the wall, producing an aspect of the most grotesque deformity. What makes these ruins the more impressive is that not only are they clothed with ivy whose huge stalks indicate a great age, but in some parts, large trees are growing out of the earth that has gathered on the top of the thick walls, and in one place, there is quite a dense grove on the roof of a ruined tower.

Among the curiosities of the Castle is the celebrated Heidelberg Tun, shaped like a hogshead laid lengthwise, twenty-three feet in diameter, and holding sixty thousand gallons. Two flights of steps lead to the top of it, and over the top, around the bung-hole, is a floor which was formerly used for dancing. This tun has been four times filled with wine, but has now been empty for nearly a century. Hard by it, is another lesser tun that holds fifty thousand gallons.

Heidelberg contains little else of peculiar interest to transient visitors. The University, which gives it much of its celebrity, is second to none of the German universities, and has one of the most valuable, though not one of the largest libraries in Europe; but its building is almost mean. The churches, though externally handsome, are meagre as to works of art. One of them is remarkable as having been occupied for centuries by both Romanists and Protestants, — a thick partition wall running between the nave and the choir, the former belonging to the Lutherans, the latter to the Catholics.

The most noteworthy building within the city is a house used as an inn, erected in 1592, the whole front of which is of the most elaborate carved work in a stone now black with age, with several finely executed medallions and busts. It was built by a French Protestant who barely escaped by flight the St. Bartholomew's massacre, and it still bears several devout inscriptions, in Latin, commemorative of his gratitude.

Heidelberg lies in the valley of the Neckar, and is surrounded by the most charming scenery. I arrived there in the midst of a great semi-annual fair, which gave me an excellent opportunity of seeing German costumes, manners, and life. On the public square and in the broader streets, long lines of wooden booths were erected, and goods of every conceivable description exposed for sale. There were also exhibitions of Punch and Judy, of waxwork, and of second-rate pictures and statuary, and booths of fortune-tellers and clairvoyants. Then there were stalls in which there was perpetual cooking, and from whose savory windows waffles and cakes, nondescript and marvellous, were urged in their smoking charms upon all passers-by. There was an untold amount of beer-drinking, undoubtedly with its concomitant stupidity and brutishness; but there was no demonstrative drunkenness, no riot, no loud talking. With thousands of people spending the night in these booths, which extended to within a few feet of my window, I should not have known, an hour after nightfall, that there was a stranger in the city. This may have been in part due to a bad cause; for beer is a soporific of no little efficacy.

The morning market at Heidelberg presents a very amusing spectacle. There is no market building or place; but for nearly half a mile on each side of the principal street, the market-women arrange themselves on the margin of the sidewalk, facing the middle of the street, almost in uniform, with coarse gingham dresses, and gingham handkerchiefs tied over their heads. Each has a basket at her feet, and each holds in her hands a specimen of her wares, — one a goose, another a head of cabbage, another a pat of butter on a cabbage-leaf. The purchasers pass between the two rows, examine the articles as they are extended for inspection, and make their purchases from the baskets.

Two hours by rail carried me from Heidelberg to Baden-Baden. Nothing can exceed the quiet **autumnal** beauty, in which I saw this city and its suburbs. Of course, in so great a watering-place there is much showy architecture, — most of it, however, in good taste; but Art here is literally smothered by Nature. Undoubtedly the same interior fires that heat the waters, intensify and prolong the summer verdure. I saw here, but nowhere else in Europe, a diversity of tint corresponding to our forest scenery in autumn. The walks and drives in and about Baden-Baden are delightful beyond description, the country being densely wooded, and undulating in surface, with distant views of the Jura Alps. The city lies on the verge of the Black Forest, most fitly so named; for the pine which forms its chief growth is almost black.

On a hill about a half-hour's drive from the city is the Old Castle, — a ruin much resembling that at Heidelberg, but less extensive, less massive, and with fewer tokens of architectural beauty. The New Castle (nearly two hundred years of age), which succeeded the old as the ducal residence, is near the foot of the hill. It is large and handsome, but in the style of a modern dwelling-house, with little of the character of a fortress. It is chiefly remarkable for certain subterranean apartments older than itself, as to which antiquaries are not agreed, whether they are Roman baths, or dungeons of the "Geheime Gerichte."

I spent two hours in the Kursaal, the celebrated gambling establishment. It is a building of great magnificence, with everything to attract visitors, and all its accommodations are opened without charge to the public, doubtless with the intent of entrapping those who have not yet acquired a passion for play. It contains a free and well-furnished reading-room, very seductive refreshment-rooms, and a room for concerts and balls, unequalled in splendor except by the ball-room in the royal residence at Munich. Throughout the season there is a free concert of instrumental music every evening, with seats enough for an audience of several hundred.

From this hall open the two gambling rooms. In one of them the game is *rouge et noir;* the other has a *roulette* table. Both are games of mere chance, with no possible room for skill. In the former, the gambler bets on the turning up of red or black cards in a pack dealt by the master of the table; in the latter, on the number against which, on a table with cardinal numbers painted all around its periphery, a little ball will rest, after an impulse given to it by a wheel in revolution. The one redeeming feature — if there can be any in a business so full of guilt and misery — is that the players do not play against one another, but against the *bank,* as the exchequer of the lessees is termed. If the player wins, the manager pushes toward him a sum equal to his stake, and he rakes that and his original venture to himself, often to risk the doubled sum on the next deal or the next revolution of the wheel, and so on till he loses his accumulated winnings. If he loses, his money is raked into the bank. Thus, although despair, utter recklessness, hopeless ruin, and suicide are the frequent results of gambling here, it does not directly produce the quarrels, feuds, assaults, duels, and murders, which are by no means rare events in the history of private gambling. Then too, except that the whole business is atrocious dishonesty, the play here is fair. There is no opportunity for fraud. The bank, to be sure, almost always comes off largely the winner, but for psychological reasons, and not by the mere necessity of the game. The fact of the ultimate success of the bank at nearly every session, is a most instructive commentary on the insanity that maddens the gambler. The bank wins, because the player hardly ever retires with his early winnings, but keeps on hazarding larger and larger sums, until a single fatal bet sweeps away his original stock and his winnings together.

Around each of the tables sat or stood some thirty or forty players, with perhaps twice that number of spectators,—some, like myself, mere spectators, with their interest, complacency, disapproval, or disgust uttered, not in words (for dead silence reigns), but in looks no less expressive; others waiting, with unconcealed solicitude, for a vacant place. Each of the players was armed with a small rake, with which he pushed his money to the spot or number which indicated the bet he intended to make, and if he won, drew his doubled money into his own custody. There were, among the players, a good many fashionably dressed women, most of them old and ugly; some, pretty and modestly attired, who may have been, a part of them at least, the stool-pigeons of the net. Most of the men had the dress and air of gentlemen; but the larger part of them showed, in countenance and manner, the fierce passions that appertain to high play. Some looked savage; some, desperate; some, brutal. I cannot be mistaken in speaking of their physiognomy; for I was not expecting what I witnessed. I thought I should see very much such a gathering of genteel-looking people as I should find in a Continental ballroom. But either their work deforms them while they are engaged in it; or else I saw a company of men and women on whom their ruling vice had set its indelible, foul, and detestable plague-spot.

The most shameful fact connected with the establishment is that it is owned by the Grand Duke, who gets an enormous rent from it.

The springs, from which Baden (*baths*) derives its name, are all hot or warm springs, a hundred and fifty-six degrees being the temperature of the hottest. They are led by conduits under the streets to supply the various baths, and at many points in the streets are gratings, at which one could easily take a vapor-bath, and at which the hands or feet might be made comfortably warm on a winter's day. Some of the springs are used for bathing only. The water of others is taken internally; but **as,** though by no means appetizing, it does not taste very badly, it is not drunk with the avidity displayed by those who seek health at more nauseous sources. There is a magnificent pump-room, where the water is drunk every morning by invalids and fashionables. This building has a very long, open portico, the walls of which are beautifully frescoed with legends of Baden and the Black Forest. The great square on which this and the Kursaal stand, is a promenade of singular beauty, — its paths lined with booths hardly less frail than those at the Heidelberg fair, certainly neither cold-proof, nor storm-proof, nor burglar-proof, yet filled with the most showy and sumptuous goods of every description.

In accordance with the rambling character of this chapter, I will again take my readers across Germany, to say a few words about a town which hardly any mere travellers from America visit, but where I found a large number of American students, among them no less than six of my own pupils, graduates of Harvard University. I mean Freiberg in Saxony, the seat of the celebrated School of Mines. The town lies in a dreary and desolate region, and has not even an edifice in which one can take any interest, with the exception of a very splendid cathedral eight or nine centuries old, in which all the Protestant sovereigns of Saxony have been interred. This church is also remarkable for a very deep portal, the vault of which is filled with hundreds of figures in relief, exquisitely carved in stone, and which has broad and massive doors called the Golden Gates, having been originally plated with gold.

The building of the School of Mines contains, of course, large mineralogical and geological cabinets, and especially — not of course — a remarkably rich collection of precious stones of every description. There is also a spacious apartment devoted to models of machinery, illustrating the several processes of mining, together with models of various mines, their shafts, and their galleries.

The Freiberg mines are commonly called the silver mines of Saxony; but they are, in fact, lead mines. The ore is not very unlike the lead ore of Galena. It yields gold, silver, lead, arsenic, and blue vitriol. None of it contains more than a fourth of one per cent of silver, and the mass has to undergo at least a dozen smeltings to coax away the silver and refine it. Yet silver to the amount of two million dollars is annually obtained from this ore, which yields also about thirty thousand dollars worth of gold annually. I doubt whether the extraction of so small proportions of the precious metals would pay for itself where wages are high. But labor is so cheap there, that they can afford to work the ore over and over, as long as any value remains to be extracted from it. The best workmen get only twelve *groschen*, or thirty cents a day.

About a thousand laborers are employed in mining and smelting. I inquired, with no little curiosity, into the condition of men who are compelled to subsist on so scanty a pittance. I learned that they live mainly on black, that is, barley bread, and potato soup, and never eat meat oftener than once a week. They are, however, contented and intelligent. Their children are sent to school, are well taught, and are not permitted to labor in the mines or smelting works till fourteen years of age.

I ought to express an opinion on such a subject with much diffidence; but I left Freiberg with impressions both favorable and unfavorable as to its adaptation to the needs of American pupils. The place is preëminently fitted for study; for there is nothing else that a young man can do, there are no distractions of any kind, and the spirit of the institution is that of hard work, deep investigation, and scholarly ambition. The scientific instruction, I am inclined to think, is all that could be desired, — elementary, comprehensive, systematic, thorough. But it seemed to me that, as a school of practical metallurgy, Freiberg must be very defective, for reasons connected with the low rate of wages. I thought I could see, in all the works, a lack of labor-saving machinery and processes, a rigid adherence to old methods, and a general looseness and slovenliness of management; while the net revenue which accrues to the government, on whose account the mines are worked, as compared with their gross products, shows that the system is not essentially less costly than where high wages put a premium on invention and economy.

My story is told. If I shall have satisfied the curiosity of any of my readers, — still more, if I shall have so awakened it as to induce them to satisfy it by following me in person where I have led them, I shall have made a happy and precious addition to my lifelong " Reminiscences of European Travel."

INDEX.

Aar, the, 110.
Acherusia Palus, the, 183.
Agnano, Lake of, 181.
Amalfi, road to, 192; site and aspect of, 194; cathedral of, 195.
Ambrosian Library at Milan, 146.
Antoninus Marcus, column of, 234.
Arc d'Etoile, at Paris, 167.
Art, ancient and modern, 76; divine element in, 77; mission of, 78; causes of the decline of, 97.
Arthur's Seat, in Edinburgh, 69.
Arveiron, source of the, 126.
Avernus, 183.

Baden-Baden, beauty of, 303; old and new castles of, 304; gambling at, 304; springs of, 307.
Baiæ, supposed temples at, 187.
Bank of England, 34.
Basle, 104.
Bellaggio, 140.
Ben Nevis, 52.
Bern, grotesqueness of, 115; clock-towers of, 116; bears in, 116; cathedral of, 117.
Bologna, site and aspect of, 225; Academy of Fine Arts at, 226; Campo Santo of, 227.
Borghese Villa, at Rome, 276.
Boston, church of St. Botolph at, 11; old houses in, 13; former and present condition of, 13.
Boulevards of Paris, 158.
Brienz, Lake of, 111.
British Museum, 46.
Brougham, Lord, 18.
Brussels, carved pulpit in, 91.

Cæsars, palace of the, 233.
Caledonian canal, 51.
Calton Hill, in Edinburgh, 70.
Campagna, the Roman, 252.
Capitoline Hill, 231.
Capri, shore of, 189; Blue Grotto of, 190; palace of Tiberius at, 191.
Capuchins, church of the, at Rome, 275.
Caracalla, Baths of, 236.
Cardinals, state of the, 270.
Castor and Pollux, statues of, on the Quirinal, 241.
Catacombs, origin of, 245; of St. Callixtus, 247.
Cavour, monument of, at Milan, 144.
Chamouny, valley of, 125; sunrise at, 129.
Chapelle Expiatoire, at Paris, 163.
Chester, aspect of, 3; cathedral of, 4.
Christ Church, in Dublin, 73.
Christmas at St. Peter's, 267; at the Ara Cœli church, 272.
Cloaca Maxima, the, 241.
Col de Balme, the, 124.
Colosseum, the, 237.
Commons, House of, 16.
Como, Lake of, 139; city of, 141; market at, 142.
Correggio's Magdalen, 84.
Costume of Italian peasants, 197.
Cumæan Sibyl, cave of the, 184.

Domenichino's Communion of St. Jerome, 266.
Dying Gladiator, the, 93.

Edinburgh, new and old city, 66; population of, 67; royal castle in, 68; scenery of, 69; Sunday in, 71.
Elysian Fields, 184.
England, love of antiquity prevalent in, 4; wealth of, 6; vegetation of, 6.
English lakes, 60.
Epiphany revels at Rome, 255.

Flegère, the, 126.
Fountains Abbey, 9.
Foyers, Falls of the, 51.
Freiberg, cathedral of, 308; mines of, 309; school of mines at, 310.
Furca, the, 126.

Geneva, aspect of, 117; washerwomen of, 118.
Giessbach, Falls of the, 112.
Glacier des Bossons, 129.
Gladstone, Mr., 16.
Goldsmith's work in the Middle Ages, 97.
Grimsel Pass, the, 109.
Grotto del Cane, 181.
Guido's Madonna della Pieta, 226.

Haddon Hall, 7.
Hadrian's Villa, 249.
Hall, Newman, 23.
Handeck, Falls of the, 111.
Heidelberg, castle of, 300; tun of, 301; university of, 301; fair of, 302; market of, 303.
Holbein's Madonna, 82.
Holyrood Palace, 68.

Inscriptions, ancient, at Rome, 243.
Interlachen, 112.
Irish mendicancy, 58.
Italian sky, the, 85.
Italy, present condition of, 197; financial and industrial state of, 198; religious toleration in, 199; progress of Protestantism in, 199.

Jardin d'Acclimatation, at Paris, 171.
Jardin des Plantes, at Paris, 170.
Judenstadt, the, in Prague, 297.
Jungfrau, the, 113.

Killarney Lakes, 54.

Lakes, Scotch, 50; Irish, 55; English, 60.
Laocoon, the, 242.
Last Judgment, the, in Sistine Chapel, 137.
Last Supper, Leonardo da Vinci's, 144.
Lausanne, aspect of, 119; cathedral of, 119.
Lauterbrunnen, 113.
Lincolnshire, fen-country of, 11.
London, municipal organization of, 25; extent of, 25; climate of, 27; police of, 28; literary associations with, 29; parks of, 31; heterogeneous character of, 32.
Lords, House of, 16.
Louvre, the, 169.
Lucerne, views from, 105; Lake of, 105.
Lugano, lake and city of, 137.
Luke, St., pictures attributed to, 274.

Madeleine, church of the, at Paris, 159.
Maggiore, Lake, 136.
Mamertine Prison, the, 240.
Manuscripts from Herculaneum unrolled, 210.
Martigny, 120.
Martineau, Rev. James, 23.
Mer de Glace, 128.
Milan, cathedral of, 95; aspect of, 144.
Mill, John Stuart, 19.
Monks at Rome, 275.
Montanvert, the, 127.
Mont Blanc, ascent of, 131.
Monte Nuovo, 181.
Mosaics, manufactory of, at the Vatican, 266.
Moses, Michael Angelo's, 94.

Naples, beauty of, 174; people of, 175; climate of, 176; museum of, 210.
Napoleon I., tomb of, 168.
Notre Dame, church of, at Paris, 161.
Nuremberg, ancient aspect of, 286; walls of, 287; fountains and

INDEX. 315

markets of, 288; churches in, 289; houses in, 290; instruments of torture preserved at, 291; old curiosity shop in, 292; churchyard of St. John in, 293.

Pantheon, the, in Paris, 160; in Rome, 238.
Paris, manysidedness of, 148; order of, 149; brilliancy of, 150; industry of, 151; manufactures of, 152; holidays in, 153; philanthropic institutions of, 155; education in, 156; paternal government of, 156.
Parliament, Houses of, 15.
Pere la Chaise, cemetery of, in Paris, 165.
Perugia, site and aspect of, 222; churches in, 223; art in, 224.
Perugino, Pietro, 224.
Pisa, site and aspect of, 216; cathedral of, 217; baptistery of, 218; leaning tower of, 220; Campo Santo of, 221; church of Santa Maria della Spina in 222.
Pompeii, destruction of, 201; streets of, 203; shops in, 204; houses in, 205; domestic life in, 206; art in, 208; skeletons found in, 209; relics of, in the museum at Naples, 211; worth of, as a commentary on the classics, 215.
Pope, the, dress of, 268; appearance of, 272.
Pozzuoli, Grotta di, 186; amphitheatre of, 186; temple of Jupiter Serapis in, 187.
Prague, aspect of, 293; worship of the Virgin Mary at, 294; cathedral of, 295; Teynkirche in, 296; Jewish population of, 297; old synagogue in, 297; peculiar church customs in, 299.
Pulpit eloquence in England, 19.

Raphael's Sistine Madonna, 80; Transfiguration, 86; Staffa Madonna, 224; St. Cecilia, 226.
Reuss, the, 108.
Rigi, the, view from the summit of, 106; storm upon, 107.
Rodgers' cutlery, 65.

Romans, descendants of the ancient, 254.
Rome, first impressions of, 229; the Seven Hills of, 230; the Capitol of, 231; the Forum of, 232; baths of, 335; Colosseum, 237; aqueducts of, 239; palaces in, 277; artists in, 277; general aspect of, 278; streets of, 279; police of, 279; environs of, 282; Protestant cemetery in, 282.
Royal Exchange in London, 35.
Rubens, character of, as a painter, 87; Elevation of the Cross by, 88; Descent from the Cross by, 89; The Flagellation by, 90; the Via Dolorosa by, 90.

St. Ambrose's church, at Milan, 145.
St. Andrew's cathedral, at Amalfi, 195.
St. Clement's church, at Rome, 244.
St. Ferdinand, chapel of, at Paris, 164.
St. Gotthard, pass of, 108.
St. John in the Lateran, church of, at Rome, 273.
St. Patrick's cathedral at Dublin 73.
St. Paul's, at London, 43.
St. Peter's, at Rome, exterior of, 258; interior of, 259; dome of 261.
St. Petronius, church of, at Bologna, 225.
St. Salvador, Mount, 138.
St. Stephen's church, at Rome, 274.
St. Vitus, cathedral of, at Prague 295.
Salerno, 196.
Saxon, Baths of, 121.
Scala Santa, at Rome, 273.
Scott, Sir Walter, monument of in Edinburgh, 70.
Scottish Highlands, 51.
Scottish Lakes, scenery of, 50 literary associations with, 52.
Sheffield, aspect of, 63; manufactures of, 64.
Sherwood Forest, 7.
Simplon, the, 132.

Sistine Chapel, the, 262.
Sistine Madonna, the, 80.
Solfatara, the, 180.
Sorrento, road to, 187; beauty of, 188.
South Kensington Museum, 48.
Spurgeon, 20.
Staubbach, the, 113.
Stufa di Nerone, 182.
Stufa di San Germano, 181.
Swiss railways, 100; carriage roads, 100; inns, 102; mendicancy, 102; women overworked, 103.

Tarpeian Rock, the, 240.
Terni, Falls of, 282.
Tête Noir, the, 125.
Thames, the, 35; navigation of, 36; bridges over, 36; tunnel, 37.
Thun, Lake of, 115.
Tiber, the, 253.
Tiberius, palace of, at Capri, 197.

Tibur (now Tivoli), classical references to, 251.
Titian's Tribute-money, 83; Assumption of the Virgin, 84.
Tivoli, Falls of, 249; temples at, 250; villas in, 251.
Tower of London, 38.
Trajan's forum and column, 233.
Trasteverini, the, 256.

Vatican, the, gallery of sculpture in, 242, 264; Etruscan Museum in, 265; hall of maps in, 265; library, 266; manufactory of mosaics in, 266.
Vesuvius, ascent of, 177; prospect from, 179.
Virgilian sites near Naples, 183.

Westminster Abbey, 40.
Westminster Palace, 14.
Wood-carving, one of the fine arts, 91.
Wordsworth, memorials of, 61.

www.ingramcontent.com/pod-product-compliance
Lightning Source LLC
Chambersburg PA
CBHW030742230426
43667CB00007B/805